D1196701

Tools for Thinking

Essentials for Thinking

Tools for Thinking

Modelling in Management Science

MICHAEL PIDD
Department of Management Science
The Management School
Lancaster University

JOHN WILEY & SONS
Chichester • New York • Brisbane • Toronto • Singapore

658.40352
P6lt

Other Wiley Editorial Offices

John Wiley & Sons, Inc., 605 Third Avenue,
New York, NY 10158-0012, USA

Jacaranda Wiley Ltd, 33 Park Road, Milton,
Queensland 4064, Australia

John Wiley & Sons (Canada) Ltd, 22 Worcester Road,
Rexdale, Ontario M9W 1L1, Canada

John Wiley & Sons (Asia) Pte Ltd, 2 Clementi Loop #02-01,
Jin Xing Distripark, Singapore 129809

Library of Congress Cataloging-in-Publication Data

Pidd, Michael.
    Tools for thinking : modelling in management science / Michael
Pidd
      p. cm.
      Includes bibliographical references and index.
      ISBN 0-471-96455-7 (cloth)
      1. Problem solving—Simulation methods.   2. Management science—
Simulation methods.   I. Title.
HD30.29.P53   1996
658.4'0352—dc20   96–32158
                                                               CIP

British Library Cataloguing in Publication Data

A catalogue record for this book is available from the British Library

ISBN 0-471-96455-7

Typeset in 10/12pt Palatino from the author's disks by
Mathematical Composition Setters Ltd, Salisbury, Wiltshire
Printed and bound in Great Britain by Biddles Ltd, Guildford and King's Lynn.
This book is printed on acid-free paper responsibly manufactured from sustainable forestation, for
which at least two trees are planted for each one used for paper production.

To my family, friends and colleagues

Contents

Preface

Since I became an academic, my teaching has been divided between two groups: specialist students of management science and operational research, and general business and management students. Students from the first group are often well qualified in mathematics, statistics and computing; those from the second tend to be very sensitive to business issues and may favour an approach to management based on well-developed interpersonal skills. This teaching experience always pulls me in two directions.

To the management science students I want to say, "Your maths and computer models are all very well, but what about the organisations in which you will work? Don't you think you think that the context of your work is worth some investigation?" But many such students are too busy grappling with their computers to worry too much about these things. In popular parlance, these are the *rocket scientists*.

To the students and others who stress the human side of management I want to say, "Hold on a minute. Yes, of course management is through people, but isn't it important to think through the consequences of possible action before doing something? Perhaps you would be better managers if you were able to use the tools to do this?" This group are often known as the *poets*.

This book is written for both rocket scientists and poets, whether they be students, academics or practitioners. It aims to give both sides a glimpse over the wall into the other playground. It argues the case for the rocket scientists to be much more thoughtful about organisational life. It stresses the need for the poets to see that methods do exist that will help them to think through possible consequences. For both camps, the idea is to stress that systematic thinking and analysis has a role to play in improving organisation life. It stresses modell*ing* as an activity and not *models*, as a noun.

The book is divided into four parts:

Part I: Modelling in Management Science. This provides the context for the rest of the book. It argues the case for rational analysis and tries to take account of some criticisms of rationality. It suggests a role for management science in contemporary organisations and proposes a few simple principles for modelling.

Part II: Interpretive Modelling: Soft Management Science. Though management science is usually associated with mathematical and statistical approaches, the last decade has seen the development of powerful approaches that are essentially qualitative. They are intended to provide support for analysts to understand and interpret people's ideas and preferences. In this way, they are used to help think through the consequences of possible action.

Part III: Mathematical and Logical Modelling. This part covers three techniques or approaches that are commonly associated with management science. There were many contenders for inclusion and the reasons for my choice are given in the introduction to Part III. They are intended to illustrate modelling, as distinct from models or techniques.

Part IV: Model Assessment and Validation. This is a single chapter which discusses how models and modelling approaches can be validated so that participants may have some faith in their results.

I am grateful to friends and colleagues from Lancaster and elsewhere who have given me pause for thought during this book's long gestation period, which stretched for many years before I finally proposed it to John Wiley & Sons. In particular, I would like to acknowledge the help provided by the comments from Vlado Ceric, Chris Chapman, Brian Dangerfield, Colin Eden, Richard Eglese, Robert Fildes, Geoff Walsham, Stephen Watson and Mike Wright. I am also indebted to a number of awkward thinkers who have stimulated my ideas, especially John Crookes, Peter Checkland, the late Steve Cook, and Ray Paul. But the mistakes are all mine.

MICHAEL PIDD
University of Lancaster

PART I

Modelling in Management Science

Introduction

Part I aims to provide a general introduction to the idea of modelling as a part of management science. The stress is firmly upon *modelling* rather than on *models*. The idea is to show how models are built and used, rather than exploring different types of models in any detail—there are plenty of books which do that very well. Thus, the approach taken is non-technical, but it does demand some stamina from readers who may not have come across the ideas before.

Hence, this part begins with a discussion of the value of modelling, taking as the theme of Chapter 1 the idea that models are convenient worlds. They are artificial worlds that have been deliberately created to help with understanding the possible consequences of particular actions. They are part of a process of "reflection before action" (Boothroyd, 1978). The models may be quantitative or qualitative, but in any case they will be simplified abstractions of the system of interest.

The modelling theme continues with Chapter 2, which looks at the role of modelling within organisations. Modelling approaches are often viewed as exemplars of highly rational schemes and it is important to consider how they can be of use within organisational life, which may be far from rational in any classical or linear sense. Thus, Chapter 2 develops a definition of rationality from Simon's work and then considers critics of this view, most notably Mintzberg and his colleagues, who argue for a more intuitive approach to the crafting of strategy. Putting these two together suggests that a role for modelling is the attempt to make sense of strategic vision; the vision stemming from processes that are, at least in part, intuitive.

Chapter 3 faces up to the common view that the main role of management science is in problem solving. But this carries with it the idea that, once solved, problems stay that way. Organisational life is rarely so kind and it is important to recognise that modelling is used as a way of coping with change and turbulence. Chapter 3 discusses various ideas about the nature of problems and suggests the role for modelling within them. It concludes with an extensive discussion of the nature of problem structuring, taking the view that this "naming and framing" (Schön, 1982) is fundamental to successful modelling.

Part I ends with Chapter 4 on a thoroughly practical note with a discussion of six principles of modelling that I (and others) have found useful. There is no sense in which this is a complete list of useful ideas about modelling, but it will at least serve as a starting point from which readers may develop their own ideas.

REFERENCES

Boothroyd H.A. (1978) *Articulate Intervention*. (ORASA text, 1.) Taylor & Francis/Operational Research Society, London.
Schön D.A. (1982) *The Reflective Practitioner. How Professionals Think in Action*. Basic Books, New York.

1
Models as Convenient Worlds

MANAGING COMPLEXITY AND RISK

Our lives are increasingly complex, whether we consider only our individual lives, sharing with our families, or working in some kind of organisation. Those of us in the western world depend on artificial aids for our survival: we travel long distances by car, boat or plane, we cook food on devices fuelled by gas or electricity, and we take for granted that computers enable us to communicate instantly across the globe. We are very much part of an interconnected world in which our decisions and those of others can have major consequences for us and for other people.

When our decisions turn out well, then we expect that we and others will benefit from what happens. But we are also aware that, when things go wrong, the consequences can be dire indeed. The same is true of businesses. For example, the costs to a manufacturer that decides to build a new factory on a greenfield site, or to re-equip an existing factory, can be huge. Clearly, the managers will make such an investment only if they expect the business to gain some return from doing so. But how can they be sure that their decisions will turn out as they intended? How can they be sure that there will be sufficient demand for the products the factory will produce? How can they be sure that the technologies used within the factory will work as intended? The consequences of failures can be very expensive and may even be dangerous. One way to help improve such planning is to find ways to learn from the failures that sometimes occur (Fortune and Peters, 1995). This learning implies that the investigators have something—a model—against which the performance of the system can be compared.

On a different theme, the high population of our planet serves to increase the awful effect that natural and man-made disasters can have. For example, modern societies rely on large-scale chemical plants for the production of materials to be turned into foodstuffs, drugs and components for goods. But these plants can be dangerous to operate, a fact which the people of Bhopal in India are unlikely ever to forget. There, in 1984, poisonous gas drifted over the town after escaping from a nearby chemical plant, killing about 3000 people and injuring another 250 000 (Fortune and Peters, 1995). We rely on electricity to power our factories and our household devices, and many of the generating plants are based on nuclear reactors. As we know from the events of Chernobyl in 1986, an explosion and a major release of radiation may have terrible consequences. How can managers of these plants try to ensure that they have minimised, or reduced to zero, the risks of dangerous accidents? How can those with the task of evacuating an area and cleaning up afterwards be sure that they are working as effectively as possible?

The effects of natural disasters such as earthquakes and floods also threaten our lives. These disasters affect both highly developed countries—for example, the earthquakes in Japan at Kobe in 1995 and in the USA at San Francisco in 1989—and poorer countries—such as Bangladesh, whose land is very vulnerable to annual floods, lying largely within the Ganges and Brahmaputra deltas. Such natural disasters not only threaten lives, but also disrupt normal life and make it impossible for people to live as they would choose. How can natural disaster experts assess the risk of such hazards? How can they ensure that they are able to warn people when a disaster threatens? How can they ensure that they evacuate people quickly and safely from danger zones?

It is, of course, impossible to be sure what will happen when we make changes in complex systems, for we can be sure of what will happen only when we have complete control over events. However, there are ways of minimising risk and of managing complexity. The complexity of modern life is here to stay and we must, therefore, adopt approaches to cope with this. The risks too are evident, as are the rewards for being able to manage those risks. The main argument of this book is that the development and use of rational and logical analysis can be a great aid in managing that complexity and in recognising and managing the inevitable risks.

Thinking about Consequences

Whenever we make a decision and take some action, there will be consequences. The consequences may be within our control, or there may be considerable risk or uncertainty. When we have full control of the consequences of our decisions and actions, we have only ourselves to blame when things go wrong and we can take the credit when they turn out well. In these cases, it clearly makes sense to think through the consequences of our actions and our decisions. For simple decisions, this process is itself simple. All we have to do is list the possible outcomes and choose the most desirable, ensuring that we know which course of action will lead to this outcome. Thus, if we wish to invest some cash in one of a small number of investments, all of whose returns are known and are certain over some defined period, simple arithmetic will help us to choose the best investment. In the terms that will be defined later, in doing so we have used a simple decision model. We have applied logical analysis to our circumstances.

Often, however, life is not so simple and we are at the mercy of other people's actions or of the intervention of events we cannot control, such as the weather. Some such cases can be regarded as "competition" and it is thus important to try to consider carefully how other people might respond to the actions which we take. As a classic example, consider the game of chess which has been much studied by students of artificial intelligence. Chess has no chance element, everything is determined and the winner is the player who follows the best strategies. There is considerable evidence (Simon, 1976) that the better players are able systematically to analyse current and possible future positions very quickly by procedures that can be modelled by computer programs. Other competitive situations are much more complex than chess. For example, a manufacturer of fast-moving consumer goods must develop marketing policies, but competitor companies will do the same and customers' responses are not wholly predictable. This situation is, therefore, more complex than that of a game such as chess.

Does this mean that logical analysis is a waste of time? Not really. Consider the example of the captain of a commercial airliner about to make a long-haul flight. Before take-off, the captain must file a flight plan specifying the intended route, timings and other aspects. However, few long-haul flights follow their precise flight plans because en-route events conspire otherwise—there may be changes in the weather, turbulence, military flights or emergencies affecting other aircraft during the flight. Nevertheless, the plan has its value for it serves two purposes. First, it serves as a standard against which progress on the flight can be monitored—which is much better than setting off in the vague hope of landing in Australia! Secondly, it allows the organisation (the airline) to build a body of knowledge of flights and how they can be affected by studying why the flight plan could not be followed. That is, it allows after-the-event audit to occur.

One major argument of this book is that rational and logical analysis is crucial in our complicated world. However, it might be instructive to think about what other ways there might be to take such decisions, and these include the following:

Seat of the pants. This term usually implies rapid decision making based on intuition, with no real attempt to think through the consequences. Sometimes this approach can be quite effective, but it can also be rather dangerous. Few of us would wish to be flown on a commercial airline flight by a crew who made no attempt whatsoever to plan their route; flying by the seat of our pants can be exciting, but some kinds of excitement are grossly overrated.

Superstition. This term is used here to indicate a mystical belief that examining some other system will shed light on whatever decision that we are facing, even when there is clearly no link whatsoever between our decision and the system that we use as a reference. This is very similar to the attitude people strike when they read horoscopes in newspapers with a view to planning their day. A similar notion is the idea that use of a lucky charm or method of doing something will guarantee a desirable outcome. For example, a soccer player might always put his left boot on before his right in the belief that doing it the other way round will cause him to play badly. It may not be stretching an analogy too far to suggest that some organisations seem to operate in a similar manner.

Faith and trust. This term is used to denote an approach which is close to superstition, but with one important difference: that there is some proper link postulated between the parallel system and the decision to be faced. Thus there is the idea that proper observance of the one will guarantee a favourable outcome in the other. Some people would argue that certain politico-economic theories could be classified in this way.

Do nothing. This is the classical "head in the sand" approach, closing our eyes and hoping that the problem will go away or that it will be sorted out in some other way. There are times when it may be best to do nothing but, paradoxically, we can only know this when we have thought through the consequences of doing nothing. An example of this might be sitting tight during an earthquake.

Probably most people use one or more of these approaches in making personal decisions that have no major consequences. But most of us would be unhappy with the thought that they were being used by others to make major decisions that might have a significant impact on us.

It should, of course, be noted that even logical approaches can fail—especially if they are blinkered. There is a wonderful example of this is in the Andalucian hills of Southern Spain. There, set among beautiful scenery about 30 kilometres from Ronda, is a dam built by the Seville Electricity Company in the 1920s. They'd found a valley into which an existing water source flowed, the valley was wide and deep and had a narrow exit—perfect for a dam. Even better, the valley was high in the hills and water flow could be used to generate hydroelectric power as well as providing water supplies. So, with Swiss engineers as main contractors, work started and continued for several years. Walls were demolished, roads rerouted and the main dam wall, the first U-shaped dam in Southern Europe, rose above the valley floor to an impressive height. Eventually, all was completed and the river was diverted back into the valley. A lake began to form behind the dam and slowly it filled with water. Over weeks, the water level rose and the Seville Electricity Company congratulated itself on its wise planning and its use of the Swiss engineers. Meanwhile, the locals were watching with keen interest, for they knew something that no outsider had thought to consider.

When the reservoir was nearly full, the water level suddenly fell and did so very quickly, leaving just a small pool behind the dam. What the locals knew, and what every visitor can see to this day, is that the hills are mainly composed of limestone. Limestone itself is impervious to water but contains many fissures through which water may pass—which is why there are many caves in this type of rock. Presumably the huge downward pressure of the water opened up small fissures and, like water in the bath, away it went. So, after all their effort, the water just drained away and the huge expenditure on the dam was wasted. Visitors can still walk across the dam and admire its fine engineering as they smile and look down at the small pool of water several hundred feet below them. The design was wholly logical, its dam was at the forefront of technology, its designers were good and conscientious people—but they forgot to ask the basic questions. Analysis without basic thought and rigour is a waste of time.

SIMPLE PHYSICAL MODELS

The Lake District is one of the most popular tourist areas of Britain, with rugged mountains and beautiful lakes. Its fells were the site of much early industrial activity that led to the growth of the small villages that scatter the landscape. Tracks that connected these villages are now the paths along which walkers explore the area. The Lake District is wet as well as beautiful and its attractive streams cascade down the fell-sides into the lakes. Many bridges have been built where the tracks cross the streams. The most appealing of these are made from a single self-supporting arch of stones (a good example is to be found behind the Wasdale Head Hotel). Figure 1.1 shows the basic design of these bridges.

A common method of building the bridges was to erect a wooden framework across the stream. This framework would be an arch on which the stones of the bridge would be placed. The builders would securely locate the sides of the bridge in the solid ground on the stream banks and would carefully place selected stones on the wooden arch, starting from the banks. Eventually the builders would reach the stage where only the keystone remained unplaced. The keystone sits at the top of the arch in the centre and would be forced into place to ensure a tight fit. If all of the stones were properly fitted tightly together then the arch should be self-supporting once the keystone is in place.

When the builders were happy that the stone arch was finished, they would set fire to the wooden arch that had been supporting it whilst it was built. The question in their minds was, would the stone arch collapse? Would it hold up its own weight and would it support the weight of the traffic (people and animals) that walked over it? Someone would have to be the first to walk over the bridge and test it. On most occasions, the arch would hold and the bridge would be safe. But there were probably occasions when it collapsed along with the plans and reputations of the builders.

Figure 1.1   *A simple stone arch bridge*

If a newly built bridge did collapse, it was unlikely to be a major catastrophe—apart from the effect on the builder's future prospects. Building such a bridge was not expensive and did not take a long time. The builders could try again until they produced a safe bridge. In the old adage of engineers, they could "suck it and see". This "suck it and see" approach does not imply that the builders did not carefully plan the bridge. Certainly they were careful to select a site and careful in their choice of stones, in preparing these stones and in placing them. They were probably working from a mental image of the bridge. They could probably envisage what it would look like and what size of loads it would bear. Hence they were able to make the bridge on site and adapt it and rebuild it until it worked as intended.

Small bridges over streams have probably been constructed in this way for centuries, but it would clearly be inappropriate to attempt work on a large-scale civil engineering project such as a motorway bridge in the same way. We take it for granted that the bridge will be planned by qualified engineers and architects who understand how to go about this job. Indeed, in many countries, bridges must be designed and their construction supervised only by fully qualified people. The work of the designers might begin with implicit mental models, their first ideas about the bridge, but we would expect them to move quickly on to formal and explicit models which would lead to a bridge that would both meet its specification and be safe to use.

There are various types of models the bridge design team might employ. The simplest to envisage are two-dimensional drawings which show, at different levels of detail, how the bridge will look and how its different components will be fastened together. These drawings may exist on paper or might be held in some form of computer-aided design (CAD) system which allows drawings to be displayed on screen and manipulated in different ways. It might also be important to test out the bridge's performance under extreme conditions, such as high winds. For this, the designers may build scale models and test-rigs, using wind tunnels and scaled tests to see how their design will perform.

The designers will also be working within cost limits. They will try to ensure that the bridge is strong enough to meet its specification, but that is not over-engineered. They will need to consider very carefully the size of the beams and supports that make up the bridge. To do this they will use well-established mathematical models and equations to describe how the components will perform. They use these different types of model as ways of managing the sheer complexity of the physical design and to minimise the risk that the bridge will not perform as intended. There is, of course, still no guarantee that the bridge will be safe under all conditions. For example, there is the well-known case of the Tacoma Narrows Bridge that collapsed in 1940 under moderate wind stress after starting to sway. But, in such cases, a model of the bridge may be used to try to discover what went wrong so as to ensure that a similar tragedy does not happen again.

BEYOND THE PHYSICAL MODELS

The designers need to go well beyond these models of the physical design for such large-scale projects. If, say, the bridge is part of a larger traffic scheme they will wish to know what effect their design has on the overall traffic flow. One way to do this would be to simulate on computer the likely operation of the bridge. Such a simulation model (see Chapter 9) would allow the designers to develop control strategies for traffic based on the capacities of the bridge and of the rest of the road network.

They will also need to assess how long it will take to build the bridge, and organise themselves to control the project properly and ensure that it runs according to plan. To do this they are highly likely to use a model of the different activities that are needed to complete the project and thus they may resort to network planning tools such as critical path method (CPM) and program evaluation and review technique (PERT) to plan the project and to control its operation. These tools allow the builders to see the effect of possible delays or accelerations in the building works. For example, what happens if the concrete cladding arrives a week late due to shipping delays? Will that delay the whole project or are there ways of rearranging the work to catch up the lost time? These are simple questions on small projects but are immensely complicated in large-scale activities.

The purpose of this book is to demonstrate how different types of model can be useful in helping to manage complexity in order to reduce the risk of wrong decisions. The book also aims to show how different approaches to developing and using models can affect their value in practice. It is perhaps obvious how models and modelling can play a useful part in large-scale civil engineering projects, but it may be less clear how they can be used in other areas of life. After all, complex models must be expensive to build and cannot possibly include the full complexity of a situation, so does this not imply that modelling is a good idea but one that always falls down in practice?

Carefully built models can be of great use in areas of life very different from the design of physical structures. An idea central to this book is that one distinguishing characteristic of management scientists (meaning operational research professionals, business analysts and others who use rational and logical methods) is their use of explicit models. Despite the analogy of the bridge builders, the work done by management scientists cannot be regarded as a type of straightforward engineering. As will become clear, it is important for management scientists to be very careful in the assumptions that they make about organisations and in their treatment of other human beings.

WHAT IS A MODEL?

There are many definitions of model in general and also many definitions of model as the term is used within management science. One of the earliest definitions simply says that *a model is a representation of reality* (Ackoff and Sasieni, 1968). This definition is appealing in its simplicity, but it ignores the question of why the model is being built. This aspect is crucial, for a model is always a simplification, and such simplification must be done with a view to the intended use of the model. If this issue is ignored a modeller could go on modelling forever in the safe and sure knowledge that parts of reality have been left out. This simple definition must therefore be expanded to consider the purpose for which the model is being built. Thus, a suitable definition for the present discussion is that *a model is a representation of reality intended for some definite purpose.*

This definition is still very wide-ranging and needs a more precise statement of purpose for the model and for modelling as an activity within management science. Management scientists aim to help managers to make better decisions and to exercise better control over the things for which they are responsible. It is, therefore, important that the definition of model (and consequently of modelling) includes this idea so as to restrict the area of discussion. That is, in management science, models are often built to enable a manager to exercise better control or to help people to understand a complicated situation. Thus a third stage definition is that *a model is a representation of reality which is intended to be of use to someone charged with managing or understanding that reality.*

This definition, in turn, could be criticised because it suggests that models in management science are only of value to those at the apex of a power structure as in a business organisation. Work in the UK in the 1980s and 1990s demonstrated that management science could also be of value to people who are not in positions of such power (Ritchie et al, 1994). It would, therefore, be sensible to extend the definition yet further so as to include these possibilities. Thus, the definition becomes *a model is a representation of reality intended to be of use to someone in understanding, changing, managing and controlling that reality.*

Any reader who is a trained management scientist may be irritated by this definition and its development. Why does it not mention the term "system"? Why not say that "a model is a representation of some system"? This is because, to me at least, the term "system" simply has too many connotations, some of which will be explored later in this book. But, what then, about the term "reality", which is included in the definition. Does this assume that everyone will agree about what constitutes reality? Suppose they are wrong? This is, indeed, an important point and this is why "system" is not used in the definition. However, it also means that the term "reality" must itself be qualified.

It is important to recognise that, in the terms used by Checkland (1981), people may have legitimately different *Weltanschauungen*. This German word, popular among philosophers, is most nearly translated into English as "world-view", but is intended to convey the bundle of "taken for granted" meanings and assumptions most of us employ in our daily lives. Some of us, for example, may take for granted that a car is a means to get from A to B with the minimum hassle. Others may regard it as primarily a status symbol, or as a hobby, or as a necessary evil that drinks money and pollutes our world. Needless to say, anyone who attempts to consider how road space should be used in our crowded world must think through these different *Weltanschauungen*. Our world-views affect what we see and how we describe our experiences. They also affect our choices. To cope with this realisation that different world-views may lead to different descriptions of reality, we need to adopt an approach to modelling which is, using Zeigler's (1984) term, multifaceted. That is we may need to accept that multiple models are possible for a single apparent reality.

We also need to accept, though it is already implicit in the definition, that no model can ever be complete. This is for two reasons. First, were a model to be a complete one-on-one mapping of something, then it would be just as complex as the real thing and we would then have two of those somethings. This may be satisfying for an art forger, but rather negates what we shall see later to be some of the advantages in modelling. The second reason is that, unless we include the entire universe in our model, then there is always the risk that something is missing. There may be some relationship between our area of interest and another part of reality that is missing from the model. This may not matter now, but it may matter later.

Our definition now becomes: *a model is a representation of part of reality as seen by the people who wish to use it to understand, to change, to manage and to control that part of reality.* A further criticism might be that this definition has no mention of improvement. Surely people engage in modelling because they wish to improve something? The only sensible answer to that question is to recall that multiple *Weltanschauungen* are possible and that one person's improvement may be regarded as a disaster for someone else. Hence our definition deliberately excludes any statement about improvement.

We have one more refinement to make. This involves the realisation that most of us operate our lives with a set of assumptions that form our mind-set. This causes us to carry around informal, mental models of our world. These models are modified by experience, sometimes because they fail to deliver and sometimes because they are challenged by other people. But these internal and implicit mental models are not the main concern of this book—here we are concerned with models that are explicit and external. Hence our definition becomes:

a model is an external and explicit representation of part of reality as seen by the people who wish to use that model to understand, to change, to manage and to control that part of reality.

WHY BOTHER WITH A MODEL?

Our definition of a model, as it is to be used in management science, includes the idea of the user, for such models are generally built with some use in mind. But what are these uses? Much of the rest of this book will explore those uses and will show how they affect the ways in which models may be built, but it would be as well to discuss here the general reasons for building and using a model. Perhaps the clearest way to do this is to think of the alternatives. What approaches might be followed if a modelling approach is not adopted?

This discussion assumes that some critical issue is being faced that requires a decision to be taken or some control to be exercised. It does not assume that the decision will be taken immediately nor that rational analysis is the only consideration. Similarly, it does not rule out the notion of "decision fermentation", said to characterise some successful Japanese companies, nor of the gradual process of dealing with issues (see Langley et al, 1995). In such gradual processes, an issue is discussed over considerable time by many people in the organisation, at different levels and with different viewpoints. Through this lengthy process a consensus emerges that develops into a commitment to act. Thus, decisions are often not taken at a definite point in time; they emerge as different considerations and are accounted for by those participating in the process. Nevertheless, when a decision is to be taken, whether immediately or by some emergent process, there are approaches that could be followed which differ from the use of explicit models as advocated here. These options will always include the status quo, that is we could leave things just as they are.

Do Nothing!

This possibility—the favoured option of the lazy and often the only option open to the powerless—has at least the attraction that the analyst will not be blamed for what happens as a result. This is not always an option to be sneezed at, for inaction can sometimes be the best initial response when faced with uncertainty. Sometimes an over-hasty response is much worse than doing nothing. However, if we do have the discretion to act then we need to ask how we know that inaction is an appropriate response and the answer, surely, is that we can only know this if some analysis has been conducted. This implies that we have either internal and implicit models, or external and explicit models.

Experiment with Reality

Considering this option takes us right back to the building of single arch bridges from stone. The same arguments apply here as they do for bridge builders. Trying possible options out for real is all very well, and can be very exciting, but it can also be disastrous for the following reasons:

Cost. In most situations in which we need to respond or to exercise some control, we have a range of options open to us. The range may be quite small (do we place the new factory in Wales, or should it be in France?) or it might be almost infinite (what control algorithm should be developed to ensure aircraft safety in crowded airspace?). Trying out any option in practice always incurs cost. The cost per option may be quite small, and if the range of options is limited this may be a very sensible way to operate. But if the cost per option is high or the range of options is almost infinite, experimentation with reality can be very expensive.
Time. There is often not enough time to try out all of the options in practice, even when the range is small. To be sure where to locate our factory we may need to see how the option works out over a ten-year

period if we are to get a realistic return on the investment. This would clearly be impossible. On a smaller scale, if we need to decide how best to route service vehicles around an urban area, there may be too many options to make it worthwhile even attempting to experiment in practice. Thus the times taken to conduct the experiments mean that experimentation on reality is likely to lead to very restricted experiments.

Replication. Linked to these two is the need, on occasions, for replication. Sometimes a case has to be argued for a change or for some control to be exercised. This can mean arguing the case at different levels within an organisation and with different groups of people. They may wish to see the effects of the policy and they may wish, entirely legitimately, to try out the same experiments themselves. Another reason for replication is statistical variation. For example, the demand for most products is variable and unpredictable, except in statistical terms. Any policy to be investigated may need to be examined under a wide range of demand patterns to check its sensitivity. Thus replication may be needed and this is both time consuming and costly on the real system.

Danger. When things go wrong, catastrophe may result. The analogy here with bridges is obvious: no one would wish a bridge to collapse, injuring hundreds of people and costing huge sums. The same is true in the realm of management science. The result of trying to cram more aircraft into a restricted airspace may be to increase the risk of collision to an unacceptable level. Most of us would rather that this were established by experiments on models of the airspace and the control policies rather than by the use of real aircraft. Especially when we are on those aircraft!

Legality. There are times when we may need to see what effect a change in the law might have. One possibility is to break the law and then see what happens. This may be very well if you are employed by the Mafia but is unlikely to endear you to the rest of society. Hence it is much better to develop a model of how things would be were the law to be different. This can be used to see the effects of various changes and allows us to see whether it might be worth pressing for a change in those laws.

MODELS AS APPROPRIATE SIMPLIFICATIONS

The Value of Simplification

It is important to understand the limitations of model building and model use, for a model will always be a simplification and an approximate representation of some aspect of reality. This is clearly true even of architects' and engineers' drawings of bridges: for example, they are not usually concerned to show the exact colour of the steel and concrete to be used to build the bridge. They are much more concerned with the general appearance and detailed functioning of the structure. Hence their models are approximations, and none the worse for that.

Models do not have to be exact to be of use. As an example, consider the problem of navigating the subway systems which are part of mass transit in many large cities around the world. The operators of these systems usually display their various routes by the use of maps displayed on the subway stations. The interesting thing about these maps is that they allow the reader to understand the possible routings by deliberately distorting reality. This is done in two ways. First, the physical layout of the subway lines is distorted on the map so as to emphasise their general directions and their inter-changes. Thus routes which may share the same tunnels in the physical world are shown as separate on the logical map. Secondly, careful use of colour allows the reader to identify the various lines from a key. As yet, despite adding coloured markers on the station walls, no subway operator has attempted to colour the steel rail track to match their maps!

Therefore it is not a valid criticism that models are simplifications, for it is precisely such approximation that makes them useful. The important question to ask is, therefore, what degree of simplification is sensible and can this be known in advance? As part of an answer to this question, consider Table 1.1, which identifies some of the important differences between a model and reality— using the term "reality" to represent the part of the real world being modelled.

Complex Reality and Simple Models: Occam's Razor

There can be no clear answer to the question of how complicated a model needs to be—it depends, as was discussed earlier, on its

Table 1.1 *Reality versus model*

Reality	Model
Complex	Simple
Subtle	Concrete
Ill-defined	Fully defined

intended purpose. One helpful idea is to consider Occam's razor. According to Doyle (1992), "William of Occam, or Ockham, b. Ockham, England, c.1285, d. c.1349, ranks among the most important philosopher-theologians of the Middle Ages". He is remembered especially for the principle of analysis, known as Occam's razor, which he used to dissect the philosophical speculations of others. Two of the many wordings of Occam's razor are as follows:

- Do not multiply entities unnecessarily.
- A plurality (of reasons) should not be posited without necessity.

A contemporary interpretation of this would be that if two explanations seem equally plausible then it is better to use the simpler of the two. In one sense, a model will be used in an attempt to provide an explicit explanation of something or other and Occam's razor supports the view that simplification is not merely acceptable, it is desirable. Consider, for example, a model that includes the arrival of customers at a service point. If observation data is available, it might show that the arrival rate can adequately be modelled by a Poisson distribution (a simple way to represent random arrivals). This simple Poisson process may be perfectly adequate for deciding what resources are needed at a service point. To people trained in queuing theory and stochastic processes, the use of such a probability distribution is a commonplace. However, in real life, the customers may have their own individual reasons for arriving when they do. Some may be earlier than they intended (less traffic than expected?), others may be later (the bus was late?) and others may have called on the off-chance. Thus a complete model of the real-life system would need to account for each of these and other factors for each customer. But this detail may be quite unnecessary unless the aim of the model is to study the effect, say, of changing road traffic patterns on the operation of a service centre.

Thus, in modelling terms, the application of Occam's razor should lead us to develop models that are as simple as possible and yet are valid and useful for their intended purpose. That is, whether an element of a model is necessary (in terms of Occam's razor) will depend on its intended purpose. This too can be difficult, for only with perfect hindsight can we be sure that a model adequately addresses the reality being modelled. Nevertheless, it is important that management scientists do attempt to assess the degree to which their models are valid. A later chapter will deal with this issue in more detail.

An Analogy about Complexity

Another reason for simplicity in modelling comes from a common joke about complexity. To a mathematician, a complex number is the square root of a negative number; it has two parts, known as the real and imaginary parts. Complex systems also have real and imaginary parts. The problem is to differentiate between the two, which is difficult because one person's reality may be another's imagination. Models, on the other hand, are simple in the sense that they are entirely explicit and can be tested by other people. Models are imagination made explicit.

Subtle Reality and Concrete Models

Though this book takes for granted that reality does exist in a form external to the observer, the modelling of reality is still not straight-forward for the reasons identified in the analogy about complex numbers. Even if we accept (as I do) that reality is "out there", we still have the problem that we must rely on our own perceptions in attempting to understand and to experience that reality. The advers-arial principle of justice that is dominant in the UK and USA stems, at least in part, from the view that witnesses to events can produce totally or partially different accounts of events without lying. Two people might enter a street at the same time to see a youth standing over an elderly person lying on the side of the road. One witness might be sure the youth is helping up a frail person who has fallen, the other absolutely certain he is stealing the old person's handbag. In reality the youth *had* knocked the woman down, but only because he dashed across the road to push her out of the way of an oncoming car.

The point of a model is to make explicit or concrete whatever aspect of reality is being investigated. In some cases, the model is being developed in order to gain some understanding about how the real world operates. In this sense, the model becomes a theory that tries to explain what has been observed to occur. One test of such a model's validity would be a Turing test of the type devised by the mathema-tician Alan Turing. He argued that a good test of an artificial system (model in our case) is to see whether a judge, knowledgeable about the aspect of the real world being modelled, can distinguish between a stream of data coming from the real world and one coming from the model. The basic idea is shown in Figure 1.2.

The problem with this kind of argument is that it assumes that the observer is both omniscient (all-knowing) and unbiased. The observer might simply be wrong in declaring the model to be acceptable or not.

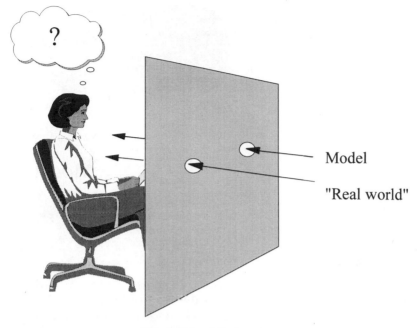

Figure 1.2   *A Turing test*

This may be because, when most of us talk about reality, what we actually mean is our own impressions about reality. Reality itself lies under those impressions and the best way to understand it may be to consider carefully many such impressions. On the other hand, the model is concrete and entirely explicit. People may also, of course, misunderstand the model or its output, but its parts can be written down and may be unambiguously addressed. This is one distinct advantage that a model, albeit a simplification, has over the real world.

Ill-defined Reality and Well-defined Model

In one familiar passage in the New Testament, the apostle Paul wrote about perfect love and ended by writing that "Now we see but a poor reflection in a mirror, then we shall see face to face" (I Corinthians 13:12). Our impressions of the world are always partial, both in the sense that we do not experience everything and also in the sense that we may well be biased. Thus our concept of what is going on in the real world will consist of ill-defined views and arguments unless they are properly codified and documented within a formal and well-

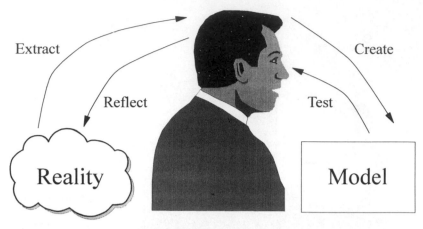

Figure 1.3 *Models and reality*

defined model. In Figure 1.3, reality is shown inside an ill-defined cloud and the model is shown as a fully defined box.

The task of the modeller is to take these ill-defined and implicit views of reality and cast them in some form well enough defined to be at least understood and argued over by other people. In the case of management science, this model may need to be represented in some computable form to allow for rapid experiments on the model so as to make inferences about the real world. This can only be done if the model is fully specified—though the specification may only emerge during the process of attempting to put them in computable forms. Thus, one major development in the 1980s was the idea of *visual interactive modelling* in which a computer is used as a device to build a model in a step-wise manner. Thus, the analyst develops a simple model by, perhaps, developing some form of representation on a computer screen. This model is then "run"—that is, used in some way or other—and it will, most likely, be found wanting. Its faults are considered and these are then remedied until the model is held to be adequate, or valid, for its intended purpose. Thus the full specification may only emerge from the modelling process.

MODELS FOR DECISION AND CONTROL

Much of what has been said so far in this chapter could apply to any kind of model, but the main focus of this book is on models and modelling in management science. That is, the attempt to use explicit models to improve decision making and control in organisations, whether they are businesses, charities, social agencies, community groups, churches, or whatever. For this purpose, the book takes the view that two important aspects of management are decision making and control. This does not mean that these are the only important aspects of management; for example, Mintzberg's early work on the realities of managerial life (Mintzberg, 1973) demonstrated that one characteristic of managerial life is a constant stream of meetings and interruptions. Time to think or to take an Olympian perspective is rare, whereas interacting with people is frequent.

Nevertheless, most organisations are made up of people working towards goals of various kinds. Those people sometimes do take decisions and also spend much of their time with other people in trying to achieve those goals. To this end, they establish policies and devise rules, which they then attempt to enforce and implement. It would be extremely foolish to argue that management is wholly about decision making and control, but some of it is and it is to these two aspects that a modelling approach can make a very useful contribution.

Decisions

A decision needs to be made when an individual, a group or whatever faces a choice in which there is more than a single option. The range of possible options might be small, or it might be near infinite. An example of the former might be the decision about whether a confectionery product is priced at 40p or 50p. An example of the latter might be the exact target weight of the pack (assuming that this is not specified in weights and measures legislation). Decisions are further complicated when they turn out to be a sequence of decisions, each of which affects subsequent options. The armoury of management science has many weapons to use in fighting this particular modelling battle. Parts II and III of this book are devoted to descriptions of some of these weapons. Some of them are based on mathematical and logical models, others are ways of helping people to think through the consequences of situations as they interpret them. As will be made clearer in later chapters, there is no need to assume that a narrow view of rationality dominates organisational decision making; the point of a model is to explore what might happen if a particular decision were to be taken. Similarly, it is not necessary to assume that decisions happen in an instant after massive and purposeful deliberation; they can occur as streams of issues are dealt with over time (Langley et al, 1995).

Control

Control is related to decision making. Often, making the decision is the easy bit! What is much harder and takes much more time and energy, is getting a decision fully implemented and then managing the continued operation of the new system. In most organisations, whatever their type, this involves a process of persuasion, consultation and argument, which can be very time-consuming. It also involves battling with the changes in the rest of the world as they occur during implementation and ensuring that the decisions taken are still sensible in the light of those changes.

For example, analysis via a model may make it clear to a group of senior managers of a supermarket chain that it would be best to concentrate their delivery system around a small number of large depots. The problem is that they currently operate with a larger number of small depots and the transition will take time. In addition, the staff in some of the smaller depots are likely to lose their jobs and so are unlikely to be co-operative in implementing the changes. The implementation of that decision, therefore, is likely to be a fraught process involving many meetings, some formal and some informal, some arranged ahead of time, others on the spot. People will need to be persuaded, to be enthused and may need to be rewarded in some way for their co-operation. All of this takes time and all is part of the day-to-day life of management.

As an analogy, consider again the task of the pilot of a long-haul aircraft. The flight may be about 14 hours non-stop, but the pilot (with computer assistance) must file a flight plan specifying the intended route and expected timings—all in advance. This is done with the aid of computer-based models of aircraft performance, computerised navigation systems and computer-based weather forecasts. This supporting technology is designed to make a difficult decision as straightforward as possible. Yet the pilot knows very well that it will be an extremely unusual flight if changes are not made to the plan en route. Winds may be unexpectedly strong, there may be air traffic control problems or the plane may be rerouted to avoid turbulence. This does not mean that the original plan is a waste of time; rather it means that the plan serves as a basis for control against which progress can be measured.

Control systems are usually based on the idea of feedback as shown in Figure 1.4. This diagram shows a mechanism controlled by the detection of its performance which is then fed back and compared with some target level of performance. This concept, though mechanistic in appearance, may also be used at a conceptual level to think

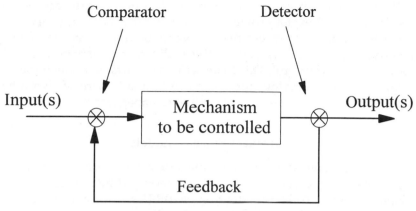

Figure 1.4   *A feedback system*

about control within organisations. Most often the feedback is negative, that is, differences between the target value and the actual are used to guide the system towards its target. Thus if the airline pilot realises that the plane is ahead of schedule, then the air speed can be reduced to bring the flight back on to schedule.

Control systems depend on the availability of information about system performance which is fed back to a manager, who is able to compare it with what is wanted and change the system's performance as necessary. In doing this, organisational managers are using models (often implicit) about what is likely to happen if they take certain action. For example, they may believe that increasing the shelf space devoted to soft drinks in a supermarket may increase sales of those drinks. If increasing sales of those drinks is one of their aims, then making such a change may seem a reasonable thing to do. But a formal and explicit model of the link between sales and shelf space would be so much more useful than a set of hunches for exercising this control.

SOFT AND HARD MODELS

Few people would disagree with the notion that some kind of formal model is involved in most management science, but many books on operational research or management science imply that only mathematical models are of interest. One of the aims of this book is to demonstrate that successful management science involves the use of other types of formal model, as well as those which are mathematical in their form. Mathematics and mathematical models are very useful, and Part III will explore some aspects of their construction and use. But it is important to realise that the value of models and modelling approaches extends way beyond the realm of mathematical models for decision and control. This issue will be discussed in much greater detail later, but some mention needs to be made here of two other types of model which are of great value in management science.

Business Process Models

Recent years have seen an increasing interest in business processes, especially in business process re-engineering (BPR) (Hammer and Champy, 1993). To some extent, such BPR is just another fashionable term for taking a fundamental look at the way a business operates—not a new idea. Yet there are some new emphases that are to be much welcomed in BPR. The first is the view that managers need to focus on business *process* as well as business *structure*. A process is a set of dynamic activities needed to get something done that will add value in the business. Thus the concern is not so much with questions such as "What departments and managers do we need to serve our customers?", but with ones such as "What tasks must we do in order to serve them?" The stress is on verbs rather than on nouns, on actions rather than on static systems, on processes rather than on structure.

These ideas are in vogue because changes in technology have made it possible to imagine ways of carrying out tasks that are radically different from the ways in which they were done in the past. For example, a national post office operates regional sorting centres in which mail is sorted for subsequent distribution. In most countries, addresses have associated postcodes or zip codes to aid this sorting and distribution. One remaining problem, however, is that many envelopes are hand-written or poorly typed and high-speed character recognition systems cannot be used to sort these automatically. People are employed to mark these envelopes with machine-readable codes to enable automatic sorting. The traditional approach to this task is to employ a number of these coders in each sorting office, but modern technology means that by using video cameras and remote keyboards, these coders could be located almost anywhere in the world. Hence shifting workloads might draw on variable pools of labour. The shifted process still involves people reading hand-written codes and marking them with machine-readable ones. This process is needed at the moment. But the changes in technology allow the process to be shifted in space (to another location) or in time (to another time zone).

Before such a process is re-engineered in this way it makes great sense to model it in order to discover the essential and sensitive components where improvement will make a difference. As another example, insurance companies in the UK must meet certain deadlines in responding to requests and in allowing leeway on contracts for different types of insurance. When launching new products, which these companies do surprisingly often, they need to plan staffing levels and computerised support to meet these legal requirements. In order to be able to operate quickly in the marketplace, the companies need rapid ways to assess the likely support levels needed to service a product. To this end they have started to use computer-based simulation models as an aid to this business process engineering (not re-engineering this time) (for an example of this see Davies, 1994).

Soft Models in Management Science

Whereas the affinity between business process modelling and the models used in engineering may be fairly clear—indeed the term "re-engineering" in BPR gives much of the clue—other types of much less concrete modelling are also carried out under the management science banner. A detailed treatment of these appears later in the book, but some discussion is important here so as to set things in context. These approaches are usually known as "Soft OR/MS"—Operational (or Operations) Research/Management Science—and they have a number of features distinguishing them from decision modelling, control modelling and business process modelling. Most of them are intended to aid in strategic management and planning, which has a number of distinctive features.

A strategic decision is one that will have a large effect on the continued survival of the organisation. Indeed, it could be argued that the development of a strategy is an attempt to take control of the future by managing or creating that future. Strategic decision making is rightly considered to be complex, and this complexity has a number of different dimensions:

- A huge quantity of both quantitative and qualitative data and information which could be considered. This does not mean that such data are immediately to hand, but that it is easy to conceive of huge amounts of data that one or more participants might consider to be important. Usually the available data is incomplete and may be ambiguous in its interpretation.
- Considerable confusion and lack of clarity about problem definition except at the basic level (we want to continue to exist). This

stems from disagreement and uncertainty about what should constitute legitimate issues for inclusion in the decision making.

● The different participants who make up the strategic team may have conflicting objectives and may be in direct opposition to one another. Within this conflict, power relationships are important and need to be considered if any kind of negotiated consensus is to be reached.

The aim of soft OR/MS is to explore the disagreements and uncertainties that exist so that an agreed consensus and commitment to action can be reached among the senior management team. In such approaches, the modeller must act in a facilitative role and cannot take for granted that the participants share the same view about reality and must, instead, work with the perceptions of those who are involved. The resultant models are used to show the consequences of these different perceptions and the relationships between them. This allows for exploration of areas in which consensus and commitment to action may be possible. A good introduction to these methods is given in Rosenhead (1989).

Part II of this book is devoted to some of these "soft" methods, which will be summarised as interpretive approaches. This is because they are attempts to enable people to understand how other people interpret their experience and what is happening. It is commonplace that different people at the same event may interpret it in quite different ways. Take, for example, the case of a scandal within the Church of England over a radical church in the North of England whose vicar is accused of the sexual abuse of women from the congregation. There were calls for an inquiry to uncover how this could have happened and to suggest what might be done to prevent this happening again. Interviewed on TV, the bishop in whose diocese the church was located said, in all sincerity, that there could be no point in such an inquiry as everything was known already. This did not satisfy those who were calling for the inquiry. Why should this be? One possibility is that those calling for the inquiry do not believe the bishop and his colleagues know all there is know about what happened. More likely it is because the bishop and those calling for the inquiry interpret its purpose in quite different ways. The bishop may well be logically correct to say that it would uncover nothing new; on the other hand, setting up the inquiry will show that the issue is being taken seriously. The two parties interpret their reality very differently, even without accusing one another of lying or of distortion.

In contentious areas of life and in strategic management, such differences of interpretation are not unusual. Part II shows that these interpretations can be modelled and can be used to help people find enough agreement and consensus to agree to action. Of course, in one sense any model can represent only a perspective on what is happening and, as mentioned earlier, different perspectives will lead to different models. The interpretive approaches are distinctive because they are deliberately designed to work with multiple interpretations and aim to make use of these differences. By contrast, though quantitative models do embody different perspectives they are usually not, of themselves, multifaceted. Multiple quantitative models can be used but this is rarely a deliberate strategy. It is an essential part of interpretive approaches.

SUMMARY—MODELS AS TOOLS FOR THINKING

In an increasingly complex and interconnected world it seems vital that we find ways to explore the possible consequences of decisions and plans before taking any action. One way of doing this is to use an approach that is based on external and explicit models that capture the essence of some situation. The models are simplifications, abstractions of features deemed to be important, and there can be no guarantee that they will be valid. But, used sensibly, models and modelling approaches provide one way of managing risk and uncertainty. In this sense, models are "tools for thinking". Just as hand and power tools add to the physical power and aptitude of humans, so these tools for thinking may be used to add leverage to human thought and analysis. But there are some obvious dangers.

The first is summarised in the anonymous comment that "if the only tool you have is a hammer then you tend to treat everything as if it were a nail". In Birmingham in the West Midlands of the UK (known as Brummagen to locals, or Brummies) a common joke is that a hammer is a "Brummagen screwdriver". The idea being that screws can always be hammered into place if you can't be bothered to do the job properly. The result is that the assembly looks OK at first, but the problems come later. In a similar way, models may be grossly misused in the name of OR/MS and there are no substitutes for intelligence, humanity and intellectual rigour in developing appropriate models and in using them properly.

The second is the danger of "nothing-but-ism". As has been repeated many times in this chapter, models are simplifications and that is part of their power and attraction. There are therefore always things missing from a model and the analyst and those using the models need to be well aware of this. Even if the model is substantially valid for the task in hand, there may be things missing from it that mean that analysis based on it can be safely and sensibly ignored. As used in OR/MS, models show the rational and logical consequences that are known or expected to follow from certain actions. Given that reality is multifaceted, then a model and its results should be as open to question as any other product of the human mind.

Despite these dangers, models within OR/MS have much to contribute to improving the worlds in which we live. The rest of this book aims to give sensible advice about how they can be built and how they might be used.

REFERENCES

Ackoff R.L. and Sasieni M.W. (1968) *Fundamentals of Operations Research.* John Wiley, New York.

Checkland P.B. (1981) *Systems Thinking, Systems Practice.* John Wiley, Chichester.

Davies M.N. (1994) Back-office process management in the financial services—a simulation approach using a model generator. *Journal of the Operational Research Society,* **45**, 12, 1363–73.

Doyle J.P. (1992) William of Occam. In *Software Toolworks Multimedia Encyclopedia.* Software Toolworks, Novata, Cal.

Fortune J. and Peters G. (1995) *Learning from Failure: The Systems Approach.* John Wiley, Chichester.

Hammer M. and Champy J. (1993) *Re-engineering the Corporation.* Nicholas Brealey, London.

Langley A., Mintzberg H., Pitcher P., Posada E. and Saint-Macary J. (1995) Opening up decision making: the view from the black stool. *Organizational Science,* **6**, 3, 260–79.

Mintzberg H. (1973) *The Nature of Managerial Work.* HarperCollins, New York.

Ritchie C., Taket A. and Bryant J. (Eds) (1994) *Community Works.* APVIC Publications, Sheffield.

Rosenhead J.V. (1989) *Rational Analysis for a Problematic World.* John Wiley, Chichester.

Simon H.A. (1976) From substantive to procedural rationality. S.J. Latsis (ed.) *Method and Appraisal in Economics.* Cambridge University Press, Cambridge.

Zeigler B.P. (1984) *Multi-faceted Modelling and Discrete Event Simulation.* Academic Press, New York.

2
Management Science—Making Sense of Strategic Vision

BACKGROUND

Chapter 1 discussed why management scientists build external and explicit models. The main reason is to support decision making and control within organisations, by helping people to see the possible consequences of their actions. The models may employ mathematics and statistics and they are an attempt to bring reason to bear on complex issues. But what do we mean by "reason" in this context? A popular book on soft OR is entitled *Rational Analysis for a Problematic World* (Rosenhead, 1989). This implies that these methods are based on a rational approach in a world that may not be wholly straightforward. This chapter will explore what might be meant by "reason" and "rationality" in an attempt to point out some of the pros and cons of using models within management science. It will do so by using ideas developed by Simon in his work in economics, psychology and artificial intelligence and laying these alongside the work of others, such as Mintzberg, who argue that factors other than reason need to be considered.

RATIONAL CHOICE

Some people see management science as a form of decision modelling that is an extension of managerial economics in which optimal choices need to be made between competing alternatives. That is, they argue that management science is an attempt to support rational choice. A concise description of this view of rational choice is given by Simon as follows:

The most advanced theories, both verbal and mathematical, of rational behaviour are those that employ as their central concepts the notions of:

1. a set of alternative courses of action presented to the individual's choice;
2. knowledge and information that permit the individual to predict the consequences of choosing any alternative; and
3. a criterion for determining which set of consequences he prefers.

In these theories rationality consists in selecting that course of action which leads to the set of consequences most preferred. (Simon, 1954)

The value of the various outcomes needs to be measured consistently and the term "utility" is commonly used in the economics and psychology literature for that purpose. Utility is some measure of welfare or of value. For the time being we will leave aside the question of how this is to be computed, though, as we shall see later, this is an issue of some importance. The decision criterion (item 3 in Simon's list) usually has two parts:

- a statement of the utility measure which will be employed
- a statement of the selection mechanism, such as choosing the most profitable or the cheapest.

Another view of the same approach is given in Figure 2.1. The ellipse depicts the environment within which the decision making

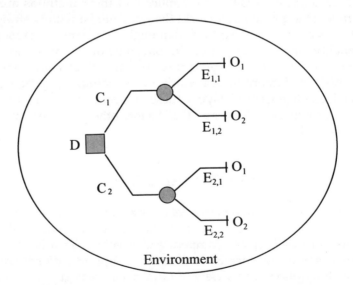

Figure 2.1 *The basic idea of classical rational choice*

process occurs. In the simplest case, as depicted, there are at least two possible courses of action (C_1 and C_2) open to the decision maker, D. In the simplest case, each of the courses of action could lead to an outcome which is desirable (O_1) or undesirable (O_2). The task of the modelling is to establish the relationships (E_{ij}) which exist between the courses of action (C_i) and the outcomes (O_j). In effect, these E_{ij} values reflect the efficiency of each choices in leading to each outcome. Some choices are more likely to get to a particular outcome than are others and therefore their E_{ij} values will be higher. For present purposes we can ignore the question of how these E_{ij} relationships can be obtained or approximated in some way or other, but this is another question which must be faced at some stage. There is no need for D to be a single decision maker, provided there is agreement among participants about the various C_i, E_{ij} and O_j values and variables. Obviously, there can be many more than two courses of action (that is, $i \geqslant 2$) and the outcome set may be rather more sophisticated than just a simple division into those which are acceptable and those which are not.

Without too much imagination it is possible to see Figure 2.1 as a form of road map or maze in which the aim is to get from one end to the other. Indeed, this notion of decision making as navigation across known terrain is, as will become clear, very pervasive. Some people refer to this view of decision making as sequential search.

A Simple Investment Decision

A simple example that fits this set of assumptions would be a straightforward choice between two alternative investments that allow you to place some cash on deposit for a known period of time. Suppose that you could place £1000 with the Reliable Bank or with the Trusty Building Society and that both institutions are guaranteed by the government should they get into difficulties. Suppose too that Reliable offers a compound interest rate of 7.5% p.a. and Trusty offers 7.0% p.a., both rates guaranteed for two years and that no other investment is available. A straightforward appli-cation of the theory of rational choice would lead you to invest your £1000 in the Reliable Bank. This fits the notions listed by Simon as follows:

1. There is a known set of choices—three in fact:

    - Do nothing.
    - Invest in Reliable Bank.
    - Invest in Trusty Building Society.

2. We have complete knowledge and can predict the consequences of each option:

   - Do nothing: producing £1000 after two years.
   - Invest in Reliable Bank: producing $£1000.(1.075)^2 = £1155.6$ after two years.
   - Invest in Trusty Building Society: producing $£1000.(1.07)^2 = £1149.0$ after two years.

3. The criterion of choice is clear: select the investment that produces the best return after two years—the Reliable Bank.

Hence, in simple cases of this type, there is little doubt that classical rational choice is a useful approach to adopt.

At the risk of labouring the point, it is important to see the how the assumptions and the example are well suited to one another. First, the set of options is relatively small and is fully known—not only now, but over the full two-year period of the intended investment. Secondly, the consequences of each option are known and are subject to no variation whatsoever—the return is fully guaranteed and will not change. Thirdly, the decision criterion is entirely unambiguous and can be directly applied by computing the promised returns over the known time period. Clearly such an approach could be entirely automated on computer and this would be wholly satisfactory if its assumptions held.

Relaxing the Assumptions

Each of these assumptions could be relaxed without entirely invalidating the classical rational approach. Considering each in turn:

1. The set of choices need not be small—computers are capable of analysing millions of choices if this is necessary. The set could even be infinite over a known range, such as when there is a need to decide how much to invest. The range might be from zero up to many millions, with every possible value in between. Such cases can be modelled by a continuous variable over that known range. This is the basis of mathematical programming models (see Chapter 8) and other optimisation approaches.
2. The information and insight needed to predict the consequences of each of the options need not be immediately known or available. Within management science much modelling effort goes into attempts to make these predictions by developing models that link options to consequences by establishing the Es (efficiencies of

choice) of Figure 2.1. This may involve the use of statistical forecasting techniques, of scenario analysis, of computer simulations or other techniques from the standard tool kit of management science.

3. The decision criterion applied need not be a simple single dimension variable; a multi-criteria choice could be made. That is, attempts could be made to find the option that does best against a whole range of criteria and, sometimes, this turns out to be possible. For example, it may be important to the investor that the investment produces a high return and is made with an ethical institution. Sometimes, both criteria can be satisfied by the same choice. A further refinement, which links this notion and also the second one, occurs when the consequences of an option are uncertain and the choice must then be made on the basis of *expected utility*. In these cases, probability theory may be brought to bear on the problem and the choice is then made on the basis of what is *expected* to produce the best outcome, though there is no guarantee that this expectation will be met. This is known as *risky choice* (Slovic, 1990) and implies that objective probabilities are known. This idea can further be refined when there are only subjective views of likely outcomes, and in such case the concern is to maximise the *subjective expected utility*. As we move from utility to expected utility to subjective expected utility, the computations grow more complicated, but the basic idea is the same.

Thus the simple classical and rational approach most certainly has its place within management science. Its application has been advocated since the early days of the subject. As an example, see Ackoff and Sasieni (1968) who, like many others at that time, suggested that modelling of this type requires the analyst to establish and to link the following:

- The set of alternative courses of action (often known as the controllable variables).
- The set of other variables relevant to the issues under consideration (often known as the uncontrollable variables).
- Some form of decision criterion which is consistent and which permits the model to be used so as to select the most appropriate course of action.

Modelling proceeds as the analyst attempts to link these sets of variables together to show their effects in terms of the decision criterion. Their suggestion fits rather well with the notions of rational choice shown in Figure 2.1. To illustrate this point, consider the following short case study, which will be used at various points in the book. As the chapters unfold, the case will be used in different ways to develop the later ideas of the book.

CASE STUDY: TICTOC

HOSE BY ANY OTHER NAME

The InCorporated Transitanian Oil Company (TICTOC) was formed around 1980 when the Transitanian government completed its ten-year programme of nationalising the oil companies engaged in extracting its oil. The oil comes from wells on the mainland and is piped directly to the supertanker port at Ventry. Here it is either refined or shipped to the consumer countries as crude oil. The Ventry port installations are controlled by TICTOC.

YOUR ROLE

You are part of a Management Science project team and are employed by TICTOC. You have just attended a meeting that may lead to a management science study. The meeting will be reconvened tomorrow so that you may sketch out your proposals for work that you believe to be worthwhile.

BACKGROUND

Today's meeting was with the Director of Port Services (DPS) at Ventry, the Controller of Pumping Operations (CPO) and the Maintenance Manager (MM). You discussed the pumping of crude oil from the Ventry storage tanks into waiting tankers. The technology used is fairly standard and involves sections of flexible hose about one metre in diameter which connect the Ventry tanks, via pumping stations, to the tankers in the harbour. Because of tidal rise and fall, the hoses are subject to shearing and twisting forces of some magnitude and this sometimes causes the hoses to fail in service. When this happens there is a large spillage of crude oil until the pumps are switched to auxiliary hose lines.

Until recently, the hoses have been bought from a UK supplier who claims to sell the best available hoses. This supplier, UKHose PLC, was the originator of these flexible hoses and has been selling its current range of hoses for about ten years. The original Ventry pumping installation was bought from UKHose and, until now, the same company has provided replacements as necessary.

Over the last two years, two new suppliers of large flexible hose have appeared. YankHose is from the USA and JapHose is from Japan. Both companies claim that their hoses are at least as good as the UKHose product—though their production technology is somewhat different and allows them to undercut UKHose prices by up to 40%. New ancillary equipment may be needed to adapt pumping operations away from the UKHose product.

The Director of Port Services is very keen to reduce his costs and has insisted that one of the pumping stations is switched to JapHose for a trial period. There have been problems during this trial and the Controller of Pumping Operations is unhappy about what he feels is a much higher rate of failure in service than was the case with UKHose products. At one stage in the meeting, the conversation went something like this:

DPS: … Yes, I know that the hoses seem to fail a bit more often, but look at the price. We save 40% on the prices charged by UKHose. I'm not bothered about shorter service lives with that reduction.
CPO: Even if the life is only 50% of UKHose?
DPS: Come on! It's much higher than that.
MM: Well, I'm not too sure about that. But I don't really know what the failure rates are. I'm sure that we could improve things by better maintenance.
CPO: But if we stop the pumping just for preventive maintenance then it costs money. There's all the demurrage to pay to the tanker owners for a start.
MM: It's still cheaper than having a hose blow oil all over the harbour when it fails. Then we *still* have to stop pumping, but we also have to replace the hose section. Then we have to clean up the harbour. We also have the Greens on our backs about pollution. I'm sure that better maintenance is the answer.
DPS: But it all costs money. There must be some way to work out what to do. What about you whiz kids in the MS Division, do you have any ideas?

APPLYING CLASSICAL, RATIONAL ANALYSIS TO TICTOC

Following the usual advice, the first task is to identify the variables relevant to the issues being faced. The primary issue of choice is the selection of flexible hoses to be used at the Ventry installation of TICTOC. An attempt to divide the various factors and variables into those that are controllable by TICTOC and those that are not reveals another issue. We need to decide which person's or group's perspective will determine whether a variable or factor is controllable or not. In this case it seems straightforward enough: you are the management scientist and the problem has been posed by the Director of Port Services (DPS) at Ventry whose perspective should therefore be taken. That is, to use common terminology, we will treat the DPS as the client for this study.

Options or Controllable Variables

There would appear to be two sets of options:

- The type of hose selected: UKHose, JapHose or YankHose.
- The maintenance policies applied to the hoses once they are in use.

That is, the decision problem is to select a hose type and to decide what maintenance it should have when in service.

Uncontrollable Variables

The most important of these would seem to be the following, bearing in mind that their identification here does not guarantee that we will be able to evaluate them:

- The expected life of the different types of hose; this may be expressed as a probability distribution.
- The likely purchase price of the hoses.
- The likely costs of spillages, should they occur; this may also be expressed as a probability distribution.
- The costs of the different maintenance policies.

Decision Criterion

Taking the perspective of the DPS at Ventry it seems as if the main idea is to control costs while still providing an adequate service to the tanker operators. Hence the problem resolves to one of cost minimisation. That is, some solution must be found to the following:

Minimise(Expected(total cost))

> Where:
> Expected (total cost) = Total [Expected(purchase price) +
> Expected(maintenance costs) + Expected(spillage costs)]

Thus, we need to compute the Expected(total cost) for each of the three types of hose, and for each one we need to do this under a range of feasible maintenance policies.

Data Requirements

In the account of the problem given above no data are provided—just as in real life. A basic principle (see Chapter 4) has to be that the model drives the data collection and not the other way round. It is, therefore, important to consider the data requirements for this simple cost model and this will help to illustrate yet more pitfalls that are open to the unwary modeller, even in simple situations.

Hose prices. To simplify matters, assume that the only point at issue here is the actual prices of the hoses and that the same ancillary equipment will fit all three types and also that all three types give identical pumping performance. Even then, the issue may be far from straightforward as there may be no "price list" for such expensive items and, instead, the prices may be negotiated between TICTOC and the hose supplier. Thus even the prices may be uncertain and it may be better to think of Expected(prices).

Expected maintenance costs. A number of factors will determine how easy it will be to get this data. First, are there any proper records of the cost of existing maintenance policies? If so, they may be used to estimate the likely cost of applying similar policies. The complications then begin. Is it reasonable to assume that similar policies will be needed for any type of hose? Probably not if we take seriously the views of the MM: "I'm sure that we could improve things by better maintenance." This means that the apparently simple decision model based on cost minimisation may depend on at least one other model which attempts to show the costs of different maintenance policies.

Expected spillage costs. This will have at least two components. First, some estimate of the likely costs of a spillage—this may be available if such an event has occurred in the past on the Ventry site or elsewhere in the world. The second component is rather more difficult and it concerns the number of spillages likely to occur. That is, some estimate of the life/ failure distribution is needed for each of the three hose types. A further complication is that it seems reasonable to assume that the service lives will depend on the maintenance policies, otherwise there is no point whatsoever in having a maintenance policy. Thus, some model showing the link between maintenance and hose life will be needed.

A further, and hidden, complication is that the hoses in question have service expected lives of several years, making it necessary to estimate long-term costs. This means that price and cost inflation need to be taken into account and also that the timing of various payments also needs to be considered. Thus, some method of comparing costs incurred at different times will be needed, for which one approach would be to use a costing model based on net present values.

Net present value

Net present value (NPV) methods involve a little algebra, but are straightforward in their basic principles. They assume that money can be invested to bring a return, which can be expressed in terms of a proportion or percentage of the capital invested. This represents an interest rate, often known as the discount rate, and the higher the discount rate then the greater the return from the investment. Suppose that we invest an amount P now, at an annual compound rate of interest i. We can compute the value of the investment in one year, two years, three years or n years ahead as shown in Table 2.1.

NPV calculations simply reverse these investment valuations so as to compute the value now of some sum in the future, assuming that any sum available now could be invested at that rate i. Hence, suppose that a sum worth, say, T would be available in n years time, then if T is its value at that time point, its present value (assuming a discount rate of i) is as shown in Table 2.2.

The present values become *net* present values when there are payments in and out to consider, the present value calculation being applied to the net flow of cash at the particular time point. Hence, in the case of TICTOC, it may be possible to compute the net cash flow (net cost) at each year over, say, the next ten. To allow for the time value of money, we then compute the NPV for each of the annual cash values, to bring the whole computation back to today's monetary values. In this way we allow for the fact that cash may be invested elsewhere if not in the hose systems. (This computation would, of course, be completely

Table 2.1   *Investment returns*

Year	Value of P at year n
0	P
1	$P(1+i)$
2	$P(1+i)^2$
3	$P(1+i)^3$
n	$P(1+i)^n$

Table 2.2   *Present values*

Year	Present value of T at year n
0	$T/(1+i)^n$
1	$T/(1+i)^{n-1}$
2	$T/(1+i)^{n-2}$
3	$T/(1+i)^{n-3}$
m	$T/(1+i)^{n-m}$
n	T

inappropriate, if the TICTOC were in an economic system which did not permit or encourage the payment of interest on investments.)

Thus, an apparently simple situation that seems to involve a choice among only three known alternatives can turn out to be more complicated than it would seem at first sight. Nevertheless, with careful analysis along the lines suggested above, it should be possible to analyse the three hose options and their related maintenance policies so as to suggest which type of hose should be purchased. Whether the analysis will be completed in time to be of use is another question.

Later chapters will return to TICTOC to show how other aspects of the decision can be considered by using some of the methods discussed in those chapters. It is clear that the problem as discussed so far is very simplistic. For example, we have taken as given that the viewpoint of the DPS should be given preference over any others and we have also assumed, with very little discussion, that cost minimisation is the agreed aim of the three participants in the discussion.

SOME POINTS EMERGING FROM THE TICTOC CASE

Linked Models may be Needed

At first sight, the issue of hose choice could be resolved by the use of a cost model that could make use of existing, or easy to obtain, cost data. The resulting computations would also be straightforward and could be based on a simple spreadsheet. However, there were complications lurking underneath because much of the data are unlikely to be available and also much of the data are not just single point estimates but are probabilistic. We cannot be sure how long a hose will last in service, even if we have data available to estimate this. It is extremely unlikely that all hoses of the same type will last for the same length of time. All we can say is that there is a probability function which seems to govern the life of a hose of a particular type, and there are likely to be different probability functions for each of the three hoses. Further, the effect of maintenance on these life distributions needs to be analysed. Thus we find that the simple cost model is like an iceberg in which most of the mass and volume is below the surface—and this is where the danger lies.

Suitable Data may not be Available

Data are rarely presented to us. Normally they must be sought, collected, analysed and carefully considered. Data collected for one purpose may not be suitable for another.

As one example of this hazard in the TICTOC case, consider the issue of the prices of the hoses. It may seem obvious that the prices of UKHose, at least, are known. But this simply may not be true. Prices are often, as mentioned earlier, negotiated and may shift over time. It seems unlikely that UKHose would remain at the same price to TICTOC if the vendors of UKHose start to believe that a small price reduction might win them the order. Most negotiations are based around such beliefs, whether they turn out to be true or false.

As another example, consider the question of the costs of maintenance. Though these may be logged in TICTOC's accounting systems, they may be collected for the purpose of assigning costs to particular pumping contracts or for a payroll system. In either case, assumptions will have been made about what to include and what to leave out in stating the costs. There may be no guarantee that the cost elements included are the ones needed for the purpose of modelling any variations from current practice. For example, the costing system would sensibly include the labour costs in its monitoring of the maintenance system. Some of these costs will be related to the scale of the operation (such as skilled manpower employed directly on the job), but others will be fixed (some office costs, for example). Thus, when modifying current costs to allow for new, possibly higher, levels of maintenance, care must be taken to scale up only the direct variable costs. Other costs, such as that for office space, may be left unchanged unless that cost will change.

Old hands at modelling often make statements such as "If you want data, then collect it yourself." This view does not stem just from world-weariness or from cynicism, but from sensible reflection on experience. Attempting to collect data oneself at least has the advantage that the collector is aware of the accuracy or otherwise of the data and of the ways in which missing data may be synthesised. The increased dependence of most organisations on computer-based information and decision support systems means that the collect-it-yourself approach is becoming increasingly difficult. This is a pitfall of which analysts need to be aware.

Changes Over Time are Important

Most decisions have only a finite life and it may be more important to select an option that appears to be robust and, contrarily, more adaptive than one which is immediately attractive. Robustness (Rosenhead et al, 1972) is the ability of a solution to stand against major changes in circumstances. Adaptiveness is the ability of a solution to be modified, or to self-modify, as circumstances change. Perversely, both attributes are valuable and may be preferable to apparently optimal solutions, which are attractive in the here-and-now but turn out to be dangerous if circumstances change.

CONSTRAINED CHOICE

The discussion so far has assumed that the decision criterion being employed is something simple, such as: maximise expected return over two years. One obvious extension to this is to consider constrained choice; that is, circumstances in which, though there exists a straightforward and agreed decision criterion, there are other aspects to consider as well. This is usually managed by treating the other aspects as constraints which will be applied before the decision criterion. Thus, the basic idea is that all options are assessed first against the constraints. Only from within this set of acceptable alternatives, usually called the feasible set, can the best option be selected by the use of the decision criterion. This is the basic idea of constrained choice.

A Simple Investment Decision Revisited

As a very simple example, consider the investment decision mentioned earlier in this chapter and suppose that it was a little more complicated. Suppose that there are now six possible investments, as shown in Table 2.3, but that you are willing to place your cash only with financial institutions you regard as ethically sound.

Table 2.3   *Six investments*

	Investment	Guaranteed annual return	Ethical status
1	Reliable Bank	7.5%	OK
2	Trusty Building Society	7.0%	OK
3	Nice Investment Trust	6.75%	Unknown
4	Triad Friendly society	10.0%	Awful
5	Mafioso Bank	10.5%	Even worse
6	Ecological Business Trust	7.25%	OK

If you were to ignore the ethical stance of the investments the most attractive is to place your cash with the Mafioso Bank. However, this is clearly unsatisfactory and your feasible set consists of {Reliable Bank, Trusty Building Society, Ecological Business Trust}. Your ethical preferences have been used to reduce the set of options down to a feasible set from which you would select the Reliable Bank if you were to apply your decision criterion of the maximum return over two years. Sometimes, of course, there is no conflict between such concerns—as would be the case if the Reliable Bank were able to offer a rate of 10.5% or more.

It is important to realise that, in any form of constrained choice, the choice is made subject to the constraints. That is, the constraints restrict the choice. This means that the use of the decision criterion (maximum return, in the above example) is subordinate to the constraints (ethical acceptability, in the above example). Only those options or courses of action that satisfy the constraints will be allowed into the feasible set. There are a number of modelling techniques associated with management science that are used to support this form of constrained choice. Two of the most commonly applied ideas are discussed later in Chapters 8 and 10. Mathematical programming methods, discussed in Chapter 8, allow the analysts to express some constrained choice problems in an algebraic form which, with the use of computer packages, can be used to find the best choice. Heuristic methods, discussed in Chapter 10, offer no guarantee that an optimal choice will be made, but they are used to search for acceptable options among the feasible set.

RISK AND UNCERTAINTY

This chapter began by stating Simon's summary of classical rational choice. This was shown to have some application in its immediate

form and also in a slightly relaxed form in which choices are constrained or may be multi-dimensional. A further relaxation of the
assumptions is needed in cases of risk or uncertainty. These conditions occur when no one can be sure that a particular choice will lead
to a particular outcome. For example, there may be no guarantee that
any of the investment options considered earlier in this chapter are
certain. There could even be the possibility that one of the banks
might fail.

To extend classical rationality to cope with such circumstances
involves the realisation that the world is not deterministic. A deterministic world would be one in which precise prediction was possible
because things run like clockwork. This may be true of some mechanical systems, but it is unlikely to be true in complex human systems. To
consider non-deterministic outcomes we must resort to ideas of
probability. That is, we need to estimate how likely it is that a
particular event, or set of events, will occur.

Some writers make a clear distinction between decisions taken
under uncertainty and decisions taken under risk, though both
assume that outcomes are non-deterministic. A risky decision would
be one in which it was possible to know the probabilities of the
different events. An uncertain one would be one in which these
probabilities cannot be known at all. This section follows de Neufville
and Stafford (1971) and regards this as a purely artificial distinction.

Uncertain Decision Making

The distinction between risk and uncertainty is based on an idea that
unless probabilities can, somehow or other, objectively be estimated,
then they should not be used. Most people are happy with the idea that
probabilities can be related to ideas of frequency for events that
happen many times. Thus we might expect that an unbiased coin
tossed 20 000 times (were anyone so patient) would result in
something like 10 000 cases of heads and 10 000 cases of tails. Most
people would not be unduly disturbed if the number of heads was not
exactly equal to the number of tails and would be happy to assume that
the probability of getting a head was the same as that of getting a tail,
i.e. 10 000/20 000 = 0.5. This is a case of a relative frequency argument
for probability. Such an approach is all well and good when events are
repeatable many, many times. However, there are events, in this non-
deterministic world, that may happen only a few times, perhaps only
once. How can ideas of probability be used in these cases?

One response is simply to say that the ideas of probability cannot or
should not be applied to these circumstances. This is the basis of

decision making under uncertainty. In these cases, the suggestion is that a pay-off matrix should be constructed to show the effects (in utility terms) of each choice:outcome combination. As an example, my wife and I have plans to camp on the Welsh coast in a few days time. At the moment, the weather is hot and fine, and has been so for about four weeks, with hardly any rain. When we go camping we can take either a tent with a flysheet, which keeps off the rain, or one without. Tents without flysheets are much quicker to erect and take less space in the car, but if it rains we may get wet, resulting in a very miserable trip. What should we do? This can be expressed in a pay-off matrix as shown in Table 2.4, where the values in parentheses represent the utilities of the four outcomes on some arbitrary scale. Note that this method of calculating a pay-off matrix is purely a way of displaying the perceived consequences of the different options and results.

The basic idea is that the decision makers should scan the matrix and select whatever option seems most appropriate in utility terms. A number of ways of doing this have been suggested, of which the two simplest are the following:

- *Maximin.* This is based on a pessimistic approach to life and suggests that the decision maker should choose the option that will maximise the minimum pay-off. In the above example, this suggests that we should take our flysheet with us.
- *Maximax.* This is based on an optimistic approach to life and suggests that the decision maker should choose the option that will maximise the maximum pay-off. In the above example, this suggests that we should leave the flysheet at home.

Which of these is correct, or might some other approach be better? The answer is that no one knows. What has been ignored is the likelihood of the different events—dry and wet. Extensions to the two

Table 2.4   A simple pay-off matrix

Option	State of nature	
	Dry	Wet
A$_1$ Take flysheet	Stay dry with flysheet (+2)	Stay dry with flysheet (+1)
A$_2$ Leave flysheet at home	Stay dry without flysheet (+3)	Get wet without flysheet (0)

simple Maximin and Maximax criteria involve weighted combinations of the utilities. Perhaps it might be better to use subjective estimates of probability. If we are really unable to say whether dry is more likely than wet, this assumes that they have the same probability.

Subjective Probabilities

Instead of assuming that probabilities are directly related only to the known frequency of events, different approaches are possible. One approach is to assume that a statement about probability relates to our belief and knowledge about events. In fact many of us may make use of this subjective notion even when assigning a probability of 0.5 to an event such as toss of a coin producing a head or a tail. As was mentioned above, 20 000 repeated tosses may not result in exactly 10 000 heads and 10 000 tails. But this may not affect our view that the probability "really is" 0.5. We could support this belief by asserting, "Well we would get the same number if we went on almost forever"—this is the relative frequency argument.

Or, instead, we might say, "I think the coin is unbiased and that the system for tossing it is also fair, therefore we should expect equal probability." This is a subjective approach. Note that "subjective" does not mean "wild", "ludicrous" or "outrageous". It simply relates the probability to our beliefs and to our information. It also allows us to change our estimates as more information becomes available. If a coin is tossed and we seem to get twice as many heads as tails, we ought to be suspicious of the coin or the tossing system and should examine these. We might also wish to revise our estimates of the probability.

Note that this argument implies that such probabilities are statements of knowledge or belief and may thus change if our knowledge improves or if our previous ideas are shown to be false. Thus a probability may be a statement about our relative ignorance of some process or other. For example, it could be argued that the process of tossing a coin is wholly deterministic—it's just that we do not understand the process. It should, for example, be possible to design a machine that could toss a coin in a wholly controlled manner within a static environment such that it would always come down with heads uppermost. In the absence of such a machine, and with our belief that the coin is unbiased we may attach a subjective probability of 0.5 to that outcome.

This same approach may be extended to events about which we have too little information to estimate probabilities in any objective sense or for events that are actually unrepeatable. This is not really very controversial, gamblers do this all the time when considering the odds in some game or race. It is the basis of decision making under risk, which seems to subsume decision making under uncertainty. From now on, the two terms will be used interchangeably. If we are really unable to make any estimates of probabilities, then it would be more honest to make all events equally probable.

Decision Trees

Probability estimates can be used to extend the idea of the pay-off matrix into that of a decision tree. Figure 2.2 shows such a tree for the simple camping decision. Decision trees show two types of node, linked by arcs. Decision nodes are represented by squares, and these represent points at which a decision can be made by the person or group facing the uncertainty and risk. Chance nodes (points of uncertainty) are represented by circles, and these attempt to show the different outcomes that may result from the prior decision nodes. Extra information in shown on Figure 2.2 in the form of the

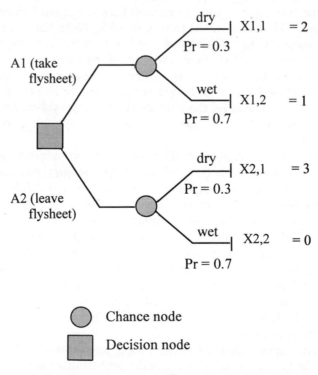

Figure 2.2   *A simple decision tree for the camping trip*

probabilities of the two weather-related outcomes, and these are placed on the arcs that stem from the chance nodes.

It is our view that there is a probability of 0.7 that some rain will fall on the campsite during the weekend, thus we think that the probability of dry weather is 0.3. The probability estimation might be based on a comprehensive analysis of historical and current weather data, or it might be rather more subjective. This form of representation allows us to conduct an analysis based on expected utility.

This type of problem can be expressed in an algebraic form by imagining that there are m possible actions (known as A_1, A_2, A_3, ..., A_m) and that each of them has several (up to n) possible consequences. That is, each action A_j ($j = 1 ... m$) has i consequences X_{ij} ($i = 1 ... n$) which depend on which of the events E_{ij} occur, there being a probability P_{ij} that event E_{ij} will occur. The expected utility of an action A_i is defined as:

$$EU(A_i) = \sum_{i=1}^{n} P_{ij} X_{ij} \text{ for all } j = 1 ... m$$

In the case of this simple example, let $i = 1$ represent taking the flysheet and $i = 2$ represent travelling without one. Thus:

$$EU(A_1) = (0.3) * (+2) + (0.7) * (+1) = 0.6 + 0.7 = 1.3$$
$$EU(A_2) = (0.3) * (+3) + (0.7) * (0) = 0.9 + 0 = 0.9$$

On the basis of expected utility, it would be better to take the flysheet with us this weekend.

Sequential Decision Processes

The same principle can be used to analyse more complex decisions that can be broken down into a sequence of more subdecisions and subevents. For example, suppose that a specialist mail order company needs to decide how to introduce a new item. They have narrowed down their choice to two options:

1. *Include the item immediately in their next catalogue.* This full launch has, they reckon, a 50:50 chance of achieving high sales, which would bring a net income of £500 000. The corresponding low sales from a full launch would bring a net loss of £400 000.
2. *Include the item only in their preview catalogue,* which is sent to a smaller group of customers before the next full catalogue. This test launch also has, they reckon, a 50:50 chance of success. High sales

in the preview catalogue would produce a small net loss of £20 000 and low sales would produce a larger net loss of £100 000. If the product achieves only low sales in the preview catalogue it would be withdrawn and would not appear in the main catalogue. High sales from the preview would lead to its inclusion in the main catalogue and a consequent chance of high sales being 70%. High sales in the main catalogue after insertion in the preview catalogue are estimated to bring a net income of £400 000 (lower than the immediate full launch because of the action of the company's competitors) and a corresponding net loss of £400 000 would result from low sales at this stage.

This problem is displayed in Figure 2.3 as a decision tree. As in the earlier, simpler example, the tree consists of a set of nodes linked by arcs. To analyse such a tree, it is normal to start from the right-hand side and compute the expected values at each chance node. It is assumed that rational decision making still holds and therefore options will be selected on the basis of maximised expected utility. This means that, at each decision node, the forward arc which produces the highest expected utility will be chosen. The usual method of computation is to start at the right-hand side of the tree and work back to each chance node, computing the expected utilities at each. In this example this works as follows, using units of £100 000.

The chance node at a full launch after the preview launch:

$$EU = (0.7 * 400) + (0.3 * -400) = 160$$

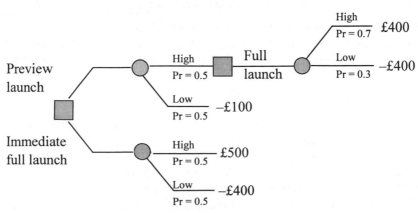

Figure 2.3   *Decision tree for the new product launch*

The chance node at the immediate preview launch:

$$EU = (0.5 * (-20 + 160)) + (0.5 * -100) = 20$$

[Note that the EU of 160 is added to the immediate return of −20]

The chance node for immediate full launch:

$$EU = (0.5 * 500) + (0.5 * -400) = 50$$

Thus the expected return from an immediate full launch is £50 000 and from a preview launch is £20 000. On this basis, the company would be best to make an immediate full launch in their new catalogue.

Some Difficulties

The computations required to use this type of decision analysis to make decisions under risk are simple enough, but the underlying assumptions deserve a brief mention here, for they are crucial. The first assumption is that it is possible to measure the utility of any outcome. The examples above carefully avoided mentioning this issue, but it is very important. If monetary values are being used, this removes one difficulty—though it may simply be untrue that, for an individual, £1 000 000 is worth ten times £100 000. For some business decisions, monetary value will, however, suffice.

When other values are being considered then things are far from simple. There are well-established techniques for attempting to build a non-monetary utility function for an individual (for details see Watson and Buede, 1987). These methods are fine for simple situations whose complication is that people may not have a monetary utility function—for example, a return of £1 000 000 may not be worth ten times a return of £100 000. However, in many complex decisions, it is important to recognise that different people and groups will have different value systems. For example, the approach could be used to investigate the value of a sequence of medical investigations. But who will determine the value of each outcome and on what basis? This illustrates that this type of decision analysis needs to be used with some care. Used sensitively, it can help you see the effects of different utility functions. This then provides a way of exploring people's preferences.

A second problem with this approach is the question of the probability values to be used. Because the events are non-repeatable, there is no empirical way of checking the values assigned to the probabilities. Instead, recourse must be made to subjective probability estimates. This should not, of course, be divorced from past experience, but they are still subjective. As in the case of utility functions, this is not necessarily a bad thing if the approach is used as a way of helping people to think about their views on the likelihood of different events. In the sense that the term will be used in Part II of this book, the approach can be used to help people to "interpret" what is happening or what might happen. A refinement is to use a Bayesian approach (for more details see Raiffa, 1968) which provide a more rigorous framework for the use of subjective probabilities.

A great degree of care is needed in using and interpreting these apparently simple methods. As was stated before, their main value may be in helping people and groups to explore their beliefs and preference systems. That is, their best use may be descriptive rather than normative.

BOUNDED RATIONALITY

So far, this chapter has introduced the classical idea of rationality and has shown how some of its assumptions may be relaxed so as to make the notions more usable. However, there have been many critiques of classical rationality and the rest of the chapter will consider two of these.

Dissatisfaction with approaches based on this classical view of rationality led Simon (1972) to propose the notion of bounded rationality. Awarded the Nobel Prize for Economics, one of Simon's main concerns was to make economics more relevant and useful to the real world. One of his justifications of bounded rationality was that "We prefer the postulate that men are reasonable to the postulate that they are supremely rational". In essence, bounded rationality is based on behavioural notions and upon observations of the ways in which decisions are actually taken in practice. It assumes that human rationality has its limits, especially when operating in conditions of considerable uncertainty.

Substantive Rationality and Procedural Rationality

In developing his case for bounded rationality, Simon (1976) discusses two alternative views of rationality which he terms substantive rationality and procedural (or behavioural) rationality. In Simon's terms, substantive rationality is dominant in classical economics and it corresponds to the basic tenets of classical rational decision making as discussed so far. Behaviour is considered, in these terms, to be substantively rational when it is goal-oriented within limits imposed by some given conditions and constraints. Thus, a substantively rational choice is one which is *the* best way to achieve a given goal. In terms of classical economics and decision analysis, this implies the maximisation of utility, which, as shown earlier, may be extended to allow for risk and uncertainty.

By contrast, procedural rationality is concerned not so much with the outcome of a deliberation but with the nature of the deliberation process. Behaviour is said to be procedurally rational when it results from some appropriate deliberation. Thus the focus is the process of decision making, on how it is done or on how it should be done. In these terms, irrational behaviour is impulsive behaviour that occurs without adequate consideration and thought. Procedural rationality is thus closer to the common-sense view of reason than might be the case with substantive rationality. In these terms, the focus is on developing procedures that may enable people to make better decisions. Thus Simon argues that, to be of use in the real world, discussions of rationality ought to focus on procedural rationality as well as on the substantive rationality that dominates classical decision theory. That is, the stress should be on the process of rational search.

Limits to Rationality

Simon (1976) proposed the notion of bounded rationality, which takes as its starting point a number of assumptions about situations in which decisions may have to be made:

1. In many complex situations there is considerable uncertainty and risk about the consequences of choices that might be made. There are a number of reasons for this. The first is that information about these consequences may simply be unavailable and may have to be forecast or modelled in some way or other. This is obviously an important issue in situations that include consider-able novelty. The second reason is that the actions of other players may influence the consequences of any action. For example, though an action to select a price for a product may seem sensible and may appear to lead to maximum profits, a competitor's promotional activity may negate this pricing policy.
2. In many situations, it is ludicrous to assume that the decision maker has complete information about all feasible options. This is

clearly nonsense for most personal decisions such as marriage or even buying a car. To take another example, buying an air ticket at the cheapest price available to you does not guarantee that you have paid less than the person in the next seat. He or she may simply have had more information than you did, or may have found some way to modify the real world so as to create more options.

3. The complexity of many decision problems means that the actor or decision maker is unable to compute the best course of action, even if all possible options are known. This is due to the limited computational capacity of the human brain. Clearly, the use of computer-based analysis allows this limitation to be pushed somewhat further away than was the case when Simon first proposed bounded rationality.

Because of these limitations and problems, Simon proposed that practical rationality is procedural and is thus bounded. Simon argued that rational choice embodies two aspects; search and satisficing.

Search

In this bounded rationality, one essential component of rational decision making is a systematic search for options which are, it is hoped, feasible. This contrasts with the classical approach, which seems to assume that a full set of feasible options is known at the outset. One implication of the inclusion of search in this view of rational choice is that account can be taken of the costs incurred in making such a search. If the search is sequential—one option after another—there may come a point at which the marginal cost of the search becomes too high. Thus none of us conducts an exhaustive search for a life partner—life is simply too short. We may, none the less, be very happy in our choice!

A second implication of option search is that there may be no need to accept only the set of options that is available and presented at the start of the decision making. When faced with options which we don't much like, many of us will engage in all sorts of behaviours to find ways to improve the set which seem to be available. In the terms of constrained choice, we look for ways to break the constraints that define the feasible set. Thus, people move house or emigrate to find jobs in the hope of a better life when they are unable to find suitable work where they currently live. We may also stall and prevaricate when making hard decisions, trying to make time in the hope that better options may emerge. It is important to note that these behaviours are highly rational in a procedural sense and, indeed, are part of good decision making.

A third implication is that decision making and problem solving can be regarded as a creative process, rather than one that is purely routine and mechanistic. This is because one aspect of decision making becomes the process of generating suitable options worthy of consideration. This can be viewed at two levels. It legitimates the use of creativity techniques such as brainstorming (Evans, 1991), which are ways of encouraging people to generate ideas. It also makes sense of the ways in which managers and other people operate. Few successful managers spend their lives isolated from other people, thinking grand and highly rational thoughts about the world. Instead they are in constant interaction with other people (Mintzberg, 1973, 1989). This is not just because they are social animals; in many cases they are in the process of searching for ways to get things done and are trying to negotiate agreement about what will constitute an acceptable, and satisficing, solution.

Satisficing

The other, better known feature of bounded rationality is the idea of satisficing, perhaps the term most closely associated with Simon in his contribution to management science. The classical approach assumes, in its most sophisticated form, that a decision maker will attempt to maximise subjective expected utility. Instead, a procedural or bounded rationality assumes that people will search for options that appear to be good enough. That is, they have in mind a level of aspiration that defines solutions and options which are not only feasible but are acceptable.

At this point, it might be argued by some that the above account of satisficing is equivalent to optimising within a set of options, the only difference being that the set of options is not believed to be complete. However, this would be to misunderstand Simon's position, for satisficing is related to search. That is, a satisficer will cease to search as soon as the first option to satisfy the level of aspiration is found. In a further refinement, the levels of aspiration may change over time. You may begin your search for a life partner with very unrealistic ideals and may need to temper them over time. In a different context, your unhappy (and squashed) experience in a small car may be acceptable when childless but lead you to look for a larger and more comfortable one when children arrive on the scene. This view of procedural rationality is close to the ways in which a designer may gradually refine a design over time, searching all the while for ways to achieve whatever is required of the design.

As mentioned above when discussing search, the notion of changing levels of aspiration makes sense of the ways in which most of us tend to operate, whether as managers or in other aspects of our lives. As we experience events, meet other people, observe what is happening and interact with the world, our views tend to change and so do our needs. In this way our aspirations may well change, effecting the search process referred to above and also affecting our definition of what may constitute acceptable, and satisficing, solutions. Nevertheless, it is still the case that bounded rationality sees choice as a form of sequential search, but based on satisficing rather than optimising.

PLANNING, INTUITION AND RATIONALITY

So far we have discussed the classical notion of rational choice, seen how its apparently restrictive assumptions can be relaxed, examined two techniques that stem from these assumptions, and looked at the idea of bounded rationality as proposed by Simon. In this way we have placed the use of rational and analytical models in the wider context of rationality. However, it would hardly be reasonable to claim that anybody acts entirely rationally, whether in a bounded sense or in the classical sense, for the whole of their lives. Fans of *Star Trek* will recall that only Mr Spock was able to do this. Acting non-rationally does not necessarily mean that we will make wrong decisions, nor that we are being fools. There is a place in life, and in decision making, for intuition. One advocate of the place of intuition in organisational life is Henry Mintzberg and it is worth exploring his argument in this section.

The Nature of Managerial Work

Henry Mintzberg was originally employed in the Operational Research Branch of Canadian National Railways. He made his academic reputation with a study of the actual working lives of senior managers, which is described in *The Nature of Managerial Work* (Mintzberg, 1973). The main findings of this early empirical research are rather a contrast to the view that senior managers are strategists who spend much of their time engaged in deep rational analysis. It is sometimes suggested that this is what they do when developing and managing strategies that will enable their organisations to prosper. By contrast, some of the findings of Mintzberg's early work in a range of organisations, public and private, in the late 1960s and early 1970s were as follows.

1. Many senior managers work long hours at an unrelenting pace. In discussing this, Mintzberg writes, "One major reason is the inherently open-ended nature of the job. The manager is responsible for the success of his organisation and there are really no tangible mileposts where he can stop and say, 'Now my job is finished.' ... No matter what kind of managerial job he has, he always carries the nagging suspicion that he might be able to contribute just a little bit more." This can seem a never-ending task.

2. Their activity is characterised by brevity, variety and fragmentation. A typical day was composed of many small, short-lived interactions with a few scheduled meetings that occupied much of the day. Though the longer meetings were often scheduled to last more than one hour, the senior manager may choose not to stay for the whole meeting. There was also variety in the tasks performed, which ranged from short phone calls, through unscheduled meetings and conversations, ceremonial tasks such as making long-service presentations, negotiations and action requests. Many of these activities and tasks were fragmented and were sometimes interrupted by other pre-empting tasks. The manager was constantly switching between tasks.

3. The managers in the sample seemed to prefer the more active elements of their workload and disliked tasks such as reading mail and reports even though they might contain "hard" data. They much preferred to spend time searching out current information, which may be "soft"—that is, based on opinion. Recently received "hot" communications would cause scheduled meetings to be rearranged at short notice. This is rather a contrast with the view that such managers are contemplative planners who spend much of their time in the type of rational analysis discussed in the first part of this chapter.

4. Linked to the point about activity, most of the managers seemed to prefer verbal media when communicating with people. Face to face was especially preferred, with phone conversations coming second. (This was before the days of e-mail.) Many of these conversations were informal, with formal meetings being reserved for ceremony (e.g. long-service awards), strategy-making and negotiation, which needed prior arrangement as they often involved many people. The verbal communications were

almost all about gaining and giving information, often soft information.

The picture is of continuous activity, of rapid decisions and consultations with individuals together with longer scheduled meetings that involve many people. Throughout this activity, the manager is continually receiving and sifting information, seeking out that which is relevant now or which might be useful in the future. It is not an image of a life of detached, contemplative reason. Mintzberg's observations, albeit based on a limited sample, shed considerable doubt on the view that management is an inherently rational activity, whether procedural or substantial. Perhaps even bounded rationality may be too idealistic.

The "Crafting" of Strategy

Later work by Mintzberg and his associates explored the process of strategy formation as it occurs within a range of organisation types and sizes. A useful summary of this work is given in *Mintzberg on Management* (Mintzberg, 1989). He argues that many earlier accounts of strategy formation attempt to place it within a strongly rational framework in which options are sought out, compared and then strategy is agreed upon. Such views stress the role of analysis and decomposition in their reliance on formal planning cycles and the development of operational plans from the strategies. They fit well with Simon's notions about search in bounded rationality. Indeed, the search for possible strategies and their subsequent evaluation is a major part of many accounts of what was once known as corporate planning (see, for example, Argenti, 1968).

By contrast, Mintzberg argues that many successful strategies are "crafted" rather than planned. What he means by this is that humans are very adaptive and can be very good at learning from what happens. Thus, strategy formation does not usually take place in some isolated ivory tower where abstract ideas are contemplated. Instead, it takes place in the current context of the organisation, which may include a host of smaller activities, some of which may develop into strategies for the whole organisation. Thus the senior managers of an organisation, as they attempt to think and debate about their strategy, may realise that they have developed some strength and expertise in certain areas of work. That is, small-scale actions from one part of an organisation may start to converge into patterns, which may then become deliberate strategy. The same could apply to external opportunities—they begin as one or more small clouds "no bigger than a man's hand", but the visionary is able to see patterns in their development and may thus develop appropriate strategies.

The term "crafted" is used as a metaphor because it reflects the ways in which, say, a sculptor begins with an idea of what he or she wishes to produce. But the variations in the material and shifts in mood lead to the development of something rather different from the original intention. The final object may be altogether more pleasing than the original idea could have been, because it fits well with the materials and with the developing expertise of the artist. In short, the vision changes because of experience.

This view has a number of interesting implications. The first is that organisations must do their best to preserve and, preferably to develop individuals with creative vision. That is, people who are able to recognise patterns, both in what the organisation already does well and in what seems to be happening elsewhere. In *Contrary Imaginations*, a fascinating book written in the 1960s, Liam Hudson (1967) describes some of his early research into creativity. This led him to suggest that the spectrum of Figure 2.4 could be proposed. This shows two extreme groups of people, with the majority (perhaps 70%) in the unclassified middle. The extreme points are the convergers and the divergers. Convergers are extremely good at analysis and at following established procedures. Divergers are more likely to be good at synthesis, at producing new ideas and seeing new patterns in things. In a prospective study, Hudson found that schoolboys who were convergers tended to study maths and science at university, whereas the divergers tended to follow creative arts and humanities degrees. Management science analysts thus tend to be drawn from the

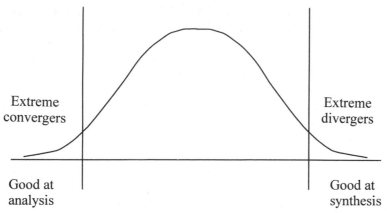

Figure 2.4 *Convergers and divergers*

pool of convergers and this suggests that many will not find it easy to fit roles which require the type of creativity implied by the "crafting" of strategy.

The second implication of crafting is that successful senior managers need deep knowledge, both of their business's internal operations and of the external environment. Useful patterns cannot be imagined if there is no understanding and appreciation of what is happening. Thus the notion that a senior (or any other kind of) manager is likely to be successful without some deep knowledge seems very dangerous. This re-emphasises the need for strategy formation to be an integral part of managerial work at all levels and not some adjunct operation performed by planning professionals. The crafting of strategy is about detecting small changes which may lead to big things, of helping emergent patterns to take a desirable shape.

This does not mean that planning cycles have no place within successful organisations, far from it. But it stresses that classically rational analysis, which tends to dominate formal planning cycles, may not play a major role in strategy formation. Much of the analysis takes place later, when the implications of possible strategies have to be explored, turning hunches into policies and plans. Thus, one role for modelling might be in making sense of the strategic vision which emerges as strategy is crafted. Other chapters of this book, especially those on "soft" management science (in Part II) will have something to say about this.

Intuition and Insight

The third relevant theme in Mintzberg's work stems from an article he wrote for the *Harvard Business Review*, "Planning on the left side, and managing on the right" (Mintzberg, 1976). This argued that, based on then current views of brain physiology, it could be argued that human brains employ two quite separate approaches to processing information. In shorthand terms, these are usually referred to as left and right brain processing. Recent research on brain function (Damasio, 1995) shows this shorthand to be misleading, as brain function appears much more complicated than this, but the ideas are interesting none the less:

Left. This is the type of processing that fits well with the notions of rationality and logic as we have discussed them so far. It refers to linear sequential processing, in which information is processed one bit after another in an ordered way. This occurs much in the same way that speech is linear, with words in a definite sequence.

Right. This is, by contrast, simultaneous processing which seems to be much more relational, more holistic. It refers to the "feeling" side of our natures, in which we sense things and experience emotion. In Mintzberg's terms, it refers to gestures rather than to speech; most of us can gesture simultaneously with our hands and our faces.

Thus, in the sense that the terms were used above, convergers tend to operate on the left and divergers on the right. To quote Mintzberg (1989), "a politician may not be able to learn mathematics, while a management scientist may be constantly manipulated in political situations". There are, of course, many exceptions to this type of generalisation, but there is some truth in it too. Awareness of emotion and intuition, alongside rational analysis, can contribute to better decision making.

Referring back to the section on managerial work, it is clear that many of the actual and preferred modes of operation of the senior managers observed in the studies could be classified as right brain rather than left. So, in the same way, can the talents required to see patterns and to "craft" strategy. On the other hand, the abilities needed to spell out the implications of different strategies may be regarded as left brain rather than right. Perhaps only the rare polymath will be good at both, and this suggests a good reason for teamwork in senior management.

Linking Reason and Intuition

It seems clear that successful management and wise decision making require the dual support of creative intuition and rational analysis. The vexing question is, how can this be achieved? The answer seems to be that neither of the two factors should be abused or downgraded. Someone, probably Russell Ackoff, once wrote that "a difference between managers and analysts was that analysts recognise every value of probability except zero and one; on the other hand, managers recognise only zero and one". Exaggeration though this may be, it does emphasise the importance of partnership in finding ways to help organisations operate more effectively.

An over-reliance on formal reason, as against intuition, can be dangerous and so can the opposite. Sometimes common sense is helpful, sometimes not. As an example, one summer weekend I planned to go hiking in the English Lake District. The previous evening, I phoned the Lake District weather service to listen to their recorded forecast for the following day. It was bad. First thing next morning I phoned again and listened to the update—bad again: rain promised, low cloud and chilly for the time of year. Looking out of our house windows it was a beautiful morning, so I cycled a short distance to a point where I could see the Lake District mountains in the distance. It looked beautiful, the sky was blue, the clouds were sparse and high and the sea sparkled in the sun. I felt good and I suspected that the weather forecast might be wrong. But I'm a rational man and I know that the weather forecast is based on all sorts of clever mathematical models, and I don't trust my feelings. So I stayed home—apparently it was a lovely day in the Lake District! I did make some progress with this book, however.

In the end, the role of analysis can only be to explore the possible consequence of different courses of action. Rational, analytical approaches do not, by themselves, provide direction nor identify alternatives. We can rarely predict, with complete certainty, that events will happen. If we could be sure of the future then there would be no problem, reason and intuition would be happy bedfellows. Perhaps the role of reason is to test out intuition and perhaps the role of intuition is to prevent paralysis by analysis. Intuitive crafting helps to provide direction and vision. Analysis helps to make sense of this vision. Each one places the other in context.

In a fascinating book, Damasio (1995) reviews evidence about brain function based on his own work and that of others, with people whose brains have been damaged in accidents or by illness. He argues that the concept of mind cannot really be separated from the body, and that to think in these terms is to fall into a false dualism. He argues that both reason and emotion/intuition are distributed across several areas in the brain and that together they constitute mind. In particular he quotes a number of sad case histories of people who, after brain damage, had not just their emotions blunted but were also unable to plan, though their day-to-day functioning seemed normal enough. Damasio argues that, in a healthy mind, emotion and reason are strongly linked through the physical body and brain. Effective and thoughtful analysis may then depend on mind, which is also steeped in the juices of emotion.

SUMMARY—MAKING SENSE OF STRATEGIC VISION

Chapter 1 made a case for taking seriously the idea that modelling approaches, as found in management science, can help people to explore the consequences of their actions and decisions. It is some-times assumed that such models must be built and used within a highly restricted view of human action—classical rationality, in which ends are clearly related to means, and in which everything is known. This chapter has pointed out that this classical rationality needs further elaboration before it can be of use. Simon's development of bounded rationality, with its emphasis on the limitations of human action and thought was one attempt to do this. Another was the extension of classical rationality into risky and uncertain decision making. However, these various extensions all seem to treat humans as information processing machines whose capacity may be limited in some way or other.

Alternative perspectives on these same issues were provided by writers such as Mintzberg who emphasise the apparently non-rational side of organisational life. It is clear from his work, and that of others, that people do not operate according to these highly rational models. It might, of course, be argued that people should operate rationally, and that those who do will always win out over those who don't. This is not an argument that will be presented in this book, for to do so would be to miss the most important point. This is that models should be regarded as tools for thinking. They provide ways in which people may reflect on what is proposed and decide whether or not certain things should be done and certain risks should be taken.

A model will always be a simplification of certain aspects of the real world. The next chapter examines how people frame the part of the real world in which they are interested—that is, how people decide what simplification and approximation might be appropriate. Chapter 4 then provides a few principles for modelling, the first of which is "model simple, think complicated". This stresses that the model and its users form a system that can help people to examine the possible consequences of their proposals. In this sense, models should be part of the process of making sense of the strategic vision; they form a link between the intuitive and the rational.

REFERENCES

Ackoff R.L. and Sasieni M.W. (1968) *Fundamentals of Operations Research*. John Wiley, New York.

Argenti J. (1968) *Corporate Planning. A Practical Guide*. George Allen & Unwin, London.

Damasio A.R. (1995) *Descartes' Error: Emotion, Reason and the Human Brain*. Picador, London.

de Neufville R. and Stafford J.H. (1971) *Systems Analysis for Managers and Engineers*. McGraw-Hill, Maidenhead, Berks.

Evans J.R. (1991) *Creative Problem Solving in the Decision and Management Sciences*. South Western Publishing, Cincinnati, Ohio.

Hudson L. (1967) *Contrary Imaginations. A Study of the English Schoolboy*. Penguin, London.

Mintzberg H. (1973) *The Nature of Managerial Work*. HarperCollins, New York.

Mintzberg H. (1976) Planning on the left side, managing on the right. *Harvard Business Review*, July–August, 49–58.

Mintzberg H. (1989) *Mintzberg on Management*. The Free Press, New York.

Raiffa H. (1968) *Decision Analysis*. Addison-Wesley, Reading, Mass.

Rosenhead J.V. (Ed.) (1989) *Rational Analysis for a Problematic World*. John Wiley, Chichester.

Rosenhead J.V., Elton M. and Gupta S.K. (1972) Robustness and optimality as criteria for strategic decisions. *Operational Research Quarterly*, 23, 413–31.

Simon H.A. (1954) Some strategic considerations in the construction of social science models. In H.A. Simon (1982) *Models of Bounded Rationality: Behavioural Economics and Business Organisation*. MIT Press, Cambridge, Mass.

Simon H.A. (1972) Theories of bounded rationality. In H.A. Simon (1982) *Models of Bounded Rationality: Behavioural Economics and Business Organisation*. MIT Press, Cambridge, Mass.

Simon H.A. (1976) From substantive to procedural rationality. In H.A. Simon (1982) *Models of Bounded Rationality: Behavioural Economics and Business Organisation*. MIT Press, Cambridge, Mass.

Slovic P. (1990) Choice. In D.N. Osherson and E.E. Smith (Eds) *Thinking: An Invitation to Cognitive Science*, volume 3. MIT Press, Cambridge, Mass.

Watson S.R. and Buede D.M. (1987) *Decision Synthesis: The Principles and Practice of Decision Analysis*. Cambridge University Press, Cambridge.

3
Problems, Problems ...

MANAGEMENT SCIENCE AS PROBLEM SOLVING?

The opening chapter of this book was a general introduction to modelling in which it was argued that, carefully used, even simple models can be of great value in helping people to manage in today's complex world. Models, as used in management science, are ways of applying rational analysis to complex issues, and hence Chapter 2 focused on the meaning of rationality and tried to locate the role of reason in decision making. With this background behind us, it is now time to think about problems and problem solving. This is because, to many people, management science is a rational attempt at problem solving. Hence it is important to understand what we mean when we use the word "problem". As will become clear in this chapter, people use this term in different ways and this can cause some confusion.

At one extreme, this is seen in the view that the main role of management science analysts and groups is to "solve managerial problems", whatever form these might take. On another dimension, it is common to hear management scientists speak of "an interesting distribution problem" when referring to work on the physical movement of goods. Another example would be when people speak of "a linear programming problem". The word "problem" is being used in three different ways here, and there are many others ways in which it could be used. What these different usages have in common, however, is the idea that problems exist and that they can be solved. The idea of solution also carries with it the notion that, once solved, a problem stays solved. As will become clear later, this particular notion of permanent solution can be very dangerous and should be avoided. The purpose of this chapter is to consider these ideas and to develop them into something which is more useful and which is intellectually defensible.

PROBLEMS, PUZZLES AND MESSES

The starting point will be to explore, in a little detail, what might be meant by the idea of a problem, especially as this is used in management science. This discussion is based on the views of Ackoff (1974, 1979), who distinguishes clearly between problems and messes. As shown in Figure 3.1, this idea can be extended to three points on a spectrum: puzzles, problems and messes, each being intended to depict a different way in which people use the word "problem". These, however, are not the only ways—they serve as archetypes on the spectrum of possible uses. Each of the three have in common the notion, made explicit in Chapter 2, that the concern is with situations in which one or more choices must be made, often in conditions of uncertainty and risk.

Puzzles

In these terms, a "puzzle" is a set of circumstances in which there is no ambiguity whatsoever once some thought has been given to what is happening or needs to be done. The issues that need to be faced are entirely clear, the range of options is completely known and there exists a single correct solution to the puzzle. Thus, in the terms which will be used later, the puzzle is fully structured and it is possible to be sure that a solution to the puzzle is correct once it has been found. The term "puzzle" is used here because common parlance refers to crossword puzzles and jigsaw puzzles. These are exercises with well-understood structures and, usually, a single correct solution. This

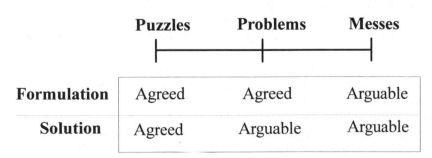

	Puzzles	Problems	Messes
Formulation	Agreed	Agreed	Arguable
Solution	Agreed	Arguable	Arguable

Figure 3.1   *Puzzles, problems and messes*

contrasts with open-ended tasks in which a multiplicity of approaches are possible. There may be various ways in which a crossword puzzle can be attacked, but the definition of the puzzle is complete and there should be only a single correct solution. The same is true of a jigsaw puzzle; some people start with the edges, some start in the centre and others start with the corners—but there is only a single correct solution. With this in mind, people who have studied mathematics will recognise that when they were told to "complete all the problems on page 42" or to "have a go at this problem sheet", they were being asked to engage in a puzzle-solving activity. In most cases, the problem sheet contains a set of similar puzzles, usually getting harder as the student works down the page. The idea is to give practice in the use of particular methods and to help students to generalise their use.

If their maths is less than perfect, such students may find them-selves turning to the back pages of the textbook in the hope of finding the answers. They are likely to be upset (and confused!) if those model solutions turn out to be wrong, as sometimes they do. Why should they be upset? There seem to be two reasons for this. The first is due to their inevitable disappointment after putting in a lot of hard work. The second that we expect puzzles to have a single correct solution and if something which purports to be such a solution turns out to be wrong, then this can cause great frustration. Most of us can often learn quite a lot by trying to work back from the given answer, if it is correct, to the question. Indeed, this is one of the strategies suggested by Polya (1957) in his book on problem solving in math-ematics and also by Wickelgren (1974).

This account of the nature of puzzles is not meant to imply that they are always simple to solve. Sometimes they are, but setters of exam papers are quick to learn how to devise puzzles that will stretch their students, whether these are first graders or postgraduates. So puzzles are not necessarily easy, but they are solvable and the correctness of the solution can be demonstrated. There may even be several different ways to get from the puzzle as presented to the correct solution. I well recall, at the age of 12, taking a geometry exam in school and being faced with the need to prove a small theorem and being totally unable to recall how to do it. In a panic I invoked a theorem which I could prove and tried (unsuccessfully) to get to the result that I needed. Needless to say, my exam performance that day was not good. However, the maths teacher took me on one side and asked how I'd thought of tackling the puzzle the way that I had. At the age of 12 all I could do was blush, mumble and apologise. Later I realised that he was intrigued by my creativity rather than angry, and that he wished to encourage me.

Problems

The middle point of the spectrum in Figure 3.1 is designated as "problems". A problem is more complicated than a puzzle, but less complicated than a mess. This complication stems from the fact that a problem has no single answer that is definitely known to be correct. At the heart of a problem is an issue that must be tackled. As they arise in real-world management science, an analyst is more likely to face a problem than a puzzle. An example might be, "How many depots do we need in order to provide daily replenishment of stocks at all our supermarkets?" As a question, this seems straightforward enough and is relatively unambiguous, however this is just the tip of the iceberg. Such a question, based on an important issue, rarely has a single correct solution, for it depends on how you, or someone else decides to construe it. Thus, for problems, in the way that the term is used here, there may be agreement about the core issue to be tackled but there might turn out to be several, equally valid, solutions.

Consider again the issue of the number of depots needed to service a set of supermarkets. One way of construing this issue might be to reformulate it as something like the following: "Assuming that the depots stay at their current size and the supermarkets do the same, how many depots would we need to meet current demand and to guarantee delivery to the each of the stores within an agreed 30-minute time window each day?" Once formulated in this, much tighter, way there may indeed be only a single correct solution. But to achieve this, a problem, with its core issue, has been transformed (some would say, reduced) to the form of a puzzle. To illustrate this point yet further, an alternative formulation of the problem might be something like: "Assuming that the supermarkets and depots stay at their current sizes and are grouped into regions as now, how many depots would be needed to meet current demand in each region and to guarantee delivery to each of the stores within an agreed 30-minute time window?" Not only is this formulation longer than the first one, it is also a little different. It now includes an extra feature, which could turn out to complicate things or might be a simplification—the depots and supermarkets must have a regional organisation. This presumably implies that a depot in region A will not normally deliver to a supermarket in region B. Needless to say, the second formulation may produce a solution different from the first one.

There is a further reason why problems, as defined here, may lead to a range of solutions that are all acceptable, and this is to do with the approaches taken in working towards a solution. As an example, consider the type of case exercises, often known as Harvard-type cases, with which most business administration students are familiar. When used for teaching, the normal mode of use is to distribute copies of a case to the class in advance of a discussion session. The case papers, which may be 20 or more pages long, give background on a company or market, provide extensive data and pose some issues. Later, possibly the following day, the class will assemble and, under the guidance of an instructor, students will propose approaches and solutions. Clearly, given a range of suggested approaches, some of them will be wrong, but more than one may be plausible. There are likely to be several possible approaches which may be used in sensible attempts to tackle the core issues in the case. Even when people are agreed about how to construe the basic issues, they may employ different approaches in an attempt to solve the problem. This may be due to their backgrounds, to their expertise or whatever. But there may be no real way of declaring one solution to be superior to all others, even after the removal of those which are obviously wrong. This is why the case method is a good way of encouraging discussion in a class of bright students. It is also the reason why the case method of teaching business administration is preferred by teachers who do not regard management as a generalisable science.

Messes

The other extreme point on the spectrum of Figure 3.1 is the "mess", as Ackoff defined it. A mess is a set of circumstances in which there is extreme ambiguity and in which there may well be disagreement. In a puzzle, there is complete agreement about the nature of the puzzle (a single correct definition) and also a single correct solution. In a mess there is a whole range of possible definitions and descriptions of what is going on and there may be no way of knowing whether a solution, as such, exists at all. Some writers (see, for example, Rittel and Webber, 1973) reserve the term "wicked problem" for this idea of a mess. In a mess, there are many issues to be faced, they are interrelated and the interrelationships are often as important as the issues themselves. A mess is a system of problems.

In most organisations, strategic decision making and management is closer to the idea of a mess than to the idea of a puzzle or a problem, as these terms are used here. Strategic decision making is often characterised by ambiguity about objectives (other than survival), uncertainty about outcomes (they may be several years ahead) and great risk if things turn out badly. A strategic decision may be one that puts all, or a significant part, of an organisation at risk. Thus what constitutes a strategic decision for a small company

("Do we move our manufacturing base to this new site?") would be considered tactical to a multinational business such as ICI. This does not mean that the decision is unimportant, simply that its scale and impact do not affect much of the company in the latter case.

It would, however, be a mistake to assume that the notion of "mess" is only of relevance in strategic decision making or analysis. Even in smaller-scale work the notion can apply. Consider again the question of supermarket deliveries. It would be reasonable to ask whether interrelated issues have to be faced. For example, is it likely that the support technologies used in the system will be constant over a reasonable time period? Recent years have seen all large supermarket chains invest heavily in electronic point-of-sale (EPOS) computer systems. These enable the managers to have rapid and accurate information about sales, stocks and receipts. This in turn affects the timing of the reorder cycle and may be expected to alter delivery requirements. As a second example, is it reasonable to assume that the type of goods stocked will be constant over the time period? Again, probably not—in the UK at least. The large supermarket chains tend to stress their fresh goods rather more than in the past; presumably the margins are higher and the goods create a pleasant ambience in the stores. Shifts in the types of goods means different storage and transport requirements. We could also question whether road transport systems will remain constant. Will vehicle sizes change? Will speed limits be reduced? Will maximum driver hours be changed? Finally, are there any new technologies which may shift the whole business? Some US supermarkets allow customers to order via the Internet—what impact might this and other developments have? The list is almost endless.

Note, too, that the various issues over which the basic depot question grows more complicated might depend on one another. This is typical of messes, even in uncontentious areas. Thus, to work with messes requires the analyst to be able to see the links as well as the separate issues. That is, the links may be as important as the separate parts of the mess and these may need just as much attention. One of the greatest mistakes that can be made when dealing with a mess is to carve off part of the mess, treat it as a problem and then solve it as a puzzle, ignoring its links with other aspects of the mess. It is crucial that the various issues are dealt with while keeping a watchful eye on the links to other aspects of the mess.

Issue streams—the dynamics of decision making and action

Further light is shed on the question of messes by Langley et al (1995), who argue that much academic research on organisational decision making has tended to stress either that decision making is highly rational or that it is highly opportunistic. By contrast, they argue, it should be recognised that meetings, discussions and debates within organisations revolve around "linked issue streams". These issues constantly recur over time and are rarely transformed into fully solved problems. Examples might include the following:

- A manufacturing company faces the constant need to keep its costs low and its quality high and consistent. Through time this has been managed in a variety of ways, initially by installing flow-line production and using mathematical stock control models, later by swapping to just-in-time (JIT) systems and so on. Around this quest swarms a number of issues such as stock control, raw material quality, process quality and management, supplies to customers and so on. These issue streams periodically throw up a series of problems such as "Should we integrate with our customers' computer systems and if so, how?", or "How can we run on minimum stocks while product variety is increasing?" Though these issues are resolved for some time, they are rarely solved in any permanent sense.
- A supermarket chain faces the constant need to have a full product offering on its shelves, to provide good customer service, to attract customers, to reduce its stocks and to make a profit. As with the manufacturing example, this throws up a continuing stream of issues through time. Examples might be the extent to which EPOS systems should be installed and used, or the question of how to get stocks from the manufacturer into the stores. At one time or another different approaches will be adopted after careful scrutiny, argument and analysis. Sooner or later these policies will be revised and others will be substituted.
- A health care system faces the need to provide emergency units which deal with walk-in casualties and people brought in by ambulance. Some of the patients may need intensive care requiring highly skilled staff and expensive equipment. Others may need only dressings or even just reassurance. How should this emergency care be provided? Should it be concentrated into a small number of large units, which forces patients to travel but which guarantees access to high-quality care? Or should there be a network of casualty units each of which can send on patients to more remote large units when needed? There is no real answer to these questions, but they must be debated and faced through time. The changes in the external environment such as technology, transport and patients' expectations will all affect what is felt to be

acceptable practice. But this view will probably change as the issues re-emerge from the issue stream.

It should be obvious why this happens. The world that provides the environment for the organisation is constantly changing: new technologies appear, competitors find other ways to operate, consumer preferences alter, and so on. Thus the same basic issues tend to occur, alongside new ones, within any organisation. Hence one of the tasks of managers is to manage these issues and their relationships. In doing so, decisions and actions tend to be mingled and may not be easy to separate.

Langley et al (1995) argue that organisational decision making may usefully be regarded as a dynamic process that emerges from attempts to manage this issue stream. The issue stream itself is a complex network of issues, linked in a whole host of ways and those linkages may result in issues that are tightly or loosely coupled. This view, which stems from organisation theory rather than from management science, fits well with Ackoff's notion of a mess as a system of problems. Whether we choose to refer to issue streams or to messes, it is important to realise that any solved problem remains solved for only a period of time. The process is highly dynamic.

PROBLEMS AS SOCIAL CONSTRUCTS

What should be becoming clear from the discussion so far is that, as they are faced in management science, problems, puzzles and messes are social constructs. That is, like beauty, there is a sense in which they are defined in the eye of the beholder. This does not mean that every aspect of the issues to be faced is within the mind of the analyst or the participants. That a business is heading for bankruptcy or that a hospital is failing to provide adequate response times may be beyond dispute. But the interpretation of those "facts" is less certain. It should, therefore, be expected that different people might interpret the same issues in different ways. Some of these interpretations may turn out to be wrong, in the sense that they cannot be defended, but reality—or people's views of it—turns out to be multifaceted. But there may be several valid views of what is happening and of what might be done about it.

Writing many years ago, John Dewey (quoted in Lubart, 1994) produced the maxim: "A problem well put is half solved." It seems as if he had in mind that a poorly posed problem will be very hard, if not impossible, to solve. If this maxim is combined with the realisation that problems, in organisations at least, are social constructs, then the importance of problem structuring becomes obvious.

CASE STUDY: TICTOC

DIFFERENT POINTS OF VIEW

Chapter 2 introduced the TICTOC case study, which revolved around the selection of replacement flexible hoses to be used to connect ocean-bound bulk tankers to crude oil storage tanks on the mainland. In Chapter 2 we treated this case as an application of the ideas of classical decision modelling. We identified the Director of Port Services (DPS) as the client or decision maker and, from that perspective, developed a cost model. The idea was to select the hose system which produces the lowest total expected cost over some time period. The preceding discussion in Chapter 3 should suggest that far more than this could be read into the text of the case. Some obvious extensions include the following, which stem from the fact that there are others who have stakes in this decision as well as the DPS. This is important, because "the selection process must also consider the distribution of the benefits and costs among the interest groups affected by the project" (de Neufville and Stafford, 1971).

INTERNAL STAKEHOLDERS

Three people, plus you as analyst, are mentioned in the text and each one will have a view about what could or should be done. It may seem obvious that the DPS is the boss, but that does not mean that everyone else's view should be ignored. We might consider why this should be, using the Maintenance Manager (MM) and Controller of Pumping Operations (CPO) as examples. It would appear that the main job of the CPO is to guarantee a continuous flow of oil from the tanks to the ships whenever this is needed. Further, this should be done in a safe way. Thus, from the point of view of the CPO it may be that a hose type that causes minimum hassle would be most desirable. Cost may not be the highest priority from this perspective, though this does not mean that cost is irrelevant. Wearing the MM hat, things may look a little different. Here may be a chance to show just how good the maintenance operation can be and there may also be the chance to boost the department's budget.

Clearly, given the brief account provided in the text of the case, the above comments are speculative, but they are not ridiculous. How then should they be dealt with? The basic principle has to be: *do not ignore these perspectives*. There are two reasons for this and they are linked. The first is that these people may know much more about some of the detailed issues of hose use than the DPS and thus much of the information needs to come from them. The same point relates to a comment made in Chapter 2 about the need for deep knowledge; such knowledge may lie with the MM and CPO rather than the DPS.

The second reason has to do with the implementation of the work if it is successful. Mintzberg (1989, p. 69) comments that management scientists are wont to complain when their recommendations are not implemented. "They have claimed that managers don't understand analysis, ..., that the politicized climates of organisations impeded the use of analysis." If analysis proceeds without taking account of significant stakeholders then it is hardly surprising that people do not co-operate; nor should it be a shock that they use political means to achieve their ends. Thus it is crucial that major internal stakeholders—in this case, the CPO and MM—are involved and consulted.

EXTERNAL STAKEHOLDERS

A fundamental, and often ignored, issue in any analysis is the point at which boundaries or limits are drawn around the mess. Later we shall look at systems approaches, particularly soft systems methodology (Checkland, 1981) to see what contribution they can make to this. In the TICTOC case, it is quite clear that there are external stakeholders who may have some involvement in the decision. Some possible examples are the following:

The tanker operators. They may have experience of collecting and delivering oil from installations elsewhere in the world at which these different hose types are used. It may be important to check on their experience and preferences.
Transitanian politicians. TICTOC is a nationalised company and there may be political pressures to buy hose systems from one country rather than another. This does not imply that TICTOC gives in to these pressures, but they should certainly not be ignored. If a careful analysis shows that a politically undesirable choice is preferable from a business perspective, then a further analysis may be needed to show what would be the financial effect of making the political choice.
The "Greens". Assuming that this label applies to local environmental activists, it may be important to gauge their reaction to the different

proposals. This would be important, whether or not the DPS, CPO and MM regard themselves as having "green" credentials.

Local residents in and around Ventry. Far fetched though it may seem to some, these people might also be regarded as external stakeholders whose views must be accounted for. Some of them will work on the terminal site and any moves to replace substantial pieces of equipment will not pass without comment.

The hose vendors. Bearing in mind the fact that prices for the equipment will be negotiated rather than taken from a published list, the likely behaviour of the suppliers can hardly be ignored.

These groups are not clients or decision makers, but they cannot be ignored if a choice is to be made which boosts TICTOC's effectiveness.

POSSIBLE RE-FORMULATIONS OF THE TICTOC "PROBLEM"

As cast at the moment, this is described as a problem of hose choice, but we know little or nothing about the history of the issue. We do not know why this group, led by the DPS, has decided to search for a possible new supplier of these expensive hoses. It could be pressure from one of the external stakeholders; it might be dissatisfaction with the existing UKHose; it might be that other pressures within the larger TICTOC organisation make it important that something is seen to be done at Ventry. There are a myriad such possibilities and the wary analyst does not ignore them, nor should they necessarily be accepted. They all form part of the "mess" with which we have been asked to work. Later we will make use of some of the "soft" management science techniques in an attempt to explore this a little further.

The use of the TICTOC case here in this chapter is intended to shed some light on what is meant by the idea of problems being organisational constructs. The idea is that "problems" do not exist in a vacuum, but exist in people's minds and relate to their experience of the world and to their expectations.

PROBLEM STRUCTURING

Given that most of the important issues in organisational life emerge as parts of systems of problems, or messes, how should we attempt to develop definitions of problems to which a useful contribution can be made? This process is often known as problem structuring and it carries with it the idea that problems are malleable and can be moulded into a variety of shapes and forms. Problems are not things which appear, as if from above, and on which the analysts must struggle until some suitable solution is found. Problems are constructs that emerge from on-going issue streams and to which attention is paid. To understand how this occurs it might be helpful to consider the views of Schön (1982) and Goffman (1974), who explain why one person might identify as a problem something other people might ignore.

Framing and Naming

Monty Python is a well-known British TV comedy series from the late 1960s, which poked fun at a number of targets. One such target was a long-running BBC Children's TV series called *Blue Peter*, which always had serious educational aims. One *Monty Python* sketch had one of the cast playing a *Blue Peter* presenter teaching children how to play the flute. "Right", he said, "You pick it up, blow in this end and waggle your fingers around. Got it? Good. Next week we'll show you how to become a brain surgeon." Some things are so simple if you know how!

The same sketch could have been applied to photography, especially with today's cameras which automate almost everything except taking the shot. Thus photography is easy, "You pick it up, look through this hole and waggle your fingers over this button. Got it? Good." However, a few minutes spent looking at someone's holidays snaps (or, even worse, their holiday video) makes it clear that things are not so simple. In photography, there is quite an art in framing the shot. What we mean by this term is that, if we look around us, there are many possible subjects within our field of view. A good photographer knows how to include in a shot only what he or she wants to see on the final picture; Figure 3.2 shows an example of this effect. To do this, the viewfinder is used as a frame which deliberately includes some things and excludes others. Photographers frame their shots very carefully to capture their selective view of the world. Poor photographers do not do this—hence the familiar shots of distant black dots against the snow: "That's Dave skiing, doesn't he look good?"

Framing is a term introduced by Goffman (1974) as a way of explaining how we make sense of events by employing a scheme of interpretation (a framework). When we come upon some new experience we tend to interpret it in the light of our existing frameworks even if we are unable to articulate what these frameworks may

Frame 1

Frame 2

Full scene

Figure 3.2 *Framing*

be. Goffman was concerned to understand how individuals make sense of events which might, to a detached observer, seem puzzling, nonsensical or even immoral. One example he quotes is the view, in most societies, that men do not handle the bodies of women with whom they have no relationship. Medics are, however, freed from this taboo in many countries and may even handle the most intimate parts of a woman's body. This does not appal most of us and we do not regard it as immoral because we have a frame of reference within which we make sense of what is happening.

Goffman argued that people develop frames of reference which are layered, with primary frames as the basic layer that makes sense of the rest. Returning to the analogy of framing in photography, a frame or framework enables us to see some things and to miss or ignore others. It is rather more than a perspective or viewpoint, being something that we have built up and which enables us to make sense of what we see and do. When people do not share common frames, then they literally see things differently. This can be the case within organisations and is often the case when people from different backgrounds come together in a team or to negotiate.

Schön (1982) is concerned to make sense of the ways in which professionals operate when they are attempting to work with and, possibly, to serve their clients. One part of this process is the way in which the professional, whether consciously or not, frames the role which he or she will fill and also frames the situation being faced. Schön calls this process "problem setting"; "a process in which, interactively, we *name* the things to which we will attend and *frame* the context in which we will attend to them" (p. 40). Problem setting is thus a deliberate and conscious process in which we choose what to study but which is guided by frames which may be unconsciously or subconsciously applied.

Taking this discussion further, Schön argues that successful practitioners strive to do two things. First they try to relate new experiences to their existing repertoire of past experiences. This may be done consciously: "Now, I recall that we saw something like this a couple of years ago", or it may be unconscious, in that we find ourselves asking certain questions and anticipating certain responses. If we do either of these things as practitioners, we are using a frame in order to make sense of a new situation. Secondly, the practitioner tries to maintain the uniqueness of the current situation. The current situation may well be interpreted in terms of prior experience and knowledge. However, the good professional does not just apply a standard response but tries to keep in mind what is different and special about the current circumstances. In this way we need not be a prisoner of our own experiences and history, instead these may be used as part of the context that enables us to set the problem.

Thus, in the terms being used here, problem structuring is a process of naming and of framing. In this sense, it is closer to an art than to a science, which should hardly be surprising given the struggle to maintain the unique nature of current circumstances. Problem structuring is a bit like setting ourselves an exam, but this is to be done with the client also involved in the process. That is, effective problem structuring is part of effective management science and this depends on active co-operation between the analyst and the client. At the very least this is because the two parties bring different insights. The analyst is familiar with the modelling approaches and may be able to think about the situation in abstract terms. The client and user know the detail and context of the situation and wish to ensure that the modelling work is of value. This suggests that their problem structuring should be a joint process of framing and naming.

In so doing it is clear that there are two obvious pitfalls to be avoided: the dangers of over-simplification and over-elaboration.

The Danger of Over-simplification

Given that problems need to be defined from messes, then one obvious pitfall is the risk of over-simplification. This can occur in a number of ways. The first is by attempting to tackle one aspect of a messy situation in complete isolation from other aspects that may be equally or more important. In this context we have already considered the case of a supermarket chain needing to reorganise its distribution to stores around the country. Within this system of problems there are many aspects that could be tackled and most of them are interrelated. At some stage, those people responsible for developing the new systems will need to carve off pieces of work that are manageable within a reasonable time period. Thus decomposition is inevitable, but it should only be done in the light of the expected links between the different issues. Ignoring the linkages may have undesirable effects on other aspects of the mess.

The danger of premature or over-enthusiastic decomposition is that resolution of one issue may worsen another aspect. These knock-on effects may be immediate or may only be apparent after some time. As an example of an immediate, but unforeseen effect, consider the case of a chain of short-order restaurants that wished to improve its efficiency. A management science consultant advised them, and his analysis concentrated on better and tighter control of foodstuffs in the restaurants. The idea was to move towards an automated system in which EPOS equipment records item usage, which permits replenishment requests to be placed with suppliers on some agreed basis. Attractive though this idea may seem, there is a down side to it. It implies a shift in the role of the restaurant manager and also in the relationship with the suppliers. Unless these other aspects are carefully thought through, there is a risk that increased efficiency of stock control may reduce the effectiveness of the service offered in the restaurant.

As an example of longer-term consequences, consider the case of a tea packing and blending company which wished to automate its blending process. Most of the packaged tea on sale in grocery stores is actually blended from up to 40 teas from around the world. The blending is overseen by blenders who, like wine-tasters, taste small samples of different teas and develop a pilot blend so as to achieve consistent tastes and appearance. The pilot blend is then scaled up for a large-scale batch production process, each batch coming from a separate pilot blend. Could this batch process not be reorganised on continuous lines so as to produce a consistent blend by the use of consistent teas? The answer is, yes it can. Analysis of the blends devised by the tea-blenders over several months showed very consistent patterns in their blends and this should lend itself to automated, continuous blending. But there is an important snag, which would only become clear after some time. The individual teas are bought on the world commodity markets where both prices and qualities vary all the time. Thus the teas needed for a constant blend may not be available in the right qualities or quantities. Also, a competitor company might realise that the tea company only ever bought certain teas and could force them into an uncompetitive position in the commodity market. Thus, the long-term consequences of a short-term improvement could be dire.

The second way in which over-simplification may occur is due to our natural tendency to see what we prefer to see, for it is very easy to be bound by frames of which we may not be aware. When we approach new situations, we bring with us our past experience and our successes and failures. Many of us are apt to apply remedies which fit well with our own expertise and we may do this while ignoring other aspects. Much of my own technical expertise is in discrete computer simulation, for example, and whenever I am asked about aspects of certain dynamic systems I envisage the system in terms that make it easy to simulate. Needless to say, this applies a set of blinkers that enables me, like a racehorse, to make rapid progress, but I do so at the risk of running in the wrong direction or even in the wrong race. This risk is almost inevitable if it is true that the notion of what constitutes a problem is socially and psychologically defined.

The Danger of Over-elaboration

As is so often the case, there is another pitfall facing the analyst, making a neat complement to over-simplification. This is the risk of over-elaboration or over-complication. A commonly expressed truism about systems is that they are interconnected internally and externally. Or, as the advocates of chaotic notions in complex systems would have it, the flap of a butterfly's wings in Beijing may trigger a hurricane in Florida (Kelly, 1994). Where do we draw the boundaries around what we are attempting? Must a study of inventory control in motor spares take in a full examination of the prospects for all kinds of transport over the next 20 years?

There is clearly no general answer to this question, but there are some principles to bear in mind when the question is asked. Probably the two most important are that it depends on the systems being studied and also on the questions that need to be answered. Later on we shall see that these two principles are highly interrelated, but they can be considered separately at this stage. Though it may be true that all systems are interconnected in some way, there is no doubt that some connections are stronger and more important than others. This is why organisations are often organised into hierarchies. Waddington (1977, p. 49) points out that it is appropriate to view a system in hierarchical terms when "having analysed the complex into a number of elementary units, we look at the relationships of those units and find that the interrelations fall into separate classes with few intermediaries". If the analysis is intended to have only short-term impact, then operating at a specific point in the hierarchy may be acceptable.

As an example, consider the job of planning an extension to the New York subway system, for which it would seem perfectly reasonable to exclude the fact that the moon orbits the earth. As far as we know, the gravitational pull of the moon is insufficient to make trains run faster or slower and we are not dependent on moonlight for the illumination of the platforms. Surely, therefore, the moon need not be considered as a component of the New York subway system.

However, things may not be so simple. Ridiculous though it may seem, knowledge about the moon and its effects may be important for the operation of the New York subway system! Consider two examples. First, the phases of the moon will affect the number of people who travel at certain times of year. Easter (a Christian festival) and Passover (a Jewish festival) are classic moveable feasts, because their calendar dates depend on the phases of the moon. Needless to say, the number of people travelling and their trip distribution may be very different from normal at those times of year. Secondly, all subway systems suffer from water seepage and in the case of New York, much of the subway is close to the sea. The sea is affected by the moon's gravitational field and this shows itself as tides of different levels. The sea defences have to be designed to withstand high tides and to pump water back at the correct times.

Hence, absurd though it may seem, from some points of view, the moon may need to be included in an analysis of the New York subway system. It is clearly not within the control of anyone who manages or uses the subway system, but it does have an influence. It may perhaps be best to regard it as part of the environment of the system, but for some purposes it cannot be ignored. Thus, one way of answering the question "how do we decide what is inside a system" is to consider its function. This is a question we shall return to in Chapter 5, which discusses soft systems methodology.

Problem Structuring as Exploration

The notion of problem structuring in management science is simple enough, though it is rather harder to put into practice. The idea is to develop some definition of the problem that is to be tackled, without losing sight of the relationship between this problem and other things. There is no need for it to carry the idea that problems are solved in any permanent sense. Because problems are constructs of the human mind and of people working together, they need to be defined. In one very important sense, they do not exist "out there" but exist within ourselves. Thus the idea of problem structuring is to come up with some problem definitions that are manageable and which seem likely to help manage the issue stream or mess. Several principles are helpful in this process of problem structuring.

In a way, problem structuring goes on throughout the life of a management science project. It is sometimes only when the project is over that we can see clearly what we were doing. This is a bit like climbing a sand dune in the dark. We struggle and slip, we may even curse and we're not too sure if we're doing things the best way. But the direction of the slope tells us that we're headed in the right direction. Once at the top, after the dawn breaks, we can see our footsteps in the sand. We see where we've been and how we got there, and we might even learn from the experience. So, throughout a management science project there tends to be a continuing questioning about the work being done. Nevertheless, the start of such a project is when most such activity takes place; this at least ensures that we are setting off in the right direction.

Some years ago a colleague and I carried out a small empirical study of how management science groups in part of the UK attempted to structure the problems that they tackled (Pidd and Woolley, 1980). We concluded that the best metaphor to describe our observations was that the practitioners whom we met and observed could be seen as "explorers". They were attempting to map out new territory in a way that would make for its later exploitation. We concluded that, as well as employing a few techniques, this exploration approach could be characterised as follows:

- The approach is *inclusive*. What we meant by this was that the practitioners were concerned with much more than the technical and "official" issues which are apparent at the start of a project. They appeared concerned to understand what was happening by exploring and discovering about the people involved as well as the problem as specified to them. This does not imply that they had a well-formulated set of notions about how their organisation functioned or about the politics of the circumstances. Far from it, indeed many of them found these considerations rather frustrating. Yet they recognised the importance of including them in their initial work on a project.

- The approach is *continuous*. What we meant by this was that, as shown in Figure 3.3, they engaged in a cycle of enquiry. Looking back on this work, we made this observation in complete ignorance of the literature on organisational and other learning (see Argyris, 1983; Kolb, 1983), with which it fits rather well as a form of single loop learning. In fact, the cycle would be better expressed as a helix through which the analyst makes gradual progress, all of the time reflecting on what has been learned and adapting his or her views at the same time.

- The work of management science groups was, in some senses, *hierarchical*, which relates to the point above about continuity. What seemed to happen was that work on one "problem" would often spawn further work as other issues of importance emerged. Sometimes these secondary issues turned out to be more important than the work that uncovered their existence and they would come to dominate the analyst's time. On other occasions, these secondary issues could just be noted and left to some later date.

- What we observed was generally *informal*, by which we meant that there was little evidence of this use of formal creativity techniques such as brainstorming or synectics. Instead there was the general

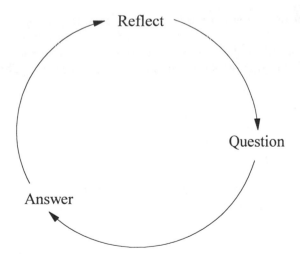

Figure 3.3   *Problem structuring as continuous exploration*

chatter and banter of people working together who bounced ideas off one another, expecting to give and to gain from the exchanges. We were a little surprised by this lack of formal technique.

Since we carried out that research, a few techniques such as cognitive mapping (see Chapter 6) and soft systems methodology (see Chapter 5) have emerged into the limelight and are used by some people in their problem structuring. It might, therefore, be the case that contemporary efforts in problem structuring are rather more formal than we observed. But this may well depend on the OR/MS group involved.

THE PRACTICALITIES OF PROBLEM STRUCTURING

In a way, much of this book is about problem structuring and this is because experience suggests that, once usefully structured, a problem may already be half solved. This section will concentrate on some of the very practical ways in which problem structuring may be made more effective. Bear in mind that these assume a backdrop formed by the features of the exploration approach as described above.

The Idiot Questions: Critical Examination—Kipling's Wise Men

One feature of method study that can be safely adopted in management science practice is the idea of critical examination. This is routine use of a standard set of questions that are well captured in Rudyard Kipling's famous verse from the *Just So Stories* ("The elephant's child").

> I keep six honest working men
> (They taught me all I knew);
> Their names are What and Why and When
> And How and Where and Who.

This gives us six lines of enquiry to be pursued at the start of a project that will help us in our structuring or framing of the problems to be tackled. They stem from the realisation that problem structuring needs to be an inclusive process that stretches far beyond the technical issues of the work. They are what I call "the idiot questions". I give them this name because they can only be asked openly at the start of the project. If asked then, they tend to make the project client, assuming one exists, think the analyst to be smart for asking such perceptive questions. However, if they are asked later in the project the client will tend to think the analyst an idiot who should know that by now. It is also important to realise that these are not intended as direct questions. Starting a project is like any other form of social interaction in which there are many ways of finding things out other than asking a direct question.

Considering each of these six in turn:

What is going on and *what* do people want? These are two very basic questions to face and they are concerned with digging into the content of the issues raised which led to the request for management science support. This is the most basic enquiry line and one that most analysts are likely to follow without thinking much about it. In effect, the analyst is operating almost as a detective or anthropologist. As with all of these lines of enquiry, it is important to ask the same questions of a number of people. A navigator fixes position by locating several reference points, and a sensible analyst will do the same.

Why have we become involved in this project? This is also a funda-mental question but may be less likely to be asked by a naive analyst. It requires digging beyond the surface and reflecting on the contri-butions management science might make to resolving the issues. As is known by experienced practitioners, their help may be sought for all sorts of reasons—some positive, but others rather negative. It may be due to their expertise; it may be due to the failure of others; it might be a result of desperation; and it might be because their involvement will postpone things for a while. Whatever the reason, it seems crucial that the analyst gives some thought to this question, otherwise there is a great risk of later misunderstanding. The analyst is, of course, free to attempt to renegotiate the implicit or explicit terms of his or her involvement and this may be an essential part of problem structuring or setting. But this is impossible unless this basic question has been addressed.

When did all this start to happen and what is the history of it all? Most interventions in organisations have a history to them and trying to understand it can shed great light on what might be done. For example, this may be a long-standing issue to which the managers of the organisation return from time to time and to which they expect to return in the future. Thus they are not expecting a once-and-for-all-time fix, but are looking for some way to operate more effectively.

The question also relates to the urgency of the work: is it to be done to a very tight timetable or can things be done at a slightly more leisurely pace? Once again this is all part of getting things in context.

How did all of this start to emerge? Clearly this and the other five "honest working men" are close relatives or friends and in this form it relates closely to the *Who* and *When* questions. But it also relates to the *What* question in facing up to how things are done at the moment or how people might envisage things to operate in the future. This depends both on the analyst's reflection and deliberation and also on the opinions of the people who are interviewed at this stage of the work.

Where is all this happening and does it have to happen here? This is another fundamental question for the analyst to face. Location can be very important even in these days of instantaneous electronic communication around the world. Physical distance can cause enormous problems and may create misunderstandings that can be ironed out only by people spending time physically together. Tasks which once had to be located in one place may now be located elsewhere in the world—for example, some large software companies are said to be locating their entire European telephone help-desks in the Netherlands because of the linguistic prowess of the Dutch. If callers talking to helpers in their own language (and the call is free), it makes no difference in which country the help-desk is located.

Who are the people involved (the stakeholders) and what do we know about them? Put in these terms this question can seem rather aggressive and intrusive but it is very important to face up to it. Organisations are made up of people who behave in all sorts of ways and analysts who ignore this do so at their own risk. To quote an extreme example, some large companies are still family owned and to treat a request from the owner in the same way as one from a junior manager may lead to an interesting situation. As with the other questions, the analyst needs to use the answer to this question as valuable information that will inform the approach that should be taken.

In a sense, these six questions are the framework for a story or narrative in which people explain what happened and why. Bruner (1990) argues that people employ narrative, that is they tell stories, to account for experiences and events that seem odd in some way or another. The storyline explains why things are as they appear to be. He argues that we do this in an attempt to relate the incongruity to aspects of our frameworks of understanding. Telling a convincing story is part of the sense making that we do as humans. In one sense, then, problem structuring is an attempt at sense making.

Spray Diagrams

Using spray diagrams is a graphical approach suggested by Fortune and Peters (1995) as part of their methodology of learning from failure. This methodology has a pre-analysis phase that corresponds, roughly at least, to the way in which problem structuring is being described here. The diagrams are intended as working tools that display relationships. They are intended to be revised and enhanced as thought, analysis, interviews and deliberation proceed. An example of a spray diagram for TICTOC is given in Figure 3.4.

The diagram has a clear focus around the main issue of hose choice, with an indication that the prime issue here is whether or not to stay with UKHose. The major preoccupations of the players are also noted on the diagram, though the central character of the Director of Port Services (DPS) is only there by implication. What is clear is the number of pressures which he is under.

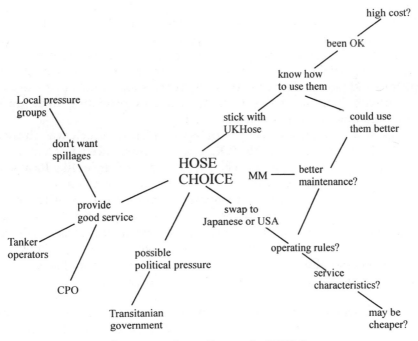

Figure 3.4   *Spray diagram for TICTOC*

Rich Pictures

Rich pictures form part of one approach to soft systems methodology (see Chapter 5), but they also can stand alone in their own right. They form part of the attempt to capture the problem situation that characterises problem structuring. As with the "idiot questions" rich pictures are intended to be inclusive and also as with the "idiot questions" they are primarily for the benefit of the analyst. They are an attempt to sketch out the main participants in the work and to show their interests and interactions. The idea is to include information which could be regarded as "soft" (such things as people's attitudes, roles and assumptions) as well as "hard" or technical data (such as numerical data and details of computer systems). In the sense that will be discussed in Chapter 5, they are intended to be holistic devices.

A moment's reflection on the notion of "framing" introduced earlier in this chapter should indicate how close a rich picture is to this idea. An artist, when drawing a picture, even a portrait, is attempting to capture what he or she "sees" as the essence of the subject and to convey that to the viewer. Barcelona is the location of the Picasso museum, of which one room is devoted to a number of studies (Las Meninas) made by the artist in his reworking of a theme of Velázquez. This series includes many studies of the small girl from Velázquez's canvas in which her shape grows steadily more and more abstract until only the essence of her form is left on the canvas. It takes skill, insight and practice to capture the essence of anything in a picture and part of this is the framing of the subject. Rich pictures are intended to help the analyst to do the same by providing an abstract representation of the problem situation.

Figure 3.5 shows an example of a rich picture which was drawn while thinking about the TICTOC example introduced in Chapter 2 and developed further in this chapter. It is clear that, unlike Picasso's paintings, this is no work of art—but nor was it intended to be. Rich pictures are devices for thinking about the problem. They differ from lists in two important ways. The first is that they make it clear that there is, as yet, no definite sequence in which the issues will be handled. The second is that they focus on relationships between issues, people and systems in a way that lists do not. There is no particular reason why an analyst should not use this device as a way of capturing the perceptions of the different people (the *Who* of the "idiot questions"). There may thus be a number of rich pictures from a range of viewpoints. Note one important feature: the analyst figures on the picture, too. This may not be obvious to the analyst, but it will

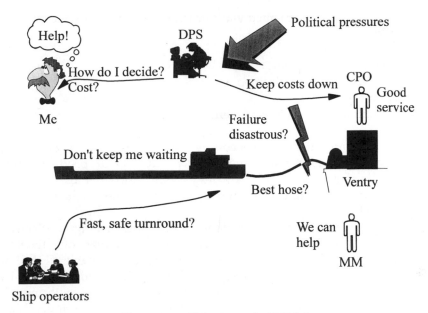

Figure 3.5   *Rich picture for TICTOC*

be very obvious to the other people involved as stakeholders in the study. It is crucial that the analyst develops this self-awareness, for organisational systems are not inanimate objects, they are made up of people, including the analyst, who react, who respond and whose views change.

Brainstorming

A third practical approach sometimes employed when problem structuring is brainstorming, a term that probably originated with Osborn (1953). According to Gilhooly (1988), brainstorming has two main principles:

1. *Deferment of judgement.* The evaluation of ideas is to be postponed until a definite time point at which idea production has ceased. This is to avoid inhibiting the person or people who are producing the ideas. Ideas that may not be useful in themselves may be a stepping stone to others that are useful.
2. *Quantity breeds quality.* The idea of this is that the more ideas that are produced then the greater is the chance that there will be some useful ones.

These are to be implemented via four rules, which are often expressed as follows:

1. Criticism is ruled out.
2. Free-wheeling is welcomed.
3. Quantity wanted.
4. Combination and improvement sought.

These rules are intended to encourage participants to freely associate positively to ideas that have been produced, to produce ideas themselves, however odd they may seem, and to look for ways to combine and improve suggestions that have already been generated.

Gilhooly (1988) provides evidence that brainstorming is effective, both for individuals and for groups. In this context, effectiveness means that the ideas produced were unique and valuable as well as the fact that the quantity of ideas was large. Other studies quoted by Gilhooly appear to show that the best way to employ brainstorming is to use "nominal groups". This approach works by having individuals use brainstorming alone and in private, thus avoiding any tendency to be afraid of criticism, whether overt or covert, in a group. The resulting ideas are then pooled (so as to increase the quantity of ideas) and there is no particular reason why the pooled ideas cannot be fed back to the participants to give them the chance to build on the ideas produced.

By relating the idea of brainstorming to management science it is possible to envisage a number of modes of use. The first is that it could be employed by a lone analyst, shut away for a period, to reflect on possible ways of shaping and setting the problems to be addressed. The second is that it could be employed by a team of management scientists who are engaged, peripherally or fully, in the particular study. If the evidence quoted by Gilhooly is taken seriously, this should be done via a nominal group. If the analyst is operating in a facilitative role (of which more in later chapters), it may be possible to engage in a nominal group with other non-management science participants in the study.

SUMMARY

This chapter serves as a bridge between the theoretical concerns of Chapter 2, which looked at rationality and how it is regarded within management science, and the various approaches advocated to help in model building, which will be the focus of later chapters. It discussed the notion of problem solving, as often used by management scientists and warned of some dangers in an over-simplified view of this. In particular it looked at the ways in which "problems" are socially defined and emerge from messes (to use Ackoff's term) or issue streams (to use Langley's term). What emerges from this discussion is the need to be aware that "problems" are socially defined; they are constructed or construed by individuals and groups. It is thus important for management scientists to be very careful and deliberate in their problem structuring.

To help with this framing and naming, a few simple techniques that have been found useful in practice were introduced. They relate to the notion that problem structuring is a form of exploration in which the analyst develops a map of what is happening and of what might be done about it.

REFERENCES

Ackoff R.L. (1974) *Redesigning the Future: A Systems Approach to Societal Planning.* John Wiley, New York.

Ackoff R.L. (1979) The future of operational research is past. *Journal of the Operational Research Society*, 30, 2, 93–104.

Argyris C. (1983) Productive and counter-productive reasoning processes. In S. Srivasta (Ed.) *The Executive Mind.* Jossey-Bass, San Francisco, Cal.

Bruner J.S. (1990) *Acts of Meaning.* Harvard University Press, Cambridge, Mass.

Checkland P.B. (1981) *Systems Thinking, Systems Practice.* John Wiley, Chichester.

de Neufville R. and Stafford J.H. (1971) *Systems Analysis for Managers and Engineers.* McGraw-Hill, Maidenhead, Berks.

Fortune J. and Peters G. (1995) *Learning from Failure.* The Systems Approach. John Wiley, Chichester.

Gilhooly K.J. (1988) *Thinking: Directed, Undirected and Creative.* (Second edition.) Academic Press, London.

Goffman E. (1974) *Frame Analysis.* Penguin Books, Harmondsworth, Middx.

Kelly K. (1994) *Out of Control: The New Biology of Machines.* Fourth Estate, London.

Kolb D.A. (1983) Problem management: learning from experience. In S. Srivasta (Ed.) *The Executive Mind.* Jossey-Bass, San Francisco, Cal.

Langley A., Mintzberg H., Pitcher P., Posada E. and Saint-Macary J. (1995) Opening up decision making: the view from the black stool. *Organizational Science*, 6, 3, 260–79.

Lubart T.I. (1994) Creativity. In R.J. Steinberg (Ed.) *Thinking and Problem Solving.* (Second edition.) Academic Press, London.

Mintzberg H. (1989) *Mintzberg on Management.* The Free Press, New York.

Osborn A.F. (1953) *Applied Imagination.* Scribners, New York.

Pidd M. and Woolley R.N. (1980) A pilot study of problem structuring. *Journal of the Operational Research Society*, **31**, 1063–9.

Polya G. (1957) *How to Solve It. A News Aspect of Mathematical Method.* (Second edition.) Doubleday, New York.

Rittel H.W.J. and Webber M.M. (1973) Dilemmas in a general theory of planning. *Policy Sciences*, **4**, 155–69.

Schön D.A. (1982) *The Reflective Practitioner. How Professionals Think in Action.* Basic Books, New York.

Waddington C.H. (1977) *Tools for Thought.* Paladin, St Albans, Herts.

Wickelgren W. (1974) *How to Solve Problems. Elements of a Theory of Problems and Problem Solving.* W.H. Freeman, Reading, Berks.

4

Some Principles of Modelling

THE PURPOSE OF THIS CHAPTER

This book discusses some of the modelling approaches that have been found useful in management science. Part I, of which this is the final chapter, is concerned with some of the general issues faced in management science. Chapter 1 developed a definition of "model" as the term is used in management science and argued that models are useful because they are tools for thinking that enable us to investigate what might happen if we (or someone else) did something. Chapter 2 was an introduction to ideas about rationality. It argued that the classical approach needs to be softened by the realisation that, in Simon's terms, practical rationality may be procedural. Further to this point, empirical studies of how managers actually manage show that other factors as well as reason are at work in decision making and control. These need to be accounted for in any ideas about modelling. Chapter 3 explored what we mean by the idea of a problem as the term is used in management science practice. It is important to ensure that, in the race to develop a useful model, an analyst takes adequate account of the circumstances which lead people to believe that there is a problem for which modelling might be of some help.

This chapter covers some general principles that can be applied when developing a model that will be useful in management science. Its focus is avowedly practical, the idea being to give you some issues to consider and some principles that may be useful to you. But it is important to bear in mind that some of these principles are almost matters of style. Such matters need to be internalised and personalised. An example I often use with students is to recall the medical training of my wife, a doctor. As a student she was taught the importance of physical examination and, as a novice, was given a strictly defined sequence of instructions to follow when examining a patient. She and her fellow students followed this to the letter until it was second nature to them. But, by that stage, each one had personalised it to some extent. One student might be rather better at hearing strange sounds, another at feeling changes in skin texture, and so on. Each slightly adapted the formula to themselves but internalised its structure and aims. The same should occur with these principles of modelling.

Finally, a caveat. This set of principles will be neither complete nor eternal. One of the hazards of writing a book is that the author's past comes back like a ghost to haunt him. Things I wrote in the early 1980s are sometimes quoted back at me—and I find that my own views have shifted and that I don't agree with what I wrote then! These principles, therefore, are not to be treated as if they were carved into tablets of stone. They are ideas that I hope will prove useful and to which I hope that others will add. Principle 5, "do not fall in love with data", could itself be subdivided into a number of principles, but it seems best to keep the number small, within the "seven, plus or minus two" rule.

PRINCIPLE 1: MODEL SIMPLE, THINK COMPLICATED

Complexity and Complicated Models

Chapter 1 argued a case for modelling which pointed out that our world is complex and that the consequences of decisions and plans can be large scale and wide ranging. Given that this is true, does this imply that models must be complicated to be of any use?

A tenet of cybernetics, the science of control, is the principle of requisite variety (Ashby, 1956), which might seem to support the view that complex systems require complicated models. The principle of requisite variety can be stated in many ways, one of which is that "variety must match variety". Its origin lies in the design of control systems that are intended to operate in complex environments. In its simplest form it suggests that, to be effective, a control system must be able to match the system it is controlling. For example, if a furnace can get too cool as well as too hot, the control system should include some way of detecting and responding to low temperatures as well as to high ones. Stated in this form, the principle of requisite variety is almost a truism. Ashby took it rather further than this common-sensical notion and developed a mathematical theory of its use.

What of its applicability to models and modelling within management science? Must a model be as complicated as the reality being modelled? Thankfully, the answer is no—for a reason that may not immediately be obvious, but which is illustrated in Figure 4.1. This shows that models are not just built, they are also used—which might be rather obvious, but is vitally important. It is crucial that the variety of the model and the user(s) combined can match that of the system being modelled. This does not mean that either one of the two components (model and user) must separately be able to do so. Chapter 5 discusses systems approaches and points that a system comes to our notice because it displays behaviour not apparent in its components. These are known as emergent properties. In the context of modelling it is important to realise that the model and the user form a system. Requisite variety is an emergent property of that human:model system and not of its components.

Model Simple, Think Complicated

The implication of this idea is captured in the aphorism "model simple, think complicated". That is, a simple model can be supplemented by highly critical thinking and rigorous argument and analysis. This view could, of course, be taken to a ludicrous extreme. For example, a verbal model might be: "The world is hideously

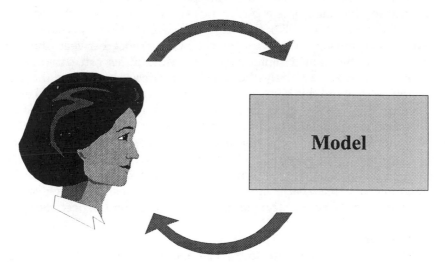

Figure 4.1 *Model and user as a system*

complicated and dangerous when things go wrong." No amount of critical thinking or analysis could take such a verbal model much further forward. At the opposite extreme, if a model itself does have requisite variety then there might be no need for much critical thinking. In such cases, the model could be built into a computer system that is used for day-to-day operation and control with no human intervention. Indeed, as Ashby pointed out in the principle of requisite variety, such complexity is essential if the model is to provide full and automatic control. Between these two extremes lies the realm within which most management science is conducted. The models are neither trivial nor fully requisite. Instead, they simplify and aggregate.

It is important to remember that simple models are easier to understand than complicated ones. Writing about the desirable features of decision models, John Little (1970) argued that one essential property was that they should be simple. This is because transparency is easier to achieve with simple models. Therefore these stand a greater chance of being used than would very complicated ones. Within management science, models are built in order to help people and organisations to become more effective in what they do. This means that their results need to be used and this requires trust on the part of the user. Trust is easier to achieve when the user is at least able to appreciate the overall workings of the model. It is important not to misread this as suggesting that a management science model must always be limited by the technical prowess of the people sponsoring the work—this, too, would be ludicrous.

Instead, the idea of simplicity needs to be linked with another suggestion of Little (1970): that the model should be easy to manipulate. As an analogy, there is a world of difference between the car driver and the skilled motor engineer. Most of us can drive cars, though we may have only the vaguest of ideas about how the car works. We can do this because we have been trained to drive and also because the car itself gives us rapid feedback about our driving. For instance, we go off the road or hit other vehicles if we steer wrongly. A motor car is, after some training, easy to manipulate and it meets our preference for personal mobility. In a similar way, a model that is easy to manipulate (for example, its user interface might be made to resemble a spreadsheet) and which produces results which seem relevant, will be used. Thus simplicity has a second aspect, ease of use.

There are, of course, occasions when this metaphor collapses. In the world of travel, if we need to traverse the Pacific then driving across is not a viable option. Instead, we climb aboard a jet aircraft and surrender control to the aircraft crew with their own expertise. Similarly, there are some models that require the user to place their trust in the skills of the analysis team, because only they fully understand its workings. But users should only do so if the model produces results and insights that are relevant and appropriate to their situations. It is the joint responsibility of the analyst and the users to ensure that this is the case. Complicated models have no divine right of acceptance.

This idea that we might "model simple, think complicated" brings us right back to the idea that models are "tools for thinking". It would be wrong to interpret that phrase as being "tools to replace thinking". Instead, they are tools to support and extend the power of thinking. Thus, a complicated model which is poorly employed may be worse than a simple model used as a tool for careful thought.

PRINCIPLE 2: BE PARSIMONIOUS, START SMALL AND ADD

The problem with the first principle of simplicity is knowing how simple or how complicated to be, and there is no general answer to this. Instead, like an army approaching a well-defended city at night, we use a little stealth and cunning. This is to employ the Principle of Parsimony, which I have long found useful in computer simulation modelling (Pidd, 1984). In its more memorable form, this principle is sometimes known as *KISS*, an acronym which stands for *Keep It Simple, Stupid*. The idea is that models should, ideally, be developed gradually, starting with simple assumptions and only adding complications as they become necessary. Instead of attempting, from the outset, a wonderful model that embodies every aspect of the situation in a realistic form, we begin with something manageable, which may have unrealistic assumptions. The intention being to learn what we can from this simple model and then to refine it gradually, wherever this is necessary. Powell (1995) calls the same approach "prototyping", as this carries the idea that it is best to develop quickly a working model, even if it is imperfect. It can be refined, or even abandoned, later.

A Simple Example: Ping-Pong Balls

Using this principle, model building should begin with the well-understood and more obvious elements of the system of interest. Once these are properly modelled and validated, the more complicated and less well understood elements can be added as required. The temptation to dive straight into the complicated aspects should be resisted, despite its siren sounds. In a fascinating book on quantitative modelling in general, not particularly aimed at a management science audience, Starfield et al (1990) develop this idea in some detail through a series of examples that increase in complexity. One of their earliest examples is the following: "Look around the room you are sitting in. How many ping-pong balls could you fit in this room?" They take the reader through a series of attempts to answer this question by a modelling approach.

Their first suggestion is that the reader should produce an answer to this in just 60 seconds. Faced with the problem put in this way, most people make a vague estimate of two volumes, that of a typical ping-pong ball and that of the room in which they are sitting. Those reading this on a palm-fringed beach should use their imagination or should go for a swim! Hence the first simple model which many people employ to tackle this is:

$$Number = RoomVolume/BallVolume$$

They use this idea to make a guess at the number. Of course, this makes a lot of assumptions. Most people assume their room to be rectangular, that there will be no furniture in the room, that ping-pong balls will not compress under pressure, and so on. Nevertheless, such a model is better than throwing up our hands in the air and crying "Oh I don't know, hundreds, thousands maybe!"

Their second suggestion is that the reader spend a further five minutes addressing the question, preferably working with a partner. What many people do at this stage is to refine this earlier model. Thus they make a rough estimate of the dimensions of the room and use this to compute its approximate volume rather than making a guess. This gives the following simple equation:

$$RoomVolume = L \times W \times H$$

where

$$L = Length$$
$$W = Width$$
$$H = Height$$

Similarly people tend to estimate the volume of a ping-pong ball and usually treat such a ball as if it were a cube. They may do this to avoid computations with π, or because they imagine that this is the correct formula for the volume of a sphere, or even to allow for the fact that there will be gaps between the balls as they are packed. Thus:

$$\text{BallVolume} = D^3$$

where

$$D = \text{Diameter}$$

Hence, after the five minutes (six in total) the overall model becomes:

$$\text{Number} = \frac{(L \times W \times H)}{D^3}$$

This has now transformed the simple guess into a symbolic model with parameters L, W, H and D. Each of these could be estimated, or even measured given more time, to provide an estimate for the number of ping-pong balls. The implicit model has been made explicit.

As a next stage, Starfield et al suggest that the modeller might spend a little more time to develop the model into one with upper and lower bounds. This is simpler than it might seem, because the cubic model developed after six minutes is one easy way of producing a lower bound on the solution. It assumes that the balls will not compress, but instead treats them as if they were cubes, which tessellate in three dimensions. If the balls actually compress, or just settle into one another, then more could be packed in than the cubic model would suggest. An upper bound, in this case, could be produced by a different simplification. This treats the balls as perfect spheres which do not compress and which, by some magic, can be packed in with no air gaps at all—clearly impossible, but that doesn't matter. In this case the volume of a single ball is:

$$\text{BallVolume} = \frac{4\pi}{3} \cdot \left(\frac{D}{2}\right)^3$$

Hence the overall upper bound model is:

$$\text{Number} = \frac{(L \times W \times H)}{\dfrac{4\pi}{3} \cdot \left(\dfrac{D}{2}\right)^3}$$

Dividing the upper bound model by the lower bound model gives an upper:lower ratio of $6/\pi$, which is just higher than 2.

Further refinements can be made by examining the assumptions made when developing these simple solutions. For example, we made assumptions about: how the balls are packed, the room being a simple rectangle, there being no furniture in the room, air pressure having no effect, and so on. Each of these is, strictly speaking, wrong. Nevertheless, our models tell us much more than would a simple guess. They are more likely to be closer to the truth and they are general symbolic statements about general rooms and general spheres. One way forward would be to develop a more realistic treatment of the way in which the balls rest on one another. A two-dimensional example of this is shown in Figure 4.2 with the balls resting on one another within a trapezium. Simple trigonometry then allows us to proceed as follows.

Suppose that, as shown in Figure 4.2, we imagine a triangle with each apex at the centre of a ping-pong ball. If the balls settle into one another without compression, then this will be an equilateral triangle if all the balls are the same size, and this enables us to estimate the packing distance P as follows:

$$\sin 60 = \frac{P}{D}$$
$$\therefore \quad P = D \sin 60$$
$$\therefore \quad P = 0.866D$$

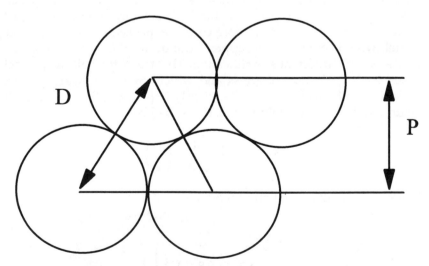

Figure 4.2   *Trapezium model for ping-pong balls problem*

The height of the trapezium that contains four balls is, therefore, $2P$, whereas the cubic model assumed that a square with sides $2D$ was needed. Hence the volume needed for four balls is rather less than might be expected using the cubic model. Working in two dimensions, as in Figure 4.2, this suggests that 13–14% less space would be needed. Or, putting it another way, we could pack in something like 13–14% more balls than the cubic model might suggest. In similar ways, the model can be gradually refined until its accuracy is suitable for the intended purpose.

A Second Example: Cloud Cover

A rather more realistic exercise is described by Miser and Quade (1990a) who discuss a model that might be used to estimate how much of a runway would be visible to pilots through partial cloud cover. This might be an important consideration for an aircraft coming in to land in cloudy conditions. There are various types of cloud, but at a height relevant to a plane seeking visual contact with an airport runway, only some need be considered. The first question is, how could these be represented in a model? As before, the principle of parsimony suggests that starting simple might be the best approach, and thus some simple geometric shape has much to commend it. One possibility is to treat discrete clouds as if they were discs. As Miser and Quade point out, using discs in this way is not ridiculous as the relevant types of cloud do tend to be compact. It is also a helpful simplification, since the geometry of discs is well understood.

Cloud cover is often measured as a percentage of the sky that is visible from points on the ground and its pattern may be specific to the location of the airport. For example, nearby hills or ocean may cause certain patterns to predominate. These patterns could then be modelled at different heights by the use of the simplified circles to represent the clouds, and in this way it should be possible to estimate the visibility of the runway from different points in the sky. Whether this model is close enough to the likely "real" distribution of cloud cover is the crucial question. This could be at least partially assessed by having an aircraft fly past different points under known cloud conditions and then attempting to compare the actual visibility with that predicted by the model. If the model is found to be too simple, it can be further refined by, for example, using shapes closer to the actual shape of clouds. For instance, each cloud could be modelled as a set of overlapping circles (producing shapes that resemble Mickey Mouse's face in one form). Again, this refinement might be chosen because the geometry of circles is simple and thus the model is tractable. In this way, the model may be gradually refined until it is adequate for its intended purpose. As with the ping-pong ball example, with this example and with real modelling in management science, the principle of parsimony has much to commend it.

PRINCIPLE 3: DIVIDE AND CONQUER, AVOID MEGA-MODELS

This is common advice given to anyone trying to understand how a complex system operates. Powell (1995) calls this decomposition, as well as divide and conquer. Raiffa has the following to say:

> Beware of general purpose, grandiose models that try to incorporate practically everything. Such models are difficult to validate, to interpret, to calibrate statistically and, most importantly to explain. You may be better off not with one big model but with a set of simpler models. (Raiffa, 1982, quoted in Miser and Quode, 1990b)

Raiffa's point is partially related to the first two principles above, but also relates to the need to build a model from components, each of which should themselves be developed parsimoniously. In a way, this principle was implicit in our treatment of the ping-pong ball problem earlier in this chapter. We developed separate, extremely simple, models of the room and of the balls themselves. Each could easily be understood and their relationship could be controlled.

CASE STUDY: LANCASTER BUS COMPANY

DIAL-A-BUS

Consider the need to provide modelling support for the Lancaster Bus Company (LBC), which is planning a new Dial-a-Bus service to a number of satellite villages that cluster around a large town. The idea being that, instead of following a fixed route, the buses would respond to phone calls from potential passengers and would pick up and drop off as required—though within some overall timetable. LBC need to know how many buses to provide and what fare levels to charge so as to cover their costs (if they are a public utility) or to make a profit (if they are a private company). The temptation is to assume that some type of all-inclusive model, possibly a large simulation, is the way to approach this. But it might be better to proceed with a series of small models that link into one another.

To simplify matters here, suppose that other towns have attempted similar systems and that they are willing to talk to LBC about their experience. However, even though the managers of LBC have some detailed data from these towns, suppose that these were heavily subsidised pilot projects. This means that, though the LBC proposal has some similarities with services elsewhere, there are some important differences. To cope with this, suppose that LBC have conducted a survey among residents to see how likely individuals would be to use the service at different fare levels.

There are major differences between the LBC project and the earlier pilot projects, not least because the pilot projects were heavily subsidised in a way that LBC cannot do. However, it may be possible to model the actual demand recorded in the pilot projects in some way that has some relevance to the situation of LBC. One approach might be to collect socioeconomic data from each of the pilot project towns. Examples might be car ownership, number of elderly people, total populations, and so on. Analysis of this data, say in a linear regression model, might reveal that ridership (the proportion of people using the service) is related to one or more of these vehicles in the pilot projects. Hence we have:

Model 1: ridership in pilot projects is a function of different variables.
e.g. Ridership = f(car ownership, proportion of elderly)

If the same data were available for the villages in the study then Model 1 could be used to estimate the likely ridership of the LBC service, if it were heavily subsidised. The resulting estimate could then be modified by Model 2, the results of the price sensitivity survey. This is likely to show that the higher the fares, the lower the actual ridership is likely to be. The Model 1 estimate could be treated as if it were equivalent to the demand at a fare level at which all interested people would use the LBC service. Hence we have:

Model 2: actual proportion of potential users at different fare levels,
e.g. Proportion = f(fare levels)

This might now lead us to Model 3, which might be related to the frequency of the service to be provided. The two extremes here would be the option of running just one circuit each day to each village and the opposite would be to run entirely on demand. The greater the frequency, the greater the proportion of the Model 2 numbers that will be willing and able to use the service. Thus, Model 3 might be a financial spreadsheet that shows the sensitivity of the revenues and costs to service frequency, given different fare levels. Hence, we have:

Model 3: financial out-turn at different fare levels and frequencies, e.g. Nett returns = f(service frequency, ridership, proportion of users)

It would, of course, have been possible to combine these three simple models into a single one, but this would be a mistake for several reasons. First, there would be a significant loss of transparency. Each of the simple models is easy to understand and its implications can be grasped by people. This is so important when it comes to persuading people that the results of a model are worth taking seriously. Another reason is that each model can be used for a sensitivity analysis. Different relationships could be tried, for example between potential ridership and socioeconomic variables and their effects should be clear.

PRINCIPLE 4: USE METAPHORS, ANALOGIES AND SIMILARITIES

Rather than being restricted to a direct consideration of the problem at hand, it can be helpful to try to get another perspective on things. This use of other perspectives should be distinguished from the use of a model to understand different viewpoints and interpretations. Here, the idea is that devices such as metaphors, analogies and related problems can be of great help in themselves.

Metaphors, Analogies and Similarities

In their early book on operations research, Ackoff and Sasieni (1968) devoted a chapter to the subject of modelling in which they discussed the use of analogue models within operations research. In such an analogue model, one property of the system is replaced by another property that is easier to represent or to manipulate. Thus, in an everyday example, hikers use maps which represent the physical property of altitude by the use of lines, or contours, on the map. Locations at the same altitude above sea level are linked by the contours and an experienced map reader may use them to gain a good impression of the physical terrain. Contours are used because they are more convenient than the obvious device of scaling the actual terrain on to the map in a relief form. Such a relief map would hardly be convenient on a hike, as its solid form means that it would be unwieldy.

Analogues of this type are sometimes employed in management science, though perhaps not as often as some introductory books might suggest. Cognitive mapping (see Chapter 6) is one example in which related concepts are drawn as a map in two dimensions. This makes their relationships visible, though it might be argued that such maps might be better represented in three or more dimensions as far as their relationships are concerned. This would, however, lose the convenience that comes from a two-dimensional map.

Another use for metaphors and analogies is to try to gain some insight into how a system may operate. In an example outside the world of management science, Gerrig and Banaji (1990) discuss this and mention some interesting experiments by Gentner and Gentner (1983). They took a group of people who were "fairly naive about physical science" and tried to help them to understand some concepts of electricity. They did this by the use of two metaphors. The first was of water flows through pumps, valves and reservoirs. The second was of a moving crowd passing through locations at different rates. The water flow analogy helped the class to use their prior knowledge of pumps and reservoirs to understand about batteries, but it did not help them to understand resistors. The moving crowd analogy helped them to understand about resistors as if they were gates restricting the movement of people between two points, but it did not help with their understanding of batteries. They found that the proper use of analogy or metaphor aided the learning process, but that a badly chosen metaphor could slow things down. We may infer, therefore, that metaphors can be useful in developing learning, if they are chosen properly.

Creativity, Analogies and Different Viewpoints

One view of creativity is that it comes from the ability to associate apparently unrelated ideas. In his book on creativity in management science Evans (1991) suggests several uses for metaphors and analogies. He quotes the early paper of Morris (1967) who also advocated the use of appropriate analogies in modelling. One approach that stresses analogies is synectics, in which analogies are used to examine an issue from different perspectives. For examples, participants in synectics sessions are encouraged to use four types of analogy:

Personal. Participants are asked to imagine themselves within the problem being discussed: "Now, if I were one of these widgets I'd have been sitting on that shelf for hours while nothing much happened." I sometimes encourage my students to devise better algorithms by getting them to imagine themselves as a bored computer who knows there must be a better way of doing things.

Direct. This is closer to the normal idea of analogies as in Ackoff and Sasieni (1968) and asks participants to think of parallel situations from real life: "Well, in some ways, the demands on emergency services are just a form of queuing system." In this way, lessons from one system may be transferred to the analysis of another. This transfer may not be complete, but it may still spark off useful ideas and insights.

Fantasy. The idea being to be totally idealist and ask for the imposs-ible. Just suppose ... What if ...: "Just suppose goods could be delivered to customers instantaneously." "Just suppose whole body scanning could be done with a portable device." This approach encourages the modeller to find ways of getting from the current position toward some idealised state.

Symbolic. This is the use of a compressed description of the problem or of its possible solution. Gilhooly (1988) quotes Stein (1974, p. 189) about a group that used the idea of the Indian Rope Trick in develop-ing a new jacking mechanism.

The idea of these analogies is to get people to take new views of things that might be too familiar or, at the opposite extreme, are not understood. In terms of management science modelling, this means trying to gain new insights which might lead to useful models.

PRINCIPLE 5: DO NOT FALL IN LOVE WITH DATA

The Model Should Drive the Data, not Vice Versa

The simple ping-pong ball exercise did not begin by suggesting a data collection exercise. A common failing of students when learning about modelling is to insist that progress cannot be made unless there is some (or more) data available. Their assumption being that examination of the data will provide some clues to extend their understanding. This may well be a mistake, even though exploratory data analysis is a very valuable technique. Modern statistical software or spreadsheets enable the rapid plotting and summary of large amounts of data and from this analysis, patterns may quickly be gleaned. Sometimes these patterns exist, but at other times they are, like beauty, in the eye of the beholder. This exploratory data analysis has much to commend it as an approach but it is no substitute for careful thought and analysis.

Some of the dangers and pitfalls that await the unwary in their treatment of data are discussed below, but there is a fundamental point that should not be missed. This is that the model should drive the data and not vice versa. This means that the analyst should try to develop some ideas of the model and its parameters and from this should think about the type of data that might be needed. One of the problems with some case-style teaching of business administration is that the cases are often intended to be self-contained. That is, the students know that all the data they may need is available in the papers issued with the case. This is quite unlike real life, in which data must be requested, justified and collected before it can be analysed. Data is not free, its collection has a cost as does its interpretation and analysis.

How then should the use of data be linked into the parsimonious, gradual approach advocated earlier in this chapter? If circumstances permit, then the best approach would be to develop a simple model and then to collect data to parameterise and test it. It may then be clear that the simple model is fine for the intended purpose or it may be that the model needs to be refined—which may need more data or different data. This new data will have a cost which should enable some rough cost:benefit calculation to check whether its collection and analysis will be worthwhile. And so on, until some point is reached at which the costs outweigh the benefits.

Of course, these ideal circumstances may not pertain and it may be necessary, especially when acting as a fee-charging external consultant to set up a complete data collection exercise at the start of the work. If this can be resisted then it would be a good idea to do so.

Data-mining and Data-grubbing

"Data-mining" has recently entered the language of statisticians and refers to attempts to develop statistical models from available data. Powerful computer packages are used to search for patterns in the data. A debasement of this is data-grubbing, which some use as a term of abuse for approaches in which many different data series are unthinkingly collected and then read as data files by one of today's powerful statistical packages. These packages allow complicated analyses to be conducted on the data in a very short space of time. Regressions can be tried, linear and non-linear. Other types of multivariate plastic surgery can be applied to the data such as by transforming the original data series by taking logarithms and the like. Most worrying, this can all be done very quickly, by someone who knows very little about the statistical tools being used in the computer software. This is rather like an attempt to bake a cake by collecting ingredients that look interesting. These might then be mixed together until boredom sets in. The resulting mélange is then popped into the oven and we wait until the smoke appears. Cakes cooked in this way should only be given to people with whom scores need to be settled.

The original intention of statistical techniques such as regression was to investigate relationships that were thought to be plausible. Old-timers can recall having to compute regressions on mechanical calculators—which was hard work (this may be why so many older statisticians were of a slim build) and very slow. Hence, data-grubbing was not a practical proposition, life was too short and the calculators were too unreliable. To stay sane, modellers of the earlier epochs would do a lot of hard thinking about possible relationships before embarking on the multivariate analysis.

This criticism of data-grubbing should not be interpreted as a call for a ban on friendly, powerful statistical packages. They are much too useful for that and they take the drudgery out of statistical modelling. However, they should not be a substitute for thought. Also, just because data is available it should not be assumed that it is useful.

Data is Useful in Model Building

This criticism of data-grubbing and of a reliance on available data might be interpreted, wrongly, to imply that modelling is best carried out in an abstract way. It is certainly not the intention that data should be ignored in this way. It might, therefore, be helpful to divide data and information into three groups. First, there is preliminary or contextual data and information. Chapter 3, which discussed the nature of problems in management science, suggested that the easy-to-remember questions of What, Why, When, Where, How and Who (Kipling's "honest working men") were a useful guide in preliminary investigation. Clearly, the results of these questions may be qualitative or quantitative. In the latter case it may be necessary to conduct significant analyses on the data that is so produced. But this data is collected with a view to understanding more about the context of the problem, rather than the development of a detailed model. It is not unusual for this preliminary analysis to reveal enough insights for there to be no real need to take a project any further.

The second type of data is that which might need to be collected and analysed in order to develop the model in some detail. This is model parameterisation, or model realisation (Willemain, 1995). But, as will be repeatedly stated under the general heading of this fifth principle, the model structure should drive the data collection and analysis, not the other way round. The third type of data is discussed under the heading "Avoid using the same data to build and to test a model".

Beware of Data Provided on a Plate

An old adage among management information systems professionals is that information is data plus interpretation. One feature of modern organisations is that computer systems collect almost every conceivable type of data about what is happening—except the data that you really need for a particular model. For modelling purposes, data is best ordered à la carte rather than table d'hôte. For example, in attempting to develop models for production control, it may be necessary to produce submodels of customer demands for the products being made. Most companies monitor their sales using data produced by the sales order processing systems that are used to take orders and issue invoices. The obvious way to get hold of demand data might be to take it from the customer order files, but there are at least three reasons why this might be a mistake. The first is that such systems often only record the actual despatches to customers and this may be as much a reflection of the available finished stock as it is of the actual demand from customers. They may request one thing, but if the company is unable to supply it the customer may either go elsewhere or accept a substitute. The second reason is that, if the customer suspects that a required item is out of stock (due to past experience) they may not even request the item. Finally, the whole idea of implementing a new production system might be to make the company more attractive to customers who normally order from other suppliers. Hence, for all of the reasons, the data from a sales order processing system might be treated with some caution.

As a second example, suppose a hospital wished to reduce its waiting lists and was proposing to model some aspects of its operation in order to decide whether to do so. Again, it might be thought that the best way to obtain data about patient referrals to the hospital would be to examine the referral data base which contains information about actual referrals. As in the previous examples, this data might be very misleading for a number of reasons. The first is that other doctors who refer patients to the hospital may have a choice of hospitals to which they could refer and may make it their business to know how long the waiting lists are. Thus they may choose to refer people to hospitals with shorter lists. Slightly more subtly, they may choose to refer to hospitals which they *believe* have shorter lists. A further point is that the waiting lists are a symptom of a problem, they are not the problem themselves. As doctors know, symptomatic or palliative treatment is given only when there are no other options, it is usually better to treat the underlying causes. Thus, it may be better to treat the waiting lists as outputs from a model rather than as inputs.

In these and other cases there may be no substitute for proper and well-organised data collection if a useful model is to be constructed. It may also be possible to take existing data and massage it in such a way as to account for some of its shortcomings. Thus, a small-scale data collection exercise might be used to reveal the discrepancies in the full, system-produced data which may then be modified to take account of this. However, it must be borne in mind that such data massage implies that a model of the data itself is being used as part of the modification process.

Data is Just a Sample

It is also important to remember that, in the vast majority of cases, data is just a sample of what could be used or might be available. This is true in a number of dimensions. First, the time dimension, this being the simplest to understand. When data is being used to build or to test a model then that data will have been collected at a particular time and over a certain period. If we say that the data is believed to be representative, we are implying that it is representative of a larger population that displays some regularity through time. We are not expecting someone to come along later and surprise us with data that differs drastically from that which we have already obtained. Nevertheless, this may happen and is always a risk which is clear when we realise that the results of a model may be used to extrapolate into the future. The future may simply differ from the past, that is the population from which the data sample comes may behave differently in the future.

Data is also a set of observations. This is the second aspect to note in the realisation that data is a sample of what might be obtained given enough time and other resources. Any observation process is subject to errors of different types. Examples might include the following:

- Recording errors—for instance a product code may be wrongly entered into a computer system. The risk of this can be reduced by careful checking, by proper training and also by the use of automatic devices such as bar codes, which may be read as the item passes a scanner.

- Transcription and analysis errors—for instance when data is transferred from one system to another or is aggregated in some way. Sales data compressed into monthly slots may mislead if the sales actually show in-week variation.

Hence it is reasonable to be very sceptical about data. Especially if it is readily available.

Avoid Using the Same Data to Build and to Test a Model

Most models used in management science make use of data in one form or another. The model, as illustrated in the ping-pong example, will have parameters that must be given values. This process of parameterisation is usually based on data, whether specially collected or generally available. The trap to avoid, if possible, is the use of the same data to parameterise the model and then to test it. As an example, suppose that a company wishes to understand the sales pattern for one of its products. Careful data collection proceeds and they eventually have a time series of their weekly sales over the last two years. A management scientist then develops a forecasting model that is intended to suggest how sales might behave, given certain assumptions, over the next few months. The idea being that the model might be used, say, monthly, each time with an updated data series, to suggest likely future sales.

There are a number of types of forecasting model that could be employed, and they have in common the fact that they are based on the analysis of historical data. Under skilful hands, computer programs are used to estimate the parameters of equations that lead to a model which is a good fit to the recent historical data. The goodness of fit can be expressed in standard statistical terms. But this goodness of fit is an evaluation of the degree to which the model fits the historical data. It is also important, where possible, to test how well the model predicts what might happen in the future. A tempting short-cut is to quote the goodness of fit statistic from the parameterisation exercise, but this might be a mistake. A better approach, is shown in Figure 4.3, in which the available data has been divided into two sets. The earlier data is used to parameterise the model and then the second set is used to test the model. This test set has not been used in the parameterisation and it is being used as a surrogate future. Goodness of fit measures can be used to assess how well the model predicts this surrogate future.

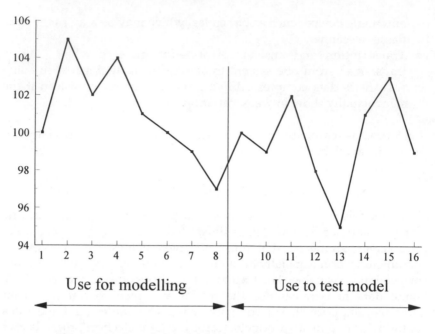

Figure 4.3 Data for model parameterisation and model testing

PRINCIPLE 6: MODEL BUILDING MAY FEEL LIKE MUDDLING THROUGH

Because a model, as used in management science, is the result of an attempt to represent some part of reality so that action may be taken or understanding may be increased, it might be thought that model building is a linear and highly rational process. There have been few attempts to investigate this issue, as it relates to management science, but the evidence suggests that modelling is not linear nor classically rational (see Chapter 2). Instead, people seem to "muddle through", making use of insights, perhaps taking time away from the modelling, trying to look at things from different perspectives and so on. This does not, of course, imply that modelling must be done this way, but it may well indicate how successful analysts actually operate.

How Expert Modellers Work

A fascinating attempt to investigate this issue is reported by Willemain (1994, 1995). He gained the co-operation of a group of 12 experienced modellers, a mixture of practitioners and academics. All had completed graduate work in OR/MS and they averaged 15 years of experience since finishing graduate school. They were not, in any sense, novices. This group were asked to do two things. First they were given the chance to describe themselves, to express their views on their own approaches to modelling, to say what experience they had in modelling and to capture something important in a short, personal modelling story. Their self-descriptions and experience showed them to work mainly in areas in which they "pursue specific objectives towards fundamental changes in complex, existing systems". Also that they "develop a unique model for each problem, though all their models involve extensive computation". From this we can conclude that their work could in no way be described as "airy-fairy", for their concerns seem down to earth.

Of their approach to actually building and developing models, Willemain (1994) summarises their responses thus: they "develop their models, not in one burst, but over an extended period of time marked by heavy client contact". Also, they are "guided by analogies, drawing and doodling, they develop more than one alternative model, in each case starting small and adding". Thus many of their claimed approaches are a good fit with the other principles of modelling discussed in this chapter.

In a second paper, Willemain (1995) reports an experiment with the same 12 people who were given modelling tasks and were asked to think aloud as they spent 60 minutes figuring out how best to develop suitable models. This is clearly an artificial task for two reasons. First, it compresses their activity into just 60 minutes, when their expressed preference was to work "over an extended period of time". Secondly, the request to think aloud as they worked might distort their normal patterns of work. Despite these reservations, this thinking-aloud protocol reveals some interesting issues.

In analysing the tapes of their thinking aloud, Willemain (1995) classifies their concerns under the following headings:

- *The problem context*, which he relates to problem structuring as defined by Pidd and Woolley (1980). That is, the exercise which aims to gain a sufficient understanding of the problem to proceed to some form of formal modelling.
- *The model structure*, which he takes to be the process of deciding what category of model to use and of analysing data prior to actually building it.
- *Model realisation*, this is the process of parameter estimation for a model and/or calculation of results.

- *Model assessment,* which is deciding whether the model will be valid, usable and acceptable to a client.
- *Model implementation,* which is working with the client so as to gain some value from the model.

The tapes show that about 60% of the modellers' time was devoted to model structure, that is, what would be regarded as the core of model building. About 30% of the time was divided equally between concerns about problem context and model assessment, with similar time spent on each issue. Just 10% was devoted to model realisation and almost none to questions of implementation.

As the study gave the modellers just 60 minutes to work on a problem it should be no surprise that so little time was devoted to model realisation or implementation. But what is significant is that so much time was spent on thinking about problem context and model assessment. What is also very important is the fact that the time spent on these three major concerns was scattered through the modelling session. The modeller kept picking up a concern for a while, dropping it, and then returning to it. Presumably this would be even more marked were it possible to follow how they operate over a much longer time period in their "real" work.

Links with the Other Principles

Perhaps it is an exaggeration to say that modellers muddle through. However, it is equally an exaggeration to assert that modelling proceeds as a linear step-by-step process. It did not in Willemain's study and it probably does not in most of our experience. The other principles presented here should be used to provide some order to the muddling through. It is quite normal for a modeller to think in parallel while working on a model. Discussing ill-defined problem solving in general, Holyoak (1990) discusses how people tend to operate in parallel lines of thought and how they are continuously restructuring their ideas. A concern to understand the problem context goes hand in hand with a desire to produce a model that will be useful, as well as technically correct.

SUMMARY

This chapter serves as a bridge between the general, fundamental ideas of Chapters 1 to 3, which underpin rational modelling. The idea was to show how some of these ideas might be put into practice by the use of a few simple principles, as follows:

1. Model simple, think complicated: there is no need for the model to be as complicated as the system being modelled, for the model will have been built with some intended use in mind. It is, however, very important that the model is critically evaluated and subject to rigorous thought.
2. Be parsimonious, start small and add: rather than attempting to build a complete model from scratch it is much better to proceed gradually, preferably from some outline model towards one that becomes realistic enough and valid enough for the purpose in hand.
3. Divide and conquer, avoid mega-models: in some ways this is an extension of the principle of parsimony. The idea is that it can be much better to build small, relatively self-contained, models that can easily be understood than to aim for an all-inclusive model that has little hope of being used.
4. Use metaphors, analogies and similarities: try to think about new things using whatever insights that previous experience may bring. One very useful way of doing this is to imagine yourself as part of the system being modelled.
5. Do not fall in love with data: this principle covers many possible sins of omission and commission. The basic idea is that the conceptual model should drive the data collection and analysis and not the other way round. Data is no substitute for careful and critical thought.
6. Model building may feel like muddling through: nobody should imagine that modelling as an activity is one in which smooth progress is made and in which everything fits neatly together. Instead, most experienced modellers jump from topic to topic while modelling and need to keep refining their ideas. But they enjoy it and produce something useful!

REFERENCES

Ackoff R.L. and Sasieni M.W. (1968) *Fundamentals of Operations Research*. John Wiley, New York.

Ashby R. (1956) *An Introduction to Cybernetics*. Chapman & Hall, London.

Evans J.R. (1991) *Creative Problem Solving in the Decision and Management Sciences*. South Western Publishing, Cincinnati, Ohio.

Gentner D. and Gentner D.R. (1983) Flowing waters or teeming crowds: mental models of electricity. In D. Gentner and A.L. Stevens (Eds) *Mental Models*. Erlbaum, Hillsdale, NJ.

Gerrig R.J. and Banaji M.R. (1990) Language and thought. In R.J. Sternberg (Ed.) *Thinking and Problem Solving*. Academic Press, San Diego, CA.

Gilhooly K.J. (1988) *Thinking: Directed, Undirected and Creative*. (Second edition.) Academic Press, London.

Holyoak K.J. (1990) Problem solving. In D.N. Osherson and E.S. Smith (Eds) *An Invitation to Cognitive Science, Volume 3: Thinking*. MIT Press, Cambridge, Mass.

Little J.D.C. (1970) Managers and models: the concept of a decision calculus. *Management Science*, **16**, B466–85.

Miser H.J. and Quade E.S. (1990a) Validation. In H.J. Miser and E.S. Quade *Handbook of Systems Analysis: Craft Issues and Procedural Choices*. John Wiley, Chichester.

Miser H.J. and Quade E.S. (1990b) Analytic strategies and their components. In H.J. Miser and E.S. Quade *Handbook of Systems Analysis: Craft Issues and Procedural Choices*. John Wiley, Chichester.

Morris W.T. (1967) On the art of modelling. *Management Science*, **13**, 12, B707–17.

Pidd M. (1984) *Computer Simulation in Management Science*. (First edition.) John Wiley, Chichester.

Pidd M. and Woolley R.N. (1980) A pilot study of problem structuring. *Journal of the Operational Research Society*, **31**, 1063–9.

Powell S.G. (1995) The teacher's forum: six key modeling heuristics. *Interfaces*, **25**, 4, 114–25.

Raiffa H. (1982) *Policy Analysis: A Checklist of Concerns. PP-82-2*. International Institute for Applied Systems Analysis, Laxenburg, Austria.

Starfield A.M., Smith K.A. and Bleloch A.L. (1990) *How to Model it: Problem Solving for the Computer Age*. McGraw-Hill, New York.

Stein M. (1974) *Stimulating Creativity*, Vol. 1. Academic Press, London.

Willemain T.R. (1994) Insights on modelling from a dozen experts. *Operations Research*, **42**, 2, 213–22.

Willemain T.R. (1995) Model formulation: what experts think about and when. *Operations Research*, **43**, 6, 916–32.

PART II

Interpretive Modelling: Soft Management Science

Introduction

SOFT METHODS

If a book of this type, addressing the subject of modelling in management science, had been written 20 or more years ago, its content would have been rather different. Most of its pages would have been devoted to descriptions of mathematical methods which were thought to be useful in helping solve organisational problems. There would also have been examples, mostly rather simple, to help the reader to understand the book. In the sense that the term is used by Morgan (1986) this would have been based on a, possibly rather naive, view that organisations are machines that must be kept well oiled and in good running order. Thus management scientists were to be one of the group of technologists who kept the machine in good shape by the use of mathematical and quantitative methods. This book does not intend to decry the value of these quantitative approaches; indeed, Part III of the book explores some of the principles of these methods in more detail. However, it is concerned to show that rational methods can also be used in other ways to help organisations, and the people within them, to work better.

In doing so, this book takes a view of rationality rather wider than simple (or even complicated) mathematics. This second part of the book assumes that different people share the same experience and yet may interpret it in quite different ways. Thus, just as quantitative models may be used to demonstrate the effect of different policies, so other types of model may be used to explore the consequences of different ways of seeing the world. This is particularly important when operating at levels above the merely operational, where the issue is not so much how to do something, but more about what should be done. That is, there is more of a concern with ends than with means. In this strategic analysis it is quite normal for people to argue and debate from different presuppositions. As this part of the book tries to make clear, modelling approaches can help people to understand one another's viewpoints and can help such a group develop a commitment to sensible action.

Therefore this part is concerned to describe three approaches which are often regarded as exemplars of "soft operational research". These three, soft systems methodology (Checkland, 1981), SODA/cognitive mapping (Eden, 1989; Eden et al, 1983) and qualitative system dynamics were developed in the belief that exploring the consequences of people's perceptions is crucial, especially in circumstances where there may be disagreement about objectives. Some writers— notably Rosenhead (1989)—regard two of the approaches—soft systems methodology and SODA/cognitive mapping—as exemplars of formal approaches to problem structuring. In one sense this is very sensible because they help us to understand how different people frame their worlds. However, this book takes the view that to regard them only as problem-structuring methods is to miss out on some of their potential.

In this chapter they are described under the heading of "interpretive modelling" because their use requires the analyst to operate in a mode rather different from that of the technological expert. The idea of the methods is that they should be used to help individuals and groups to think through the consequences of their beliefs and preferences. They are thus ways in which the analyst may facilitate this, by recording what people say or claim and playing this back to them inside a formal structure. The formal structures of the "soft" methods provide a language to talk about these things and may also take some of the heat out of a conflict-ridden situation by forcing the debate to operate at a different level of abstraction. In essence, they may separate a viewpoint from its advocate. The soft models are partial interpretations of how an individual or group believes things to be. This does not mean that the analyst must collude with someone whose views of the world may be clearly ludicrous. Rather, the idea is to open people's interpretations to a more public scrutiny. Needless to say, this must be done with some tact and care.

SOFT VERSUS HARD

Several places in this book have already used the term "soft" in contrast to the word "hard" and it is now time to unpack this a little.

Checkland (1981) devotes considerable space to this question and, rather than duplicate that effort, a slightly different approach will be taken here. Table II.1 summarises the main differences between "hard" and "soft" approaches, though it must be borne in mind that the differences are intended to isolate the distinctions between two stereotypes and that there are many shades in between.

Problem Definition

First, soft approaches begin with the assumption that problem definition is not straightforward but is itself problematic. As discussed in Chapter 2, problems are social or psychological constructs that are the result of framing and naming (Schön, 1982). This contrasts with the view, common in engineering, that work begins once a need is established. Thus, as mentioned before, in soft analysis, the work focuses on ends as well as means to those ends. In hard systems engineering, the idea is to provide "something to meet the need" and the concern is with "how ... not what?" (Checkland and Scholes, 1990). Soft approaches are based on an assumption that people's perceptions of the world will vary and that their preferences may also differ. Thus it is important to try to understand the different ways in which the different stakeholders may frame the issues being addressed in the study.

As an example, in the TICTOC case introduced in Chapter 2 we saw, in Chapter 3, that there are internal and external stakeholders and these may each frame the issues somewhat differently. Soft approaches see problem definition as multifaceted—much as a jewel has facets which sparkle in the light and which create different appearances from different angles. Thus soft approaches are pluralistic in their assumptions about problem structuring. Linked

Table II.1 *"Hard" versus "soft" approaches*

	Hard approaches	Soft approaches
Problem definition	Seen as straightforward, unitary	Seen as problematic, pluralistic
The organisation	Taken for granted	Has to be negotiated
The model	A representation of the real world	A way of generating debate and insight about the real world
Outcome	Product or recommendation	Progress through learning

to this, they must therefore assume that problem definition is not straightforward in many cases but will only emerge through debate and discussion. They therefore provide ways of helping such debate.

The Nature of Organisational Life

Secondly, soft approaches do not take the nature of organisations for granted. In particular, they do not assume that organisations are just "human machines" in which people are organised according to their functions, all of which are geared to some unitary objective. Instead, they assume that people may, rightly or wrongly, fight their own corner rather than be subsumed into some overarching objective. Thus these approaches make different assumptions about the nature of organisations.

The soft systems methodology (SSM) of Checkland is based on the assumption that human activity systems are a useful way of thinking about organisations. Thus SSM takes a systems view of organisations. On the other hand, the SODA/cognitive mapping approach developed by Eden and his colleagues is individualistic as it focuses on how individual people see their world. In doing so it takes account of the fact that people behave politically within organisations. Neither assumes that an organisation is a machine which grinds on its way regardless of the people who compose it.

In the case of system dynamics, this feature may not be so obvious, based as the approach is on an analogy with physical systems. However, the focus of a system dynamics analysis on active organisational processes forces the analyst to consider what people are doing or proposing, rather than what roles they occupy.

Models as Representations

Thirdly, hard and soft approaches differ in the view they take of models themselves. In a hard approach it is typically assumed that a model is a proper representation of part of the real world. It is accepted that the model will be a simplification and an abstraction of the real world. In this view it is vital that the model is properly representational and that its operation must therefore be thoroughly validated against the part of the real world being modelled. By contrast, such assumptions are unnecessary in soft approaches. In these, the idea is that models are developed so as to allow people to think through their own positions and to engage in debate with others about possible action. Thus, the main concern is that the models should be useful in doing this and in supporting the cyclic nature of their supporting methodologies.

As will become clear in the final chapter of this book, this means that the question of model validation is problematic for soft models. In what sense can confidence be placed in the model if the main criterion is its immediate utility?

Outcome as Product or as Learning

The final feature of these soft approaches is that they stress the importance of organisational and individual learning. They do not guarantee that a set of recommendations, or a definite product (such as computer software) will emerge from a project. They stress that, when people face problematic situations, this is a chance for them to learn how to cope with such circumstances in such a way that their performance is improved. This does not mean that there will be no tangible product or recommendation from such a project, just that such may emerge from the learning that occurs. Hence their exponents tend to present the approaches as, in some sense, cyclic and as part of an on-going stream of organisational life. They are closer to the view, expounded by Langley et al (1995) that this stream of issues may, at times, deposit decisions and new systems on the banks as it flows past. The aim is to find ways of operating with this rather dynamic and loosely structured view of organisational life.

COMPLEMENTARITY

Though there are clear differences between soft and hard approaches, some of which are discussed above, this does not mean that the two cannot be used together. If soft methods are viewed as problem structuring devices then this is clearly the case, the intention being to proceed with appropriate hard modelling if the problem structuring shows this to be necessary.

REFERENCES

Checkland P.B. (1981) *Systems Thinking, Systems Practice*. John Wiley, Chichester.
Checkland P.B. and Scholes J. (1990) *Soft Systems Methodology in Action*. John Wiley, Chichester.
Eden C.L. (1989) Using cognitive mapping for strategic options development

and analysis (SODA). In J.V. Rosenhead (Ed.) *Rational Analysis for a Problematic World*. John Wiley, Chichester.

Eden C.L., Jones S. and Sims D. (1983) *Messing About in Problems*. Pergamon Press, Oxford.

Langley A., Mintzberg H., Pitcher P., Posada E. and Saint-Macary J. (1995) Opening up decision making: the view from the black stool. *Organizational Science*, **6**, 3, 260–79.

Morgan G. (1986) *Images of Organisation*. Sage, London.

Rosenhead J.V. (Ed.) (1989) *Rational Analysis for a Problematic World*. John Wiley, Chichester.

Schön D.A. (1982) *The Reflective Practitioner. How Professionals Think in Action*. Basic Books, New York.

5
Soft Systems Methodology

BACKGROUND

The term "system" is in common use. We rarely think deeply about terms such as digestive system or nervous system when we talk about our bodies. Similarly, we speak of transport systems, of economic systems and of systems of government. We also may speak of the solar system, of mechanical systems and of computer systems. In fact, in some ways, the word system has almost lost its meaning it has become so commonplace. We generally use the term to describe something in which we are taking an interest and whose behaviour we wish to study. It seems that the ideas which are usually included under the banner of "systems approaches" originated in the study of biological and mechanical systems. Later they were applied to management science, but this required some significant modification. The reasons for this should become clear in this chapter.

Soft systems methodology (often abbreviated to SSM) was developed by Checkland (1981) because he felt that "hard" systems analysis was of limited use. Having worked for about 20 years, many of them as a senior manager, he could see few points at which management science had been, or could have been, of value to him. This worry was increased by the term "management science", for he could see little in management science that justified the use of the word "science". When he moved to academic life at Lancaster University he set out to see if it were possible to develop other systems approaches that could be of demonstrable value to managers. The main text on SSM is Checkland's own (Checkland, 1981), but others have followed and readers may also wish to look at Checkland and Scholes (1990), which addresses some of the criticisms levelled at the Checkland's 1981 account of the approach. Another book which may be of interest is that by Wilson (1984), which is mainly concerned with the application of SSM, rather than with its justification.

A slightly different perspective on similar issues is to be found in Vickers (1983), who was concerned with rather more than the development of a methodology. Vickers showed how the development of ideas which first emerged in biology can be used, with major modification, in the world of human systems. Indeed, both he and Checkland are concerned to show how careful use of systems ideas can be of great value in helping people to manage and govern themselves better. Equally, both of them are insistent that the inappropriate use of some systems ideas can do great harm. Rather like the old joke: "How do porcupines make love?" Answer: "Carefully", so must the user of systems ideas take great care. A useful, but gentle, critique of systems views is to be found in Morgan (1986) who places systems ideas alongside other ways of understanding the workings of organisations and the people within them.

SYSTEMS, WHOLES AND HOLONS

It is important to develop some terms that can be used in this chapter and elsewhere. The most important of these concerns the word "system", for which Vickers (1983) uses the term "whole" and Checkland and Scholes (1990) prefer "holon". The basic definition of system, whole or holon is independent of the type of system with which we are concerned. Later in this section it will be developed into a concept suited to human systems (Vickers' term) or human activity systems (Checkland's term).

Basic Ideas of Open Systems

There are many books and papers which devote considerable space to defining what is meant by system; clearly written examples of these are: Ackoff (1971), Bertalanffy (1971) and Boulding (1956). As far as human systems or human activity systems are concerned, we need to consider open systems—that is, ones that exchange with their environments. Such systems have the following features:

1. A system has more than a single component and these are organised in some way. One part of the study of a system is to consider the component parts of that system and their organisation, what Vickers (1983) terms "the internal relations of the

whole". These internal components interact with one another and may themselves be considered as systems. Thus a production control system may include computer programs, computer hardware, shop-floor data capture instruments, the people who operate the system and the set of rules that defines its operation. To study a system we need to investigate its components and also their organisation and relationships.

2. Systems have boundaries—that is, they are wholes. Some things are inside the system, others are not, and those which are not constitute the environment of the system. In an open system, the boundary is permeable in both directions and there is communication and interaction across the boundary. The way in which the system interacts with its environment constitutes the external relations of the system. As mentioned above, we usually define the boundaries by thinking about the relationships between the components being considered for membership of the system. The production control system mentioned above may sit within an organisation which markets products to customers and which buys materials from suppliers. Thus the production control system might be expected to communicate with other systems within the organisation. In addition to studying the internal relations of a system, we must also account for its external relations.

3. Systems behave—that is, they display behaviour that is recognisable and distinctive in some way. This behaviour is a consequence of the interaction and organisation of the internal and external relations of the system. Indeed, it may well be the behaviour of a system that brings it to our notice. It is also usually argued that the behaviour of the system will, in some way, be different from that of its components. Thus the production control system as a whole displays behaviour that cannot be expected from any of the individual components. These behaviours, which differ at distinct levels of analysis, are sometimes known as emergent properties. A concern for these emergent properties is one part of holism (sometimes written as wholism).

4. Systems of this type exist only for a finite time, they are not eternal and they continue to exist by virtue of their internal regulation. Thus a characteristic of an open system will be a process of regulation, control or governance which maintains it through time. These systems may be in equilibrium but this stability is not the same as stasis. A stable system may persist, but it will also undergo changes both in its internal and external relations. Hence the production control system will be sustained by a constant inflow of information and will be operated accord-

ing to certain rules which may change over time. A static system undergoes no changes and does not respond to changes in its environment. At some point, though, any human system will cease to exist.

It follows from the first three points that systems are nested. That is, any system may be regarded as a component or subsystem of a higher level, or supersystem. Thus it is possible to regard any system as also being a subsystem and a supersystem. The production control system contains components and is, itself, part of the system which we may choose to call the organisation. It is not necessary to assume that this nesting implies hierarchical organisation.

Human or Human Activity Systems

In this chapter, the terms "human system" and "human activity system" will be used interchangeably. As far as such systems are concerned there are two more considerations that we must note. At one level, the difference between human systems and non-human (for example, biological or electrical) systems is obvious—human activity systems involve action by humans. It is the implications of this commonplace observation that matter, for this is what distinguishes them from systems that are merely biological or man-made.

They differ from biological systems because they have, in some sense, been created and designed by humans. Any stability which they possess should be a consequence of that design, as should their behaviour. By contrast, biological and ecological systems come into being as a result of happy accident (for atheists) or divine intervention (for believers). Their stability is a pleasing result of their interaction with the world around them. Therefore, in human activity systems, the question of system design is a central issue, since neither accident nor divine intervention is invoked. Sadly, human activity systems are not always well designed. There are, for example, many examples of production control systems which have turned out to be useless, despite massive expenditure. This is often because the design has concentrated on computer hardware, software and control algorithms, sometimes at the expense of any real thought about how the system would be used and about its consequences for the rest of the organisation. The same is true of computer-based management information systems.

Thus, in human activity systems, design is a key feature. The criteria that will guide the design will often be a subject of great debate and even of some controversy. For example, is this to be a system that will "guarantee ex-stock delivery on the next working day"? Or is it to be one that "meets customer requirements, where these include guaranteed ex-stock delivery on the next working day"? A key feature of SSM is that it aims to provide a way for those involved in a human system to address the design of the system and the criteria that will guide that design.

However, the same argument about design clearly applies to technological systems. They do not appear by random mutation or by divine intervention, they are designed by humans. The difference is that human activity systems include humans who have freedom to act and for whom their actions have some meaning. If people are treated as if they are machines, they tend to find ways to show that this is a gross distortion of their humanity. Workers treated as machines tend to act in that way—which is probably not what their managers intended. Hence successful human activity systems must be deliberately designed with their human actors in mind. Well-designed production control systems take careful account of the ways in which people form part of the system and are not just machines who can operate keyboards. Properly thought-through management information systems do the same—they consider who need what information when.

There is a further aspect of the "humanity" of human activity systems. Checkland (1981) points out that the person describing or defining a human activity system must also be accounted for. That is, any description of a human activity system will depend on the viewpoint of the observer and there are many different ways of seeing and describing the same thing. To a production manager, the production control system may be a way of ensuring that routine manufacturing plans are fulfilled with the minimum of hassle. To the marketing manager it may appear as an obstacle to his important customer getting that special order as promised. Similarly, a corporate information system may be seen as a great boon to people at the centre of the organisation, but to those at the sharp end it may seem less of a blessing. This is one reason why, though they are nested, we need not regard human activity systems as hierarchically organised.

We can highlight the important features of human activity systems as being:

- They are deliberately designed by human beings with some purpose in mind.
- They include human beings.
- They are open systems with internal and external relations.

- They have a finite time span and, to continue to exist, they employ internal regulation which permits dynamic equilibrium.

Any systems methodology which is intended for use with human activity systems must take account of these features.

Do Human Activity Systems Exist?

This may seem a strange question, but it is a very important one to face. Is the world actually composed of interacting sets of entities which combine to create systems? Or is the notion of a system simply a convenient way of describing the world? In the final analysis, we simply do not know. We do know that people, ourselves included, experience a world separate from themselves—of that we can be sure. However, we have no really effective way of ensuring that our own perception of the external world is the accurate one and that others are wrong. In a sense, objectivity can be considered to be a consequence of different people agreeing that their perceptions are similar. They could, of course, all be wrong (see Janis (1972) on this point), but our confidence tends to increase as others agree with us.

The standpoint taken in this chapter is that it is safer to argue that the real world can be usefully regarded as composed of systems of interacting entities. This allows us to accept that the question of system definition is at least partially arbitrary. That is, we define a system because we are looking for something and the notion of a system provides some way of explaining what we have observed. For instance, if we arrive in a subway station from another planet we would probably try to understand what was going on by noting the different entities—passengers, trains, station, tracks, and so on—how they interact, and why this should be. But our description of this system would be somewhat different from that given by the person responsible for the subway network as a whole. In the sense that this notion was introduced in Chapter 3, we employ our existing schemata to make sense of what we experience. Thus our own position as observer cannot be ignored when considering the whole question of system definition.

Therefore, to understand SSM we must add to our notion of human activity system the idea that systems are artefacts. They are a useful creation of the human mind. There is no need to argue that the world is systemic, we need only argue that it is useful to envisage it as a set of interconnected systems. Further to this, different people may define a system in quite different ways and each may be, in some sense, correct. Consider, for example, a student bar. Is this: a pleasant place for students to socialise, a money machine for the brewery, a way of the university making money from its students, a useful service to summer conference visitors, a den of iniquity, or something else? Each of these stereotypes is a way of describing a student bar and each may, in some sense, be regarded as a valid point of view. It is important that any notion of system can cope with the fact that different people may, quite legitimately, have different points of view.

AN OUTLINE OF SSM

Methodology and its Underpinnings

Soft systems methodology is both a methodology and an approach. *Chambers Concise Dictionary* gives several definitions for methodology including the following: "a system of methods and rules applicable to research or work in a given science or art".

Within management science the term has come to have two quite distinct meanings. The first, common in the USA, uses the term methodology to refer to what people in the UK would describe as techniques—academics from the USA sometimes refer to the methodologies of linear programming (see Chapter 8) or of forecasting. That is not the usage intended within SSM.

In SSM the word "methodology" is used in two ways. The first is that it provides a set of rules that guides the conduct of a study using soft systems ideas. Figure 5.1, which will be discussed in some detail in this chapter, provides a common way of describing some of the main features of the approach. It depicts a sequence of activities in which an SSM study might be conducted. As an example of this, the methodology suggests that before a system can be modelled in some way its essence should be captured via a set of root definitions. In this sense, SSM includes a method of enquiry, though it should not be assumed that the method has to be followed in a rigorous, step-by-step manner.

The second sense in which SSM provides a methodology is that it embodies a set of guiding principles and beliefs which, while not rules for action, embody the basic ideas of soft systems. Thus, it assumes that there are many ways of defining a system and that, if root definitions are to be employed, then multiple definitions may be produced. In this sense, SSM prescribes outcomes which might result from its use. Referring back to the introduction to Part II, it is clear that its methodological underpinnings are very definitely soft.

The SSM Approach in Outline

This section briefly describes the approach of SSM. There will be more detail in later sections. Figure 5.1 shows a commonly used diagram which summarises the approach, based on the one in Checkland (1981). A different one is used in Checkland and Scholes (1990), but the one shown in Figure 5.1 seems to be more commonly used by practitioners. Remember that this is intended as a framework to guide action and it is not intended to be a step-by-step recipe for success.

Several things are immediately apparent in Figure 5.1. The first is that this is not intended to be an approach that is started at one point (number 1) and ends at another definite point (number 7). Instead, it is a cyclic approach rather like the learning cycle of Kolb (1983). This should be no surprise given that soft approaches tend to stress the learning that will emerge from their use. Checkland (1981, p. 162) claims that the approach can be started, in principle at least, at any of the points in the cycle. He also stresses, sensibly, that real-life use will involve backtracking (going back to do the same thing again, even though it had been hoped to have finished that activity) and iterating around the loop.

The second thing to notice is the line which runs more or less diagonally and separates stages 1, 2, 5, 6 and 7 from stages 3, 4, 4a

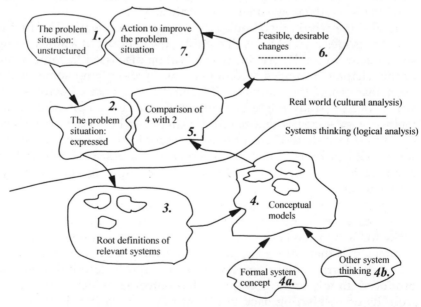

Figure 5.1　*Soft systems methodology (adapted from Checkland 1981)*

and 4b. This line indicates that the analyst using SSM must wear two hats: one for the real world and the other for the realm of systems thinking. The term "real world" is meant to indicate the everyday world in which people live and to which they relate. To use SSM we must investigate this world by working with at least some of these people, hoping to be of use to them and hoping to understand how they interpret the world. This requires what Checkland and Scholes (1990) call "cultural analysis". Thus, this work in the real world must not ignore the meanings that people attach to what they and others do. Indeed, these meanings are fundamental to the cultural analysis.

By contrast, the realm of "systems thinking" represents the deliberate withdrawal from the real world during which the analyst uses systems concepts to try to understand what is happening in the real world. This requires what Checkland and Scholes (1990) call "logical analysis". In doing so, however, it is important to maintain a defensible view of the real world. Checkland's (1981) account of SSM was criticised for taking a view of organisational culture that was naive; the methodology is stated in somewhat different terms in Checkland and Scholes (1990) to counter some of those criticisms. In particular this affects the across-the-line links between the real-world activities of SSM and the realm of systems thinking. Nevertheless, the analyst must, at some stage, think about the system in terms that may well be rather different from those used by the people who are part of the system itself.

The earlier criticisms of Checkland's (1981) presentation of SSM led to its re-presentation in Checkland and Scholes (1990). The effect of this re-presentation is shown in Figure 5.2. The idea is that the approach must be multi-dimensional throughout its application. They suggest that three linked analyses should run in parallel as shown on the figure. The idea is to pre-empt the criticism that SSM is purely concerned with system logic and ignores the cultures within which it will be used. The three analyses are primarily concerned with the across-the-line linkages between the real world and the world of systems thinking as follows:

1. The analysis of the *roles* people are playing or might be expected to play. This is an attempt to think about the intervention in which the analyst and others are engaged. There will be at least three roles—client, would-be problem solver, and problem owner. These roles may coincide and it is clearly important to identify the people occupying them.
2. The analysis of the *social system* in terms of the roles, norms and

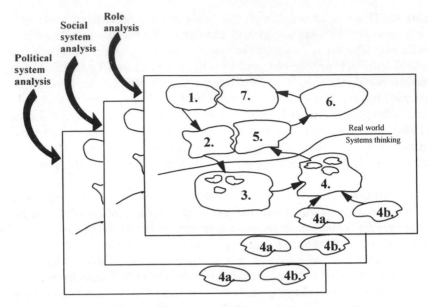

Figure 5.2   *Three analyses*

values that are evident. Roles are taken to be the social positions people occupy, which might be institutional (teacher) or behavioural (clown). Norms are the expected, or normal, behaviour in this context. Values are the local standards used to judge people's norms. The idea of this analysis is that the analyst should try to understand how people play out their roles.

3. The analysis of the *political systems*, which is an attempt to understand how different interests reach some accommodation. This is an explicit recognition that power-play occurs in organisations and needs to be accounted for. Needless to say, this analysis needs to be undertaken carefully and, maybe, covertly. There is little point asking people what their power-ploys are!

SSM: Exploration and Finding Out

The first two activities in Figure 5.1 are labelled as "The problem situation: unstructured" and "The problem situation: expressed". Note that the concern is with the circumstances, the *situation* in which someone feels there is a problem to be tackled. These activities aim to uncover different perceptions of why the intervention is needed and what it is that appears to be going on. Keeping in mind the view that the world can be regarded as systemic, rather than assuming that the world is composed of systems, the idea is to find some way of understanding and exploring the presenting context. In a way, this corresponds to problem structuring as it was described in Chapter 3, and this is why some people regard SSM as an aid in problem structuring. This exploration is rather like a first attempt to drill for oil: the ground must be surveyed and trial bores will be drilled, but there is no real intent to build a production rig at this stage. Instead, enough information will be gained to allow proper and detailed work to proceed. Continuing with this analogy, circumstances may change (e.g. oil prices) which may mean that this stage of the work has to be scrapped or reworked. Hence the need, sometimes, to revisit this exploration stage.

Checkland (1981) provides remarkably little guidance about the conduct of activities 1 and 2 in the approach. One suggestion is the use of "rich pictures", which were discussed in Chapter 3. It is also clear that any of the other approaches listed there could also be of use. At this stage there is no particular need to use systems terminology in the exploration of the problem and its context. The aim is to ensure that the exploration digs into a number of aspects, of which the following deserve special mention:

The structure of the situation. This refers to the relatively static aspects, such as physical layout, official and unofficial power hierarchies, communications systems (whether formal or informal). To use an analogy, until about five years ago, soccer players wore numbers on their shirts, which more or less indicated their playing position. Lower numbers were defenders, higher numbers were attackers. In addition, the captain often wore an armband to indicate his status. Useful though such information is, it does not tell us much about the dynamics of what might happen on the pitch. It does not describe the tactics employed nor their shifts during the different stages of the game. The numbers do, however, have their value—they allow us to recognise the players by linking the number to that in the match magazine. In the same way, structural ideas do not tell the whole story, but they can be useful.

The process of the situation. In addition to the structure, we need to understand how things are done and what people are trying to do. In our analogy of a football game, this corresponds to the ways in which the game is actually played and the roles that people actually occupy. In a newspaper report of a soccer match, this is much more interesting than the team sheet or a list of the rules of the game. However, it is probably true that, in many situations, it is easier to make sense of the process when something is known about the structure of the situation. The reverse is also true.

The climate of the situation. Here we wish to capture the attitudes of the people involved and we start to consider the question of organis- ational culture. How does the situation feel? Is it exciting or rather boring? How do people value what they do? What meanings do people ascribe to their actions? In Checkland's terms, climate is the relationship between process and structure. Thus, the three aspects are, like a three-legged stool, a stable way of thinking about the problem situation.

These three aspects need to be considered, bearing in mind that the aim is to think about roles, social systems and political systems by the three streams of enquiry. Figure 5.3 shows the basic idea. At the end of the exploration phases, the analyst should have captured the essence of what appears relevant. The next stage is to enter the realm of systems thinking in order to reflect on what is happening and what might be done about it.

SSM: Root Definitions of Relevant Systems

The situation has not been explored just out of intellectual curiosity, but because we wish to understand it more and, possibly, to improve things. We need, therefore, to take our structured exploration and

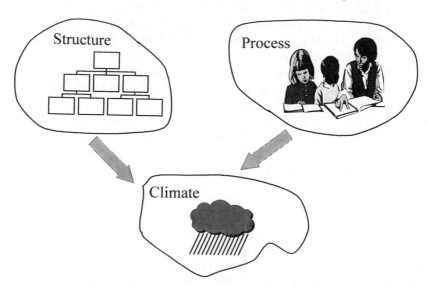

Figure 5.3 *Structure, process and climate*

express some aspects of it in systems terms. In particular, we need to think about what systems might be put in place to achieve what people want. This means we need to develop hypotheses about how things might be—that is, hypotheses about possible systems. SSM's soft credentials are very clear at this point, for we are invited to develop root definitions of relevant systems (both plural). This assumes that different people and different groups may see things in different ways. Root definitions are interpretations of these viewpoints. Thus a root definition is an attempt to capture the essence of a system which might be useful, given the problem and its situation. There is no need for the root definitions to map on to existing organisational systems. The root definition is the first stage of an idealisation of what might be. This is quite different from the question of what is.

A root definition, as a verbal account, is usually reckoned to have six components which are summarised in the mnemonic CATWOE, which stems from the initial letters of the following six terms:

Customer. This is the immediate beneficiary or victim of what the system does. It can be an individual, several people, a group or groups. It is very close to the total quality management (TQM) notion that the customer is the next person to receive the work in progress. It indicates what happens to the output from the system and forms part of the external relations of the system.

Actors. In any human activity system there are people who carry out one or more of the activities in the system, these are the actors. They form part of the internal relations of the system. There may be several actors or several groups and their relationships also form part of the internal relations of the system.

Transformation process. This is the core of the human activity system in which some definite input is converted into some output and then passed on to the customers. The actors take part in this transformation process. The process is an activity and its description therefore requires the use of verbs. Ideally, a root definition should focus on a single transformation.

Weltanschauung. This is the, often taken for granted, outlook or world-view which makes sense of the root definition being developed. It is important to specify this because any system definitions can only make sense with some defined context. The Weltanschauung provides a context within which the rest of the root definition makes sense. Thus a root definition should have only a single Weltanschauung.

Ownership. This is the individual or group responsible for the

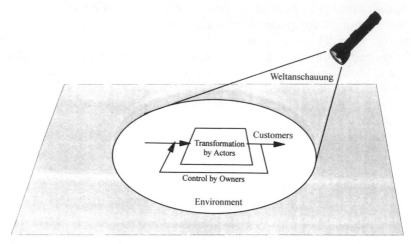

Figure 5.4 *CATWOE as an input:output system*

proposed system in the sense that they have the power to modify it or even to close it down. This can overlap with the actors of the system.
Environmental constraints. All human activity systems operate within some constraints imposed by their external environment. These might be, for example, legal, physical or ethical. They form part of the external relations of the system and need to be distinguished from its ownership.

One way of understanding CATWOE and the idea of Weltan-schauung is captured in Figure 5.4. This shows a simple input:output process, a black box. The process involves a transformation, carried out by the actors and the results of the transformation pass through to the customers. External control is maintained by the owners and the whole system sits inside an environment. The Weltanschauung, shown as the beam of a flashlight, illuminates the picture and enables things to be seen in context.

CASE STUDY: TICTOC

ROOT DEFINITIONS OF RELEVANT SYSTEMS IN TICTOC

The best way to understand the creation of root definitions and the use of CATWOE is to consider an example. For this purpose we will use the

TICTOC case study introduced in Chapter 2. The initial dialogue of the case introduces four people: the Director of Port Services (DPS), the Controller of Pumping Operations (CPO), the Maintenance Manager (MM) and you—the would-be problem solver. In a real situation we could interview the other three people, but here we will need to infer things from the dialogue. For simplicity's sake we will assume that each person's viewpoint can be expressed in their own, single root definition. Clearly there will be cases where one person may exemplify several root definitions. Bear in mind that the following root definitions are what I infer from the dialogue. You may read things somewhat differently.

The DPS is responsible for the entire operation of TICTOC at Ventry; we have discussed in earlier chapters that he is concerned to keep down his overall costs. We might thus develop a CATWOE for him, as follows, taking the hose system as the relevant one. The easiest place to start is with the transformation, which is probably that the hose takes crude oil from storage tanks to tankers at minimum overall cost. The customer for this transformation may be, in the DPS's view, TICTOC itself—it benefits. The actors are TICTOC workers, plus workers on the tankers. The system is owned by the government of Transitania and operates under constraints set by pumping rates, sea conditions and environmental concerns. Finally, what is the Weltanschauung of the DPS which makes sense of all this? This is presumably a belief that there is a need to supply world markets with Transitanian oil. Hence the CATWOE of the DPS might be as follows. Note the obvious point that there is no need to develop a CATWOE in the sequence of its letters.

Customers: TICTOC
Actors: TICTOC workers and tanker operatives
Transformation: transfer crude oil from storage tanks to tankers at minimum overall cost
Weltanschauung: need to supply the world markets with Transitanian oil
Ownership: Transitanian government
Environmental constraints: pumping rates, sea conditions and environmental concerns.

Alternatively, we might capture this in the following sentences:

A system owned by the Transitanian government and operated by TICTOC staff, with the co-operation of tanker operatives, to transfer oil from the Ventry tanks to waiting bulk carriers at minimum cost. It must operate within physical constraints such as pumping rates and sea conditions, plus environmental constraints. The system is needed so that Transitanian oil can be supplied to world markets.

What about the other two principal internal stakeholders, the CPO and MM? Considering the CPO next then, it would appear that he sees the hose system as follows. Once again, your interpretation of the CPO's position as you look back to Chapter 2 may be slightly different. Checkland stresses the need to be aware that the analyst is one of the players in the drama of SSM. This is why it is much better to involve the participants in developing the root definitions, then there is less chance of these being your misinterpretation of their interpretation! A CATWOE for the CPO's view is:

Customers: tanker operators
Actors: TICTOC workers and tanker operatives
Transformation: hose takes crude oil from storage tanks to tankers as reliably as possible
Weltanschauung: my job is to provide a service to tanker operators
Ownership: TICTOC
Environmental constraints: pumping rates, sea conditions and environmental concerns, need to keep costs down.

Note that there are some differences between the CPO and DPS root definitions. The CPO sees the tanker operators as the customers and he treats cost as a constraint imposed from outside. His view of "outside" differs from that of the DPS, for he sees the ownership as vested in TICTOC itself—whatever that may mean. Thus the CATWOE can be expressed in something like the following form:

A TICTOC-owned system to transfer oil from the Ventry tanks to waiting bulk carriers as reliably as possible, operating within physical constraints such as pumping rates and sea conditions; plus environmental constraints and within cost limits. The system is operated by TICTOC workers and tanker operatives, and is needed because my job is to provide a service to tanker operators.

Finally, in this example, we need to consider the Maintenance Manager (MM). His CATWOE is:

Customers: TICTOC
Actors: TICTOC workers and tanker operatives
Transformation: improve service life of hoses
Weltanschauung: better maintenance helps provide a better service and saves money
Ownership: TICTOC
Environmental constraints: pumping rates, sea conditions and environmental concerns, need to keep costs down.

This third CATWOE includes yet more differences. The MM's Weltan-schauung stresses his belief that better maintenance is a help in providing a better service and should also save cash. The transformation is, therefore, the process of improving the service life of the hoses. He sees TICTOC and the tanker operators as customers for this transformation. Thus, this CATWOE can be expressed as follows:

A TICTOC-owned system to improve the service life of hoses used to transfer oil from the Ventry tanks to waiting bulk carriers at low cost. It must operate within physical constraints such as pumping rates and sea conditions, plus environmental constraints and within cost limits. The system is operated by TICTOC workers and tanker operatives for the benefit of TICTOC.

Looking at the three root definitions it is clear that any attempt to resolve this will need to take account of these three different perspectives. The DPS is interested in low-cost operation; the CPO wants to provide a better service with minimum hassle; and the Maintenance Manager thinks that better maintenance could help all this. Of course, things get even more complicated if we attempt to develop root definitions for the external stakeholders, which were identified in Chapter 3. It may also be the case that other root definitions could be developed for the DPS, CPO and MM. As an exercise, you may like to do this now.

SSM: Conceptual Modelling

Fascinating though the production of root definitions may turn out to be, it is not intended as an end in itself. This is why it is wrong to regard SSM purely as an approach to problem structuring. Root definitions are a means to an end, and that end is the development of conceptual models which are intended to embody, in outline terms, what a system *must* include in order to meet the root definitions. Note the word "must": conceptual models are intended as minimal descriptions of the subsystems or components that would be neces-sary in any embodiment of the root definition. They are intended to take the verbs included in the root definitions and to show how they might relate to one another. These conceptual models are not intended to refer, at this stage, to any particular implementation within any particular organisation. Remember, at this stage we are in the realm of systems thinking and not in the real-world domain.

In the terms of SSM, a conceptual model is a diagrammatic representation of the interconnections of the activities that must be present for the root definition to make sense. It thus focuses on the verbs from the root definition and links them logically in quite conventional ways. Checkland and Scholes (1990) suggest that a conceptual model should contain between five and nine activities, though the examples in Checkland (1981) do not meet this criterion. Any more than that and some aggregation is needed, any less and the model is too simple to be of use. The activities *must* include processes for monitoring and control as this is a fundamental part of the notion of an open system. Thus, the models are validated against systems concepts and not, at this stage, against any notion of "reality".

Figure 5.5 shows a first attempt at a conceptual model for the root definition which we have ascribed to the Director of Port Services in the case study. It includes the following activities:

- Pumping of oil from Transitanian sources to tankers via Ventry.
- Financial control.
- Monitoring of the needs of the tanker operators as customers.
- Monitoring of available technologies in addition to UKHose.
- Monitoring of environmental demands and constraints.

It also shows the DPS in there, under political pressure from the Transitanian government.

In Checkland's terms, the "pump oil via Ventry" activity is the operational subsystem of the DPS Hose System and the other activities are subsystems that support or control this. Clearly, conceptual models for the other two people would be a little different

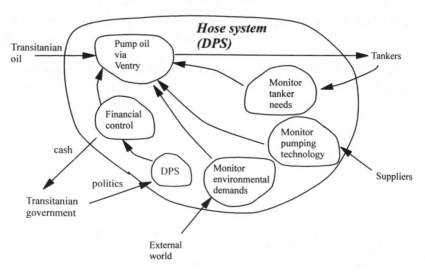

Figure 5.5 *DPS: conceptual model for the hose system*

from this. The next stage in conceptual modelling is to consider each of the activities in the broad-brush conceptual model by looking "inside" them. For example, the activity of monitoring environmental constraints might be separated into those that are legally imposed and those that seem sensible for other reasons. Once again, it is important to note that this part of SSM assumes that the analyst is currently within the realm of systems thinking—there is no need to consider whether such systems really do exist (though this is a hard temptation to fight).

Looking back to Figure 5.1, there are two subsidiary activities linked to number 4: the use of the formal system concept, and the use of other systems thinking. These were briefly mentioned earlier when discussing the validity of such models. If there is no concern, at this stage, with the real world, how can they be validated? Answering this question requires the analyst to fall back on the notion that open systems ideas provide a useful way of regarding the real world. Thus, a conceptual model within SSM is to be judged against the formal definition of open systems and of human activity systems in particular. Clearly this means that there must be ways for the system to communicate across its boundaries with the outside world. That is, there must be established relationships between the activities and subsystems and there must be control systems which guarantee that the system will continue to operate for some time. In addition, the model can be checked against other systems ideas such as the notion of a viable system model (Espejo and Harnden, 1989). If it can be made to fit none of them, then its validity, in systems terms, must be in doubt.

Checkland and Scholes (1990), in their revision of SSM, suggest that there may in fact be no need to use formal system concepts in developing the conceptual models. Instead they argue that it is sufficient that the pairing of the root definition and model be defensible. That is, each activity in the model should be traceable back to words or concepts within the root definition. That is, the model is validated against the root definition. As Figure 5.4 suggests, this still falls back on notions present in formal definitions.

SSM: Comparison—Conceptual Models versus What is There Already

The purpose of developing the conceptual models is to ensure that the system as defined through people's perceptions is captured in terms that fit the notion of open system. This is done in the belief that this is an effective way to design human activity systems in the real world. Hence it is important to compare the current, as-is, situation with the conceptual models, with a view to thinking through what action and changes may be needed. Checkland (1981) suggests four ways of doing this:

1. Using the conceptual models to support *ordered questioning*. The models are used as a source for a set of questions which can be asked of people involved in the actual situation. In effect, the analyst should keep the conceptual models under wraps and should use them to open up debate about change, to get people to think whether it is needed, and if so, in what form. This is an attractive way to proceed for it permits the analyst to work with the people in developing possible changes and it avoids the accusation that he or she knows a lot about systems but little about "what goes on here". Only the analyst need be aware of the conceptual model.

2. By *walking through* the conceptual models with sequences of events that have actually occurred in the past. The idea here is to investigate how they would have been handled, had the systems of the conceptual model existed, compared with what did happen in practice. It is obviously important to realise that people's memories of events can be very selective when doing this. Needless to say, this approach needs to be used with some care so as to avoid antagonising those who might have been involved in whatever led to the request for a soft systems study.

3. By *conducting a general discussion* about the high level features of the conceptual model vis-à-vis its comparison with the present situation. This requires the analyst to spend time with the major actors explaining the models to them and discussing with them the differences and similarities. Unlike point 1 above, in this case, the major actors must be made aware of the conceptual model. As ever, this may require some tact.

4. By *model overlays*, which means an attempt to compare the detail of the conceptual model with the detail of what is. It must be noted that this really means a comparison of the conceptual model with another model of what currently exists and operates; hence the term model overlay.

Of course, if the study is focused on a novel system which is known not to exist, none of these methods can be used. In such cases the conceptual models serve to focus people's attention on what might be done to implement their vision.

It cannot be stressed too highly that, in crossing the boundary from the systems thinking to the real world, we are re-entering a world in which considerations other than just the cerebral and logical apply. Hence, Checkland and Scholes (1990) emphasise the crucial importance of maintaining two streams of enquiry, and this becomes especially important at this stage in the work. The first stream they term the *logic driven stream*, by which they refer, primarily, to the analysis carried out below the line in the realm of systems thinking. Here rigour and logic are needed to develop conceptual models which are valid in systemic terms. In addition, though, a second stream, the *cultural enquiry stream* is also vital and this features most strongly in the first two stages of SSM (exploration and finding out) and these latter phases (comparison and implementation). Implementation, especially, is not just a cerebral act. Deciding to do something in such a way that the outcome will be as desired, demands commitment and agreement. This takes time and is an emotional and psychological response at least as much as a logical one. Thus the three enquiry levels mentioned earlier must be maintained with especial vigilance at this stage and the following ones.

SSM: Implementing Feasible and Desirable Changes

This stage in SSM encompasses activities 6 and 7 in Figure 5.1. This is the stage at which the client for the study may be expecting a pay-off. This is, however, not entirely straightforward with soft methods. In these, one outcome should be the learning that accrues as a result of the study. In most cases, however, there are also changes recommended as a result of such a study. The changes might be large scale, such as the implementation of a planning and control system where no such effective system existed prior to the study. On the other hand, they might be smaller in scale and may require adjustments to existing ways of doing things.

During the exploration stages of SSM, three important aspects were the investigations of the structure, process and climate of the situation (see Figure 5.3). It should be no surprise, given the cyclic nature of SSM, that these should loom large at implementation time. Indeed, there are many similarities between the exploration and implementation stages of a methodological approach (Pidd, 1988). Thus we might expect possible changes in the ways in which people are formally organised and controlled (the structure, which changes slowly); in the ways in which work is done and the people interact to do the work (the process, which is always in flux); and in people's attitudes about their work, the customers and one another (the climate).

The definition of these changes should emerge from activity 6 of the SSM approach, the comparison of the conceptual models with the real-world problem situation as it was expressed. Whether the production of a set of feasible and desirable changes and the implementation process can be fully separated from that comparison seems dubious. It may be better to regard this part of the approach as explicitly cyclic, as in Figure 5.6. That is, there is likely to be explicit to-ing and fro-ing between these three activities in an effort to ensure that the client gains from the study.

In deciding whether a change should be made, Checkland (1981) and Checkland and Scholes (1990) argue that any change must be systemically desirable and culturally feasible. This statement is unfortunately open to misinterpretation. What it seems to mean is that, taking the notion of a human activity system as an ideal type, then any changes should be ones that can be defended in terms of that ideal type. If the change cannot be defended in systemic terms, it should not be recommended. Alongside this, the idea that changes should be culturally feasible is a swipe at impractical ideas of optimisation and rationality. They are arguing that, no matter how attractive an idea may seem in the realm of systems thinking, unless it is acceptable given the culture of the organisation at that time, there is little chance of it being implemented. This, of, course, could be taken as an argument for a form of short-term, fudge and mudge approach. However, major changes often do take years to put into place and having an acceptable, or feasible, plan for their implementation is crucial.

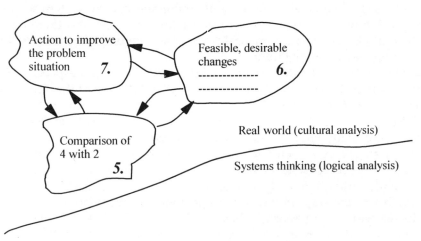

Figure 5.6 *Cyclic activity in the "real world"*

SUMMARY—SOME REFLECTIONS ON SSM

In his book *Images of Organisation*, Morgan (1986) compares different metaphors in common use for the idea of organisation. Of these eight metaphors, three are in everyday use:

- the organisation as a bureaucratic machine
- the organisation as an organism or system
- the organisation as the expression of a culture.

The first metaphor, that an organisation is a machine deliberately designed to perform certain functions, is extremely pervasive. It stresses the structural aspects of organisations, the formal roles people take and the explicit rules they may follow in carrying out their work. In manufacturing it is most strongly expressed in the approach of "scientific management", often known as Taylorism, which stresses the need to organise work so that interchangeable people can carry out well-defined and highly structured tasks managed by explicit co-ordination. The aim of management is to design the machine so that it works, to maintain it so it remains in good condition, and to co-ordinate the different tasks on which people are engaged. This mechanistic approach fits well with highly bureaucratic organisations that are governed by rule books and in which task and role divisions are clearly defined.

The second metaphor, the idea that the organisation is a form of organism, is virtually the same as regarding it as a system. The idea is that the organism does not need to be pre-programmed to respond to different, rather limited, circumstances. Instead it expresses its organic nature by interacting with its environment in an adaptive way. Hence the role of management is to develop appropriate systems that will support that adaptation and which will have some form of internal control. These are the same assumptions, in fact, that underlie many systems approaches. Morgan writes that the organismic view is really that of a machine in soft focus. What he means by this is that both metaphors, when used, pay scant regard to the nature of the social world. Both tend to take it for granted and assume that it can be dealt with in intellectual and logical terms. This was one of the criticisms made, fairly or not, of Checkland's (1981) account of SSM.

By contrast, his third metaphor, also in common use, is that an organisation is an expression of a culture that is shared by its members. This culture might be co-operative, action-oriented, research-based or whatever. As an example, in the week in which this is being written, the British Home Secretary has sacked the Director

General of the British Prison Service. Commenting on this, a spokesman for the association that represents prison governors described the Prison Service as a "command culture". This was not intended as a criticism, merely a recognition that the service is organised on a military model in which orders are not to be questioned, they are to be obeyed. This could, presumably, be contrasted with the notion of a co-operative culture in which people were highly self-motivated. Use of the idea of organisational culture implies that changes will only be made if they can be accommodated within the culture—apart from deliberate efforts to change the culture.

How does this relate to SSM? Perhaps it is best to regard SSM as a way of taking a systems or organismic approach and adapting it to fit with the idea of organisational culture. Hence the stress in Checkland (1981), which is increased in Checkland and Scholes (1990), on the need to engage with the culture of the organisation. Mingers and Taylor (1992) report on a postal survey of people who know of SSM and who might be expected to use it in some way. The proportion of users was quite high and, of these, the majority claimed to use SSM with a view to easing a problem situation or to develop understanding. They also claimed that a main benefit of SSM was that it provided a strong structure within which they could achieve these aims. These findings seem to support the view that SSM provides a formalised approach to gaining understanding within an organisation, paying due regard to cultural issues.

The next chapter explores another "soft" approach, cognitive mapping and SODA, developed by Colin Eden and his colleagues. It takes a rather different view of the same issues, though some of its outward appearances look similar.

REFERENCES

Ackoff R.L. (1971) Towards a system of systems concepts. *Management Science*, **17**, 661–71.

Bertalanffy L. von (1971) *General Systems Theory: Foundations, Development, Applications*. Allen Lane, London.

Boulding K.E. (1956) General systems theory—the skeleton of science. *Management Science*, **2**, 3.

Checkland P.B. (1981) *Systems Thinking, Systems Practice*. John Wiley, Chichester.

Checkland P.B. and Scholes J. (1990) *Soft Systems Methodology in Action*. John Wiley, Chichester.

Espejo R. and Harnden R. (1989) *The Viable Systems Model: Interpretations and Applications of Stafford Beer's Viable Systems Model*. John Wiley, Chichester.

Janis I.L. (1972) *Victims of Groupthink*. Houghton Mifflin, New York.

Kolb D.A. (1983) Problem management: learning from experience. In S. Srivasta (Ed.) *The Executive Mind*. Jossey-Bass, San Francisco, CA.

Mingers J. and Taylor S. (1992) The use of soft systems methodology in practice. *Journal of the Operational Research Society*, **43**, 4, 321–32.

Morgan G. (1986) *Images of Organisation*. Sage, London.

Pidd M. (1988) From problem structuring to implementation. *Journal of the Operational Research Society*, **29**, 2, 1–7.

Vickers G. (1983) *Human Systems are Different*. Harper & Row, London.

Wilson B. (1984) *Systems: Concepts, Methodologies, and Applications*. John Wiley, Chichester.

6
Cognitive Mapping and SODA

INTRODUCTION

The introduction to Part II stressed that "soft" methods are pluralistic and aim to be interpretive. That is, they do not assume that there will be agreement about objectives when working within an organisation. They assume, instead, that there may be different perspectives on the same situation for all sorts of reasons. The last chapter described the soft systems methodology (SSM) developed by Checkland and his colleagues. SSM requires the analyst to develop root definitions of alternative systems. It accepts that there will be alternative viewpoints and it tries to express these in systems terms. A criticism of SSM is that it provides little guidance about how such conflict or disagreement might be handled. Indeed, Checkland and Scholes (1990) argue that the aim of an SSM study, in situations where there is disagreement and conflict, should be accommodation between the parties, not consensus. Presumably this is because the idea of consensus so often contains an image of flabby compromise which satisfies no one. It would appear that, if SSM is used, this accommodation will, if all else fails, be achieved by an appeal to the logic of systemicity—effective systems *must* be designed this way.

A Technique and a Methodology

The second interpretive approach to be considered here, cognitive mapping and SODA (strategic options development and analysis) was proposed and used by Eden and his colleagues. It goes rather further than SSM and starts at a different point. It consists of a technique (cognitive mapping), which sits within an enclosing methodology (SODA). The technique stems from cognitive psychology, the discipline that is concerned with trying to understand how humans think and make sense of their experiences. Whereas SSM is deliberately systemic, albeit in a "soft" way, cognitive mapping has no truck with these ideas and is avowedly individualistic in its stance. Thus its starting point is an attempt, via established techniques, to build a cognitive map of someone's ideas based on what they have to say about them. If there are several individuals involved, then the SODA methodology is invoked with the aim of generating a debate, based on the individual maps, which will lead to a commitment to act. This chapter will explore cognitive mapping and SODA.

Process and Content

Eden's approach is to use a cognitive map as a way of capturing people's views so as to develop an explicit model of them. The idea is that the analyst should interview people in a semi-directed way and try to sketch out a map of their thinking by trying to understand the concepts that they use and how they are linked together. It also assumes that individual people work together, sometimes co operatively, sometimes not, and that, to be effective, team members need to appreciate one another's thinking enough to develop a joint commitment. Thus, the technique, cognitive mapping, is linked to a methodology, SODA, which aims to support this process of shared appreciation. In doing so, it is important to note Eden's (1989) point that the outcome of any attempt to work with people results from both the content of the help and the process through which it is delivered and experienced. This is captured in the notional equation:

$$\text{Outcome} = \text{Process} \times \text{Content}$$

Thus if the analyst concentrates only on the content of the help that is given—which might mean the techniques used or the responses gained from people—the outcome of the intervention is unlikely to be of much use. Similarly, any attempt to offer help which focuses only on a process of some kind is likely to be vacuous and is unlikely to produce anything of much value. The analyst, therefore, needs to master technique, but also must be consciously managing the process of what is happening. Though Checkland places rather less stress on this in SSM, it is clear that the same argument must hold if SSM is to be of much use. This is one reason why the introduction to Part II refers to these two approaches as interpretive.

Varieties of Cognitive Maps

As a term, cognitive mapping has a number of meanings. In the wider literature of psychology it usually denotes attempts to depict a person's mental image of physical space. For example, most people have a very distorted (i.e. non-physical) map of their surroundings; that is, our spatial memory is not just evoked by conjuring up an image of a scene in our minds. Other factors are at work while we collect, organise, store, recall and manipulate information about our spatial environment. In fact, we tend to distort things in different ways according to our interests. For a brief discussion of this issue see McNamara (1994), and for more substantial coverage see Downs and Stea (1977).

This chapter will focus on the term "cognitive mapping" as it is used by Eden et al. These maps are intended for use by someone who wishes to understand elements of the thought of another person or group, leaving aside for the moment the question of whether groups have thoughts as such. It would be hopelessly over-optimistic to describe the maps as models of thinking or as maps of thought. Instead they are "tools for reflective thinking and problem solving" (Eden et al, 1992). They are to be developed during interviews by a mapper who tries to capture the ideas of the interviewee, using the words used by the interviewee. Hence they represent the mapper's interpretation of the views of the interviewee. They are preferable to verbal accounts because they enable the links between the concepts used by the person to be shown on the map in an unambiguous way. Verbal accounts of many linked concepts tend to be ambiguous.

A number of mapping approaches have been devised for use within organisations, especially for helping senior managers with their strategic thinking. A short overview of these is given in Fiol and Huff (1992) and a longer discussion is to be found in Huff (1990). The different approaches are based on a range of assumptions, which for Eden and his colleagues (Eden, 1989; Eden et al, 1979, 1983) stem from personal construct theory (Kelly, 1955). It is not necessary to fully understand this theory to appreciate how the maps might be drawn and used. But some understanding may help to prevent their abuse. The next section summarises the essence of personal construct theory in an attempt to clarify the intellectual underpinnings of Eden's approach.

PERSONAL CONSTRUCT THEORY

The motivation for cognitive mapping was the realisation that, even though people may have different perceptions of the same situation, the different perceptions can often be understood rationally. To do this implies enough time and also a language in which they can reliably be described. Hence, what was needed was an acceptable way of understanding people's perceptions and of describing them. The method of understanding had to be intellectually defensible and the language had to be one which could, itself, be easily understood. Personal construct theory was developed by Kelly and is thoroughly described in two volumes (Kelly, 1955). It is one of the frameworks used in cognitive psychology and is based on some deceptively simple ideas. A discussion of the basics of construct theory is given in Bannister and Fransella (1986) and some idea of other applications of the theory can be found in Adams-Webber and Mancuso (1983). Eden's cognitive mapping is based on Kelly's construct theory and it makes use of some of the theory's ideas, but not of all of them.

The Basics of Personal Construct Theory

Construct theory was intended to be a reflexive theory that explains how, as human beings, we make sense of our world. It is reflexive in the sense that it can be used to make sense of itself. It assumes that, as humans, we have no direct contact with an interpretation-free reality. That is, we have no way of distinguishing between our experiences and our interpretation of them. This does not mean that all interpretations of experience are equally valid—that would be nonsense. However, it does mean that to understand what someone is thinking we need to understand their interpretation of the world. In one sense it assumes that there is a world external to our own experience; however, it recognises that our contact with the world is through a series of filters based on our prior experience.

The theory as expounded by Kelly is based on a formal postulate and a number of corollaries, which are clearly summarised in Bannister and Fransella (1986). Kelly postulates that humans strive to make sense of their world—that is, they attribute meaning to events and experiences. This is formally stated as the postulate: "A person's processes are fundamentally channelised by the ways in which they anticipate events." The meaning of this postulate may not be crystal clear. It means that as we enlarge our experiences in daily life, we try to make sense of them. We do this by using our imagination in anticipating what the consequences might be of what we have experienced. This notion is sometimes described as "man the scientist", because it implies that we are continually trying to understand what we experience. It is a cognitive view because it relates to cognition, another word for thinking. It assumes that even apparently irrational behaviour can be understood in rational terms.

Constructs and their Organisation

The theory is developed from the postulate, through a set of corollaries, which follow from the postulate one after the other. They are as follows, as expounded by Bannister and Fransella (1986):

1. *Construction.* Cognition is a process of discrimination in which people anticipate events by construing their replication. This process of construing results in a set of constructs, which are used to make sense of things. In our daily lives we are faced with a range of events which we experience and categorise in some way or another. The basis of that categorisation or discrimination is the system of constructs that we develop. As an example, the pleasant experience of a first holiday spent in the mountains in a week of good weather may lead someone to favour mountain holidays in the future.

2. *Individuality.* Each human develops an individual set of constructs with which to make sense of experience. Thus, people who have lived similar lives might be expected to make similar interpretations of experience, though their interpretations will be similar and not identical. We each interpret experience through the filter of our own personal construct system. As an example, a family may choose to spend a holiday in a very quiet location. But the teenage children, preferring rather more action, may construe its quietness in ways somewhat different from the way their parents see it.

3. *Organisation.* Within our minds, these constructs are organised in an ordered way such that some constructs are more powerful and wider ranging than others. Thus, they form a type of hierarchical system. This organisation is also a personal matter, and, even if two people share the same constructs, their system of constructs may differ.

4. *Dichotomy.* A person's construct system is composed of dichotomous constructs; that is, they each have, or imply, two poles. Thus a construct can be represented as statements, one pole of which denotes agreement and the other which denotes the opposite. As an example, a person may believe that a pleasant holiday involves a relaxing time; its opposite, which may be implied and not stated, is that a holiday that is not relaxing will

not be enjoyable. This is based on Kelly's view that we cannot affirm one thing without explicitly denying something else within a particular context. It is important to note that the poles are psychological rather than logical. There is, for example, no particular logical reason why a person should not enjoy a strenuous holiday as much as a relaxing one.

5. *Choice.* When interpreting experience, people try to move from confusion to understanding by developing their construct system in such a way that it reinforces itself. That is, they do not seek to upset their construct system but instead seek to elaborate it and to extend it. Bringing down the whole house of cards can be a very destructive experience and we try to avoid this.

6. *Range.* A person's constructs need not apply across their full range of experience but may be limited in range to particular contexts. For example, we may have a construct system which fully supports truth telling, but we may be very relaxed about violating this when asked to comment on someone's newly purchased clothes.

7. *Experience.* As a person has new experiences, their personal construct system undergoes continuous revision. This change may be slow, but sometimes it might be very fast and it occurs in relation to the value of their constructs in anticipating events. There is thus continual learning. Though people seek to confirm their systems this may not always be possible.

8. *Modulation.* Though a person will vary their construct system, this variation is limited by the "permeability" of the constructs in use. A permeable construct is one that we use to make sense of novelty, whereas an impermeable construct is one that we use to force our experience of events to fit our existing system. Some people have much more permeable constructs than others and seem much more adaptive—but this is not an argument that this is necessarily a good thing. A person's core constructs, the basic principles on which they build themselves (Rowe, 1983), are likely to be very impermeable in adult life.

9. *Fragmentation.* Though each person develops a construct system, this will contain construction subsystems which might be logically or inferentially incompatible. Thus, referring back to corollary 3, not all new experiences can be resolved by reference to a logical hierarchy of beliefs. This means that we might even find ourselves drawing several conclusions about the same events. The idea of fragmentation clearly relates to the range corollary.

10. *Commonality.* If two people employ constructions of experience that are similar, we can infer that their psychological processes are similar. This might be because they interpret similarly those events that have the same meaning for them. People who do not share the same experiences may, nevertheless, have similar construct systems.
11. *Sociality.* People are able to understand one another's construct systems and this is the basis of social interaction. If we are unable to share in another's construct system then opportunities for interaction or joint action will be very limited indeed.

Techniques Associated with the Theory

From this fundamental postulate and its 11 corollaries, Kelly went on to construct a consistent theory of cognition. Personal construct psychology is "an attempt to understand the way in which each of us experiences the world, to understand our 'behaviour' in terms of what it is designed to signify and to explore how we negotiate reality with one another" (Bannister and Fransella, 1986). Associated with this theory are techniques such as repertory grids, which are attempts to develop ways of isolating and representing people's personal constructs. The techniques can become an end in themselves for some people and may obscure the insights to be gained from the rest of the theory (Rowe, 1983). From the point of view of this chapter, these techniques need not be discussed. Here we are concerned with the ways in which the theory can be used to help people understand and interpret other people's views of reality. Eden developed the cognitive mapping technique with this in mind. Unlike some of the other techniques, it is intended to be simple, transparent and flexible in use.

ASSUMPTIONS OF COGNITIVE MAPPING AND SODA

Eden has provided a number of accounts of cognitive mapping and SODA, the most straightforward of which is Eden (1989), where it is conveniently placed alongside Checkland's (1981) own description of soft systems methodology. At first glance there are many similarities between the two approaches, which is interesting because they are based on different assumptions. There are also some major differences in the two approaches. The specific assumptions underlying cognitive mapping and SODA are discussed in this section.

Action Orientation

Fascinating though it can be to explore people's perceptions via cognitive maps, this is not an end in itself. Instead, Eden takes an action orientation in which the aim is to help people decide what to do and how to do it. Indeed, there is a specific assumption that people are working towards a commitment to action and they are not taking part just to understand themselves. This is not intended to belittle the need for analysis and understanding—indeed, finding ways to help other people understand one another's perceptions is at the heart of the approach. However, the aim is to move people towards some commitment to act.

Individualistic Focus

Whereas SSM assumes that it can be useful to regard organisations and their parts as if they were human activity systems, SODA and cognitive mapping make no such assumption. Instead the view is thoroughly individualistic. That is, organisations are taken to be composed of human beings, individual people who may or may not choose to operate within systems. Each of these individuals is assumed to hold views on what is happening to them and about what they would like to see happen. The idea of the cognitive mapping is to model those perceptions and desires. The aim of SODA is to find ways for groups to develop a commitment to action despite those differing perceptions and desires. Given its roots within construct theory, this view of individualistic perception should be no surprise.

The idea is to work with the construct systems people employ, and to use these to engage in a debate about possible action. In this sense, the approach assumes that problems are artefacts of the human imagination. Therefore, individuals who have different perceptions will tend, as discussed in Chapter 3, to frame problems differently. Different construct systems will lead to different framing. To work as an effective group or team, these people need jointly to define the problems on which they will work. This involves negotiation and this may include power-play and argument. SODA aims to support that negotiation and argument and to help the people move to a joint commitment to action.

Stress on Cognition

Being based on construct theory, Eden's approach has at least some of its roots within cognitive psychology and therefore assumes that humans try to make sense of their environment and of their experiences. The approach therefore requires the analyst to work with the "sense-making systems" people use rather than with the world as the analyst sees it. Hence the stress is upon linked constructs, which are psychologically based rather than logically based. The idea, in the cognitive mapping stage, is to develop a graphical scheme of the linked constructs that people seem to employ when thinking about whatever the problem situation happens to be.

COGNITIVE MAPPING

A cognitive map is a form of influence diagram, similar to the ones used in system dynamics (see Chapter 7). It is considered by Eden et al (1992) to be a subset of cause maps, or causal submaps to use the terminology of Fiol and Huff (1992). The map consists of nodes, known as concepts and similar to constructs, linked by arrows. The arrows may carry a sign at the arrow head, though the absence of a sign is usually taken to indicate a positive link and a negative sign indicates a negative link. The basic idea is shown in Figure 6.1. This shows two abstract concepts linked in a positive way. The direction of the arrow is intended to represent the causal direction of the relationship. This means that as expressed, concept 1 tends to lead to towards concept 2.

Concepts (Nodes)

As mentioned earlier, a concept stems from the idea of a construct in construct theory. Therefore, a concept is expressed as a pair of

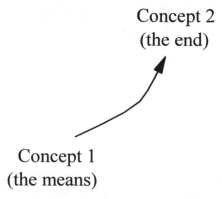

Figure 6.1 *Concepts and links*

psychological opposites, and these opposites need not be logical. The idea of the concepts is that they should capture the views and outlook of the person for whom a cognitive map is being drawn. Hence it is important to use labels for them that somehow capture the words used by that person. A concept is expressed as a pair of poles because an apparently similar concept could have different interpretations and its expression as a pair of opposites helps to clarify what the person means by this concept. The second pole is not simply the negative of the first pole because "psychological opposites are rarely as simple as simple negatives" (Brown, 1992).

As an example, someone may be planning their holiday and part of their thinking might be that they would prefer to stay in a hotel. Thus, if the concept were expressed as a single pole, we could capture it as "Prefer to stay in hotels". However, that statement makes more sense against some opposite such as "don't like camping". If the concept is expressed as "Prefer to stay in hotels ... don't like camping", this opens up the possibility that a rented cottage or gîte accommodation might be acceptable. Or, again, the positive pole might be contrasted with something like "no wish to self-cater". In which case the concept becomes, "Prefer to stay in hotels ... no wish to self-cater" and this allows the possibility that bed and breakfast accommodation might be OK, or even a rented house that is close to acceptable restaurants. Whereas, if the concept is expressed as "Prefer to stay in hotels ... don't like anything else" then there is much less psychological room for manoeuvre.

Ideally these bipolar concepts should be expressed in a way which itself is action oriented, thus "Prefer to stay in hotels" expresses a desire to act in a particular way. This does not mean that this action will eventually be taken, because other concepts may interfere with this. For example, the person's thinking might include a concept such as "Wish to spend less than £300 on accommodation". This concept, whatever its opposite pole, might mean that the preference for hotels must be moderated in some way or other. Both concepts are geared towards action and their interaction is what will, eventually, lead to some action.

Though concepts on these cognitive maps should be bipolar, it is sometimes the case that the second pole is unclear. There can be two reasons for this according to Eden. The first is that neither the individual being interviewed nor the analyst is clear about this. In this case, further discussion of the concept is needed in order to clarify this. "From what I understand, you say that you prefer to stay in hotels. It would help me if you could be a bit more precise about this. You say that you prefer to stay in hotels, but this implies that you prefer them to other options. Perhaps we could briefly discuss what these other possibilities are?" A second reason for the missing opposite pole is that the concept may really be a subsidiary (or even final) goal rather than an action intended to get to some goal. Continuing with the example, it may become clear that "Prefer to stay in hotels ..." should be stated as "I really want to stay in a hotel" and this is one of the goals which the person wishes to achieve. As will become clear later, it is important to distinguish these goals from the bipolar concepts.

Sometimes it is not necessary to state both poles of a concept since the opposite is so clearly logical that there is no ambiguity. The concept "Wish to spend less than £300 on accommodation" is one of these. Such a concept is closer to the idea of a constraint than a goal even though it needs no second pole.

Arrows (Arcs)

The arrows are intended to show the links, as expressed by an individual, between pairs of concepts. The concept at the start (or tail) of the arrow is to be thought of as the means to achieving the concept at the end (or head) of the arrow. The concept at the head is a consequence of the one at the tail, this one being an explanation of the one at the head. Therefore, the means concept is subordinate to the end concept. The map should ideally be drawn so that it flows upwards towards the higher level goals. As an example, consider Figure 6.2, which relates to some of the concepts employed by someone in deciding where to go on holiday.

An arrow head carrying a negative sign is intended to show that there is negative causality between the two concepts. This does not mean that the means:end relationship is reversed. It means that the second pole of the means concept is psychologically linked by the person to the first pole of the end concept. Thus the person believes that a self-catering holiday is likely to be cheaper than one based in a hotel. The negative sign system is employed because the concepts ought to be expressed with the desirable pole as the first of the two in the concept. Thus, this person would prefer to stay in a hotel but would also prefer a cheap holiday. Notice that, at this stage at least, there is no need to force the person to be more specific about what they mean by cheap or expensive. The use of a negative or positive link should be a feature of the concepts expressed by the individual and should not be a reflection of the views of the consultant. For example, Figure 6.2 shows a negative link from "No cooking ..." to "No illness ...", this being the view expressed by the person whose

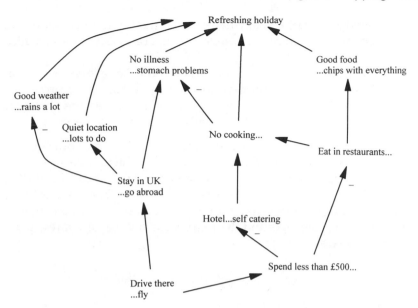

Figure 6.2 Cognitive map—holiday choice

map this is. Other people, particularly those whose cannot cook, might see things differently! In addition, there is nothing to prevent the consultant from developing his or her own map of the situation—indeed this may be a good idea in some cases.

Drawing the Map

Eden et al (1995) suggest 12 guidelines that people should follow when attempting to draw cognitive maps. Rather than repeating them here, I will draw out a number of the main points, which might be of value when drawing a map while interviewing someone.

- Try to get the structure of the map sorted out. This means making an effort to distinguish between three types of concept:

  (i) Goals should be placed at the top of the map, since these are the things at which people are aiming.

  (ii) Place the other concepts below the goals, but leading into them. Be sure to spot concepts that might turn out to be "strategic issues". They may have long-term implications, high cost or irreversibility. They may require a portfolio of actions to make them happen, or they may even require a change in culture. In essence these are pivots around which the map is centred.

(iii) The other, normal, concepts should be expressed in an imperative, or action-oriented way. That is, express the concepts with the preference of the person as the first pole even if this means that a negative arrow will be needed.

- Be careful to ensure that the arrows have the correct direction of causality. If unsure then check carefully with the interviewee.
- If the map is drawn during the interview it will need to be tidied up later and this is advisable for reasons other than just neatness. Working through the map again after the event allows the analyst to think about the links and their structure and to check any aspects that are unclear.

Software Support for Mapping

Any attempt to understand and interpret people's ideas will produce information that must be organised and analysed. Though this can be done by hand, it gets rather tedious when a map consists of a large number of constructs. Though it is arguable whether computer software should be used interactively during a client interview to develop a map of the ideas expressed, there are uses for computer support.

- As a map is developed, its appearance can grow increasingly scrappy and untidy, with lines that cross, writing that becomes nearly illegible, attempts to fit in a space more than was originally intended, and so on. Thus the first use for software support is in making a sketch map rather neater, better organised and easier to read. According to Eden and his colleagues, there is little to be gained from a map with only a few concepts that cannot be achieved by a straight verbal account of the ideas and their links. However, they argue that many useful maps may contain over a hundred concepts and considerable layout skills are needed to draw these legibly.
- Once a map has been developed and is properly drawn, it needs (as will be seen later) to be analysed. This is to link together any concepts that seem to have similar meanings and, possibly, to prepare the maps for aggregation with other maps in the SODA process.

Eden and his colleagues have developed the software system, COPE (Ackermann and Sweeney, 1995), as an aid in drawing and using these maps. COPE runs on PCs and compatibles with versions for different operating systems.

Accounts of the use of SODA and cognitive mapping often assume that COPE, or some similar tool, will be used in helping to draw the map and to analyse it. This does not necessarily mean that the software will be used during the early interactions with the person whose ideas are being captured in the map. That is a question for the analyst to consider when consciously planning the process of interaction.

Consulting Styles and Consulting Processes

Schön (1982) argues that many professionals employ what he terms "technical rationality" in justifying what they do and what they offer to their clients. This embodies a view that professional knowledge sits in a hierarchy in which "'general principles' occupy the highest level and 'concrete problem solving' the lowest" (Schön, 1982, p. 24). In this model, the professional aims to apply the general principles to specific problems. This implies that professionals have a systematic knowledge base which is specialised, firmly bound, scientific and standardised. Hence most professions require their members to sit exams designed to test their understanding of this knowledge base. Further, the professional is consulted because of this expertise. Schön argues that most professions recognise that the use of this knowledge to give specific help is far from straightforward but tend to subsume this under "craft skills" or something similar. Technical rationality implies that professionals function best as experts who themselves define the problems of the clients on which they work.

A different approach is, however, possible and this is what Eden et al (1983) term the *negotiative approach*, which they contrast with other approaches as shown in Figure 6.3. They argue that three styles of helping or consulting are in common use, the first of which is a *coercive approach*, which has some of the features of Schön's technical rationality. In this coercive approach consultants use their professional power to persuade and convince clients of how their problems should be framed and how they should be tackled. In this approach, problem definition is the responsibility of the consultant, though this may be cloaked in an approach that is apparently based on consultation. An *empathetic approach* is the opposite of a coercive one, and this refers to an approach in which consultants set out to fully understand the problem as the clients see it. The consultants work with the clients to help them to frame their own view of the problem. In one sense, the consultant is a passive reflector of the client's concerns.

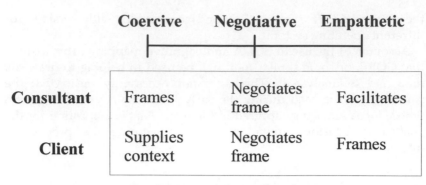

Figure 6.3 *Consulting approaches*

Rather than these two, Eden et al recommend a *negotiative approach* which is based on a period of negotiation between consultant and client. The idea is to negotiate a problem frame in which both parties are interested and to which both are committed. This approach sits between the other two and it assumes that both parties have something they bring to the venture and that both may have something to gain from it. It accepts, as given, that the problem as initially expressed by the client may not be the one on which the consultant eventually co-operates and vice versa. Thus, problems are seen as negotiated.

This assumption underlies the process advocated by Eden and his colleagues with respect to cognitive mapping and to SODA. It assumes that the aspects technical rationality would relegate to "craft skills" are fundamental to a successful intervention using cognitive mapping. The cognitive maps should not be the consultant's imperious interpretation of what the interviewee has said. This partly explains the stress laid on expressing concepts in the words used by the interviewee. Nor should the maps result from the consultant acting like a bland tape-recorder who just plays back what the interviewee has said. It is important for the mapper to interpret what the client has said and it is important that the two of them discuss this interpretation.

CASE STUDY: TICTOC

AN EXAMPLE MAP

The TICTOC case was introduced in Chapter 2 and features four main players: the Director of Port Services (DPS), the Controller of Pumping

Operations (CPO), the Maintenance Manager (MM) and you—the consultant. The account of their views provided in the dialogue is rather short, but it can be used to develop some cognitive maps. Strictly speaking, an example such as TICTOC cannot be used to simulate the SODA process since the only data that we have is the "transcript" of the meeting. What we really need to do is interview the other three people as individuals. Nevertheless, it is still possible to develop cognitive maps for the participants. As with the application of SSM, we will start with the DPS and will attempt to consider a map of our interpretation of his view of the situation. This is shown in Figure 6.4.

The example is deliberately simple and includes rather fewer concepts and links than would be the case in real life. It is also a double interpretation of the DPS's views, being an interpretation of an interpretation! Nevertheless, it serves to illustrate a number of features of these maps. The first is that the map is deliberately drawn to run from bottom to top. "Minimum total cost", which seems to be his ultimate goal, is placed at the top and will presumably be expressed in whatever terms the DPS would use. At the bottom are the initial, basic explanations or causes, which should lead through a causal chain to this goal. The DPS is faced with considering whether to make changes to the ways in which the Ventry pumping operation is conducted. He could "Change the hose

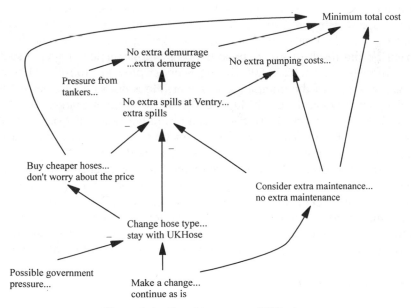

Figure 6.4 *Cognitive map – DPS's views*

type" (which has a second pole, "Stay with UKHose") and/or he could "Consider extra maintenance … no extra maintenance". This concept needs a second pole since another possibility might be "no maintenance at all". If he decides that a new hose type should be used, he would prefer this to lead to "Buy cheaper hoses" rather than to its alternative pole of "don't worry about the price". But he wishes this to lead to another outcome of "No extra spills at Ventry … extra spills at Ventry". Note that this too needs a second pole since another possibility might be "no spills at all at Ventry". This in turn is hoped to lead to "No extra pumping costs …" as is the option of increasing the maintenance, but the latter of itself would tend to increase the total cost. Finally, he is aware that "Possible government pressure" may lead to not changing the hose type. The directions of causality are shown on the arrows and correspond to the argumentation.

The second feature of the map is that each concept, initial ones apart, is expressed with the desirable outcome (in the DPS's view) stated as the first pole, and this forces the direction of causality of some of the links. Thus, even though he believes that changing hose types may lead to more spillages at Ventry, the first pole of the spillage construct is expressed as "No extra spills at Ventry". This use of the positive pole first is part of the action orientation of these maps. They are intended to stress the actions that people state they would prefer to take.

Figure 6.5 shows a possible cognitive map for the CPO, whose concerns seem somewhat different from those of the DPS. He seems preoccupied with the need to maintain a steady supply of oil to the tankers. Also, he wishes to avoid any more spillages of oil which he fears might be the result of using cheaper hoses whose service characteristics are unfamiliar to TICTOC staff. But he is under pressure from the DPS to reduce the cost of the pumping operations. He is not sure whether extra maintenance would help—it depends on whether he is charged for the cost of this extra work. Thus, his map looks rather different from that of the DPS's in Figure 6.4. Most of the concepts on the CPO's map have implied negative poles, as their meaning seems fairly clear.

Figure 6.6 shows an attempt, under the same synthetic conditions as the other two, to provide a cognitive map of what the maintenance manager (MM) seems to be saying. His concerns seem to be to demonstrate that more maintenance would help whichever hoses are used in the future. Thus, though he may agree that total costs ought to decrease, he is hoping that a greater share of operating costs will be spent on the service provided by his department. He argues that this would keep the tanker operators and the Greens happy.

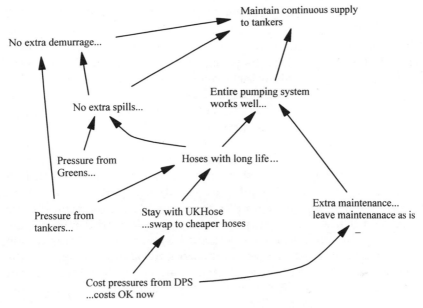

Figure 6.5 Cognitive map—CPO's views

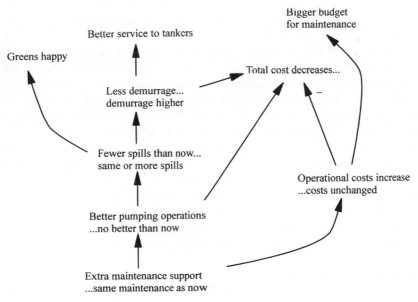

Figure 6.6 Cognitive map—MM's views

WORKING WITH COGNITIVE MAPS

Given that these cognitive maps are intended to help people to think through the actions that they might take, it is clearly of some importance to consider how these maps might be used. A later section of this chapter will discuss the SODA methodology, which is the process by which Eden and his colleagues suggest that the maps might be used to negotiate problem definitions leading to agreed action within teams of people. In this sense, SODA is a form of group decision support and COPE, the software system referred to above, forms part of a group decision support system (Eden and Ackermann, 1992). Note that the software is only one part of this system, human beings and their interactions are also important. Before discussing SODA, however, it seems sensible to consider how these maps might be understood and analysed. The first part of this section will consider how the mapper might work through the map with the interviewee, clarifying and working towards some agreement about possible actions. The second part will discuss ways in which more complex maps can be handled.

Working Through a Map

Eden (1989) suggests that there are two ways of working through a map with the other person. Later, it will be clear that a similar approach applies if SODA is invoked when working with groups of people. The two approaches are *top-down* or *bottom-up*. Both have the same aims in mind: to check whether the map is complete enough to be used, and to move the discussion from expressing ideas (the mapping phase) to considering actions that might be taken. It is important to note that working with and through a map is part of the negotiative approach advocated above. The map serves as a vehicle by which the two people can move towards aspects on which they can agree and on which they might co-operate. It thus serves as a vehicle for negotiation by separating, for a time at least, the interviewee from his or her thoughts and ideas. This must be done with some care, for people's ideas can seem a bit trivial and rather banal when sketched out. The idea is not to show how foolish the client is; the idea is to find some way to move towards sensible action that can be defended in rational terms. This relates to the view that the outcome of the work is a product of the content and the process by which the people work with that content.

In a top-down approach, the idea is to start with the concepts at the top of the map and to work back down through the others. If the map has been drawn as suggested earlier, then the concepts at the top will be an attempt to capture the goals of the interviewee. Hence, in the case of the Director of Port Services in TICTOC the discussion might start with asking why he is so concerned about the overall costs of the Ventry operation. Note that this can seem dangerously close to an "idiot question" (see Chapter 3) and needs to be approached carefully, but it cannot be ignored. Presumably the DPS is not really wanting to minimise total cost—this would be easy, just shut everything down. This concept may need further elaboration to consider service levels offered to the tanker operators and so on. The idea is that each refinement of the concept moves the map further up its hierarchy until some point is reached at which the new top concept is "self-evidently a good thing" (Eden, 1989, p. 31). At this point, the idea is to work back down the hierarchical network by asking what actions might be taken to change and improve things other than the ones already placed on the map. The idea is to identify actions that might be taken. The discussion can then, if this is desired, shift to considering how these actions might be taken.

In a bottom-up approach, the two people work together by examining the tail of the map, that is those concepts at the bottom of the hierarchy which have no predecessors. As with the top-down approach, the idea is to search for options which might provide ways of taking action. For example, the DPS's map contains "Possible government pressure ..." as one of the driving forces. What action might be taken to deal with this? As in contact sports, there are two ways to deal with pressure: roll with it and find some opportunity to turn it to your advantage, or stand your ground and accept the hit. There may be some way in which the pressure being applied could be used to improve other things at Ventry as part of a deal that could be struck. Working up the map by examining each concept should lead to similar discussions, for there may be other ways of keeping costs under control and yet not increasing the splillages of oil. The idea, in each case, is to examine the concepts to see if there are other opposites which could be considered. In this way, the co-operative thinking of the client and consultant can be expanded.

Analysing a Map: Loop Analysis

As mentioned earlier, cognitive maps look very like the influence diagrams used by system dynamics modellers (see Chapter 7). As with the system dynamics diagrams it is possible to examine cognitive maps for loops, the idea being to see if there are any which may be self-reinforcing (positive feedback) or self-maintaining (negative feedback). A loop occurs when arrows leading out from a concept end up back where they started, if followed forwards through intervening concepts. An abstract example of this is given in Figure 6.7. This hypothetical map contains two loops, both of which start from concept 2. The larger of the two loops starts at concept 2 and returns there via concepts 9, 10 and 11. The smaller of the two loops goes to concept 9 then concept 11 and back to concept 2 again. Checking a large map for these loops is rather time consuming; however, this task is simple to automate and can be managed by tools such as COPE if the map data are in a computer-readable form.

Having found loops on a map, what do they signify? The first possibility is that they may simply indicate a mistake—either by the person being interviewed (they were muddled) or by the mapper. Thus the first check is that the loops are intended to be there. If so, then the next stage is to check their sign so as to consider what this might imply in dynamic terms. Checking the sign of the loop allows the mapper to see in what direction the causality lies. As with normal multiplication, an odd number of negative signs indicates that the loop has negative feedback. In terms of control theory this means that a system will be self-controlling in the sense that it will tend to

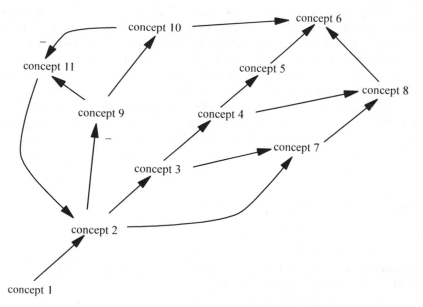

Figure 6.7 *Abstract map segment showing loops*

dampen down fluctuations. The small loop which links concepts 2, 9 and 11 is an example of such negative feedback. An even number of negative signs implies positive feedback, which will therefore be amplifying—precisely what would be expected from a set of concepts linked by positive relationships. The larger loop linking concepts 2, 9, 10 and 11 has two negative signs, making it a positive feedback loop.

The aim of the loop analysis is to check for mistakes and then to check the direction of causality of any remaining "correct" loops. These can then be discussed by the mapper and the client to try to understand their implications. The loop analysis is best conducted before any attempt to cluster the concepts.

Analysing a Map: Clusters

Given the fact that practical cognitive maps may contain a hundred or more concepts, even when produced for a single person, some way is needed to support this process of using the maps. The software system COPE provides some support in this, but the basic principles need to be understood so as to avoid the risk of inappropriate use of such a tool. One important feature of such analyses is the idea of a cluster of concepts. These are sets of concepts that are similar in some way and could, in some sense, be more-or-less separated from the rest of the map. Clearly, if a map contains concepts that are all strongly interlinked, it may not be fruitful to attempt this sort of analysis. This might be the case if the ratio of links to nodes is high.

A cluster indicates that there is an issue of some importance which may have an effect rather greater than just on a single input and output link. Underlying cluster identification is the notion that "language is the common currency of organisational life". That is, people's words have meanings and a good starting point is to assume that, though the meanings will change over time, the same words may have more or less the same meaning. Clusters can be formed around the names and words that are used—this explains the importance of capturing the words used by the interviewee. Note that this question of meaning is crucial and will be revisited when considering SODA and the question of how to merge the maps of different people. This is less of an issue when working with a single person.

Eden et al (1992) suggest two approaches to cluster formation.

Linkage clustering. In this approach, the labels given to the nodes (that is, the words employed in the concepts) are examined for their similarity. Nodes with similar labels are aggregated into clusters, with the proviso that each node can inhabit only one cluster. Once developed, such clusters should identify issues of sufficient importance to warrant further discussion. As mentioned above, this relies on the mapper capturing the words used by the interviewee and then coding them in a consistent way. If the map, its nodes and its links, are captured in a computer data file, it should be possible to parse the text into separate words and to subject it to a semantic analysis. Then some scoring system could be used to establish the similarity of different labels. This could then be used as a stopping rule to indicate when a concept should or should not be added to a cluster. The resulting clusters should provide a summary of the overall map.

Hierarchical clustering around core constructs. This approach relates back to the ideas of Kelly (1955) that constructs are organised in a hierarchical way. If this is so, and if the mapping concepts relate to these constructs, it may sometimes be useful to examine the map for hierarchies. In one sense, each node will have a supporting hierarchy, apart from those at the very bottom of the map. However, the purpose of the analysis is usually to show the linkages from certain "core constructs" (Eden et al, 1992). These can be identified by a count of the in and out arrows at each node, as it might reasonably be supposed that important nodes will have more such links. A single node may well appear in more than one hierarchical cluster, indeed if it does so, then this may well indicate that the concept is of considerable importance in the map. In Eden's terms, such concepts are regarded as "potent". This process of hierarchical clustering can also be automated if the map data is held in some suitable form. It may be easier to implement in computer software than is linkage clustering as the need for a semantic analysis is less urgent.

SODA: STRATEGIC OPTIONS DEVELOPMENT AND ANALYSIS

Cognitive mapping also provides the basis for helping teams of people to commit themselves to suitable actions. One criticism of much management science is that, though valuable at a tactical level, many of the methods and techniques turn out to be of limited value at the strategic level in most organisations. This is, as has been argued in this book so far, because strategic decision making and planning is characterised by great uncertainty, not just about how to do something, but often also about what should be done. That is, there is debate about ends as well as about means. In the terms used in the introduction to Part II, this suggests that "soft" methods might be able to make a useful contribution. SODA is an approach developed by Eden and his colleagues with the intention that it should provide a way of enabling groups of people to commit themselves to action by careful and rational consideration of the possibilities they can envisage. As with SSM, SODA is a methodology in two senses. It provides an approach that should be followed, but it also embodies a set of assumptions, those which have already been discussed when introducing cognitive mapping—it is individualistic, it stresses action and it works with people's expressed ideas. This section of the chapter will focus on the SODA approach.

Merging Maps: Working towards a Strategic Map

The first stage of the SODA approach is to interview the individual participants in order to develop their cognitive maps of the situation. This should be done as described earlier in this chapter. The next stage is to look for links, differences and similarities between the maps of the participants. This process is referred to as merging by Eden and his colleagues and the result—an aggregation of the individual maps—is known as a strategic map. A slightly subtle point underpins this merging process: to whom does the strategic map belong and whose views does it express? When we have described how the merging process works we shall return to this point.

The rationale behind this merging is to produce a strategic map with which the participants can all identify. The idea is to move the group towards a position where its members are committed to some appropriate action. It is therefore vital that this is done in such a way that they do not feel compromised. Agreement may not be complete, it may be slightly grudging, but each member is willing to work at the actions that emerge from the process. Hence, as has been said several times before, this means that the processes involved in SODA must be carefully managed.

Eden also stresses, very sensibly, that it is important to ensure that some of the words individuals used and which appeared on their own maps are preserved on the strategic map. There are two reasons for this. The first is that words may have several meanings and the substitution of apparent synonyms may obscure the original meaning. The second is that it may help the individuals involved to be committed to the outcome if they see their own words on the strategic map. Of course, if a large number of people are involved, the consultant may need to decide which are the key people whose views must be shown. In this sense, SODA recognises the reality of power in organisational life.

There are four processes in merging the individual maps into a strategic map:

1. By examining the individual maps it should become clear that at least some of the participants are using similar concepts. If there were no such similar concepts, then this would indicate that the participants are framing the issues in radically different ways that this may be the most important observation that can be made. The fact that the concepts are presented as pairs of opposing poles helps the recognition of the similarity. So does the fact that the analyst has worked with the individuals in drawing their maps. The similar concepts can be overlaid on one another in the strategic map, much as transparent sheets may be overlaid, one on the other.

2. Once overlaid in this way, it may be possible for the consultant to add extra links between the concepts used by individuals. This is a way for the consultant to suggest to the team that their ideas can fit in a synergistic way. The strategic map is to be used as a device to enable the team to negotiate with one another and with the consultant. Any links which are added are created with this in mind because the consultant is not just a disinterested observer or referee.

3. While overlaying and linking, the analyst needs to ensure that the strategic map preserves any hierarchies of links that were present in the individual maps. This may be difficult to achieve, but the dependencies are important.

4. The strategic map needs to be analysed for loops and clusters as described in the previous section. This is a crucial part of the process for it helps to identify the issues paramount in people's minds to which attention must be paid.

Earlier we asked: to whom does the strategic map belong? After the merging, the answer is presumably that it belongs to the consultant, but is intended to reflect the views of the participants. The approach is, as mentioned earlier, negotiative and does not assume that the consultant acts only in a bland, facilitative role. The strategic map is the result of a deliberate attempt by the consultant to pick out what seem to be crucial issues from the mess or issues stream (see Chapter 3) with which people are working. If the individual maps are subjective statements about these issues, the strategic map is an intersubjective statement. That is, it shows where people's subjective views are close or distant. Whether the group will accept this is another matter, and this too requires careful process management via SODA workshops.

SODA workshops

Chapter 3 developed the idea that, rather than working on self-contained and well-understood problems, it is more common for people to find themselves working with messes or issues streams. These are systems of interconnected problems and issues that are hard to pull apart without losing some of the meaning. The strategic map is the first stage in helping the group to develop their own views of that mess. The core of SODA is one or more deliberately planned SODA workshops which employ the strategic map. The aim, as mentioned several times before, is to enable negotiation between the team members so that they, and the consultant, can agree on some action to which they are committed. Hence, the vital prerequisite for a SODA workshop is a strategic map that has been analysed and clustered to show the important issues. Discussions of the conduct of the SODA workshops are to be found in Eden and Ackermann (1992) and Eden and Simpson (1989).

The analyst needs to be aware that she is taking on a difficult, though manageable, task in attempting a SODA workshop. Most teams of managers have a shared life or culture of some kind if the team is at all cohesive and may not be over-welcoming of attempts to question their ideas. It is thus vital that the consultant starts these workshops in a carefully planned and facilitative mode. The strategic map is to be used as a vehicle for discussion and negotiation—led by the consultant. Eden (1989) suggests a number of principles for the conduct of the SODA workshops:

- The room, the seating, lighting, ventilation and other comfort factors must be carefully planned. The idea is to create an atmosphere that is workmanlike and yet enables people to relax a little. If the COPE software is to be used and its output is to be displayed via some kind of computer projection system, then controllable lighting is very important. All participants need to be able to see one another and see the screen on which the strategic map is being displayed. Hence, banal though it may sound to some, the ambience is important.
- The consultant needs to remain in control of the proceedings. Given that many senior managers are extremely powerful personalities then this may be easier said than done! Perhaps the best approach is for the consultant to be explicit with the group about his or her role as chair. But, even having done this, the consultant must try to retain control without losing credibility.
- The consultant *must* come to the workshop with an agenda to be

addressed. This *must* focus on the concepts, issues, problems and relationships which have to be addressed if progress is to be made. These should emerge from the strategic map and should be identifiable on that map.
- The workshop should consist of a two-pass approach:

(i)   *The introductory pass.* This should be led by the consultant with little or no opportunity for the group to comment or to discuss. The consultant should take the group through the strategic map so as to identify the key goals that have emerged, the different problems that have been identified and their relationships, the options for action which people seem to have identified, and the assumptions which seem to have been made. As when working with individuals, this could be done in a top-down or bottom-up mode. Discussion needs to be limited to points of clarification. The idea of this first pass is to start a process in which the participants see their views as part of a larger picture and also start to understand the concerns of other people. The map is a neutral device that separates concepts and concerns from the people themselves. They may recognise their own concepts on the strategic map, but other people may not. People can think about the concepts rather than judging the person who has proposed them.

(ii) *The second pass.* This may take a considerable time, depending on the group and the complexity of the map. The idea is to take the individual clusters and issues and work on them in more detail by encouraging discussion. This second pass fits into the notion of cyclic learning mentioned in the chapter on soft systems methodology (Chapter 5). The idea is that people usually learn new ideas gradually and at different rates and may need to return to them as their understanding gradually changes. In this second pass the consultant may need to extend or elaborate the map as new issues or linkages emerge in the discussion. It is important that these are visible to the participants so that their commitment may be obtained.

The idea of the SODA workshop is to gain commitment to agreed and negotiated action. The consultant is, as would be expected in this negotiative approach, not just a neutral facilitator, but also has interests and may have other expertise. One outcome of the workshop may be that there is scope for traditional management science of the type discussed in Part III. In this sense, SODA can be regarded as an approach to problem structuring. However, it is not uncommon for people to find that, once they have negotiated an acceptably common perspective on the issue stream, the action needed is fairly clear.

SOME REFLECTIONS ON COGNITIVE MAPPING AND SODA

Part I introduced the general idea of modelling as used in management science and discussed its advantages and disadvantages as a way of anticipating the consequences of events. It also discussed views of rationality, given that these models are part of an attempt to use rational methods in managing organisations. Finally, it covered the idea of problems and decisions to try to relate what are often abstract ideas to the world of organisational life. Part II, of which this is the second chapter, addresses the question of soft or interpretive model-ling. How does cognitive mapping and SODA sit within all this?

First, there is great stress laid on the need for facilitation skills. Thus the analyst, or consultant, is not seen as exercising the form of "technical rationality" identified by Schön (1982) in which these skills are reduced to the notion of "craft". Instead they are seen as central to the success of the approach. Hence, unlike SSM, SODA makes concrete suggestions about how to generate commitment from individuals who, initially at least, take up positions different from one another. Thus, to slightly distort the views of Simon (1976), SODA provides a way of implementing procedural rationality in social or organisational terms. That is, SODA is a form of social heuristic, which can give no guarantee of success, but which has been found to be very useful. It employs a rational and explicit tool-set based, at least partially, on Kelly's Construct Theory.

SODA is also, like SSM, pluralistic in its outlook and assumptions. It thus recognises that, in some situations, there may be conflict and disagreement and, in helping to generate a debate it also implicitly recognises that conflict is not always dysfunctional. Sometimes, change can only occur through conflict, but when conflict gets out of hand, the results are very uncertain. With this in mind, there is no assumption in SODA that organisations are systems designed to achieve some goal. Instead there is the idea that they are composed of people with all sorts of mixed agendas who choose to co-operate for some reason. Uncovering the areas of common interest so as to enable progress to be made is one of the goals of a SODA workshop.

The approach is also explicitly cyclic and multilevel. In working with both individuals and the groups that they form, the approach recognises that people do operate in both modes and that their work in both levels needs to be acknowledged. This links in with the idea in the previous paragraph that people bring mixed agendas to their work. The cyclic nature of the approach may be less clear as, unlike SSM, there is no argument that one study leads into another, nor that the approach could be started at any point. Instead, Eden and his colleagues are firm in their view that strategic maps should stem from individual maps. Nevertheless, the approach is cyclic in that the individual gets at least three chances to develop their understanding. They are interviewed for their own map, they hear the consultant's views in the first part of the SODA workshop and they take part in the debate that forms the second part of the workshop. They therefore have the chance to reflect on the different issues as they are returned to.

Finally, SODA is organisationally sophisticated. It makes no assumption that an organisation is a machine or even that it is an organism. Instead, as pointed out in Pidd (1995), it is closest to the view of organisation that Morgan (1986) characterised as "flux and transformation". This is a view of organisation that stresses verbs rather than nouns. There is thus an interest in how they develop and are changed rather than in the positions and roles that people fill within them. Thus the focus is on the development of methods that will help to manage that change rather better than they might do if they were fire-fighting the whole time. This view of organisations takes for granted that things are constantly changing within and without the organisation and that people will employ all sorts of strategies to achieve their ends.

SUMMARY

Cognitive mapping is an approach, based on Kelly's theory of personal constructs, that may be used to try to help people to think through the options that face them. Its basic technique involves drawing a graph of ideas or concepts that are linked together in means:end relationships. The approach is individualistic and makes no claims to the rest of explicit systems ideas, unlike soft systems methodology (Chapter 5). The originators of the ideas stress the need to ensure that it is used as part of a negotiative approach in which the role and views of the consultant or analyst are not ignored. Instead the idea is to use the map as part of a process of helping the client or group to commit to some action that will help achieve whatever their goals are found to be.

REFERENCES

Ackermann F. and Sweeney M. (1995) *Graphics COPE User Guide, for Version 2.* University of Strathclyde, Glasgow.

Adams-Webber J. and Mancuso J.C. (1983) *Applications of Personal Construct Theory.* Academic Press, Toronto.

Bannister D. and Fransella F. (1986) *Inquiring Man: The Psychology of Personal Constructs.* (Third Edition) Croom Helm, London.

Brown S.M. (1992) Cognitive mapping and repertory grids for qualitative survey research: some comparative observations. *Journal of Management Studies*, 29, 3, 287–308.

Checkland P.B. (1981) *Systems Thinking, Systems Practice.* John Wiley, Chichester.

Checkland P.B. and Scholes J. (1990) *Soft Systems Methodology in Action.* John Wiley, Chichester.

Downs R.M. and Stea D. (1977) *Maps in Mind. Reflections on Cognitive Mapping.* Harper & Row, New York.

Eden C.L. (1989) Using cognitive mapping for strategic options development and analysis (SODA). In J. Rosenhead (Ed.) *Rational Analysis for a Problematic World.* John Wiley, Chichester.

Eden C.L. and Ackermann F. (1992) Strategy development and implementation—the role of a group decision support system. In R.P. Bostrom, R.T. Watson and S.T. Kinney (Eds) *Computer Augmented Teamwork: A Guided Tour.* Van Nostrand Reinhold, New York.

Eden C.L. and Simpson P. (1989) SODA and cognitive mapping in practice. In J. Rosenhead (Ed.) *Rational Analysis for a Problematic World.* John Wiley, Chichester.

Eden C.L., Ackermann F. and Cropper S. (1992) The analysis of cause maps. *Journal of Management Studies*, 29, 3, 309–24.

Eden C.L., Ackermann F. and Cropper S. (1995) *Getting Started with Cognitive Mapping.* Supplied with Graphics COPE v2. Banxia Software, Glasgow.

Eden C.L., Jones S. and Sims D. (1979) *Thinking in Organisations.* Macmillan, London.

Eden C.L., Jones S. and Sims D. (1983) *Messing About in Problems.* Pergamon Press, Oxford.

Fiol C.M. and Huff A.S. (1992) Maps for managers. Where are we? Where do we go from here? *Journal of Management Studies*, 29, 3, 267–86.

Huff A.S. (Ed.) (1990) *Mapping Strategic Thought.* John Wiley, New York.

Kelly G.A. (1955) *The Psychology of Personal Constructs.* Volumes 1 and 2. Norton, New York.

McNamara T.P. (1994) Knowledge representation. In R.J. Steinberg (Ed.) *Thinking and Problem Solving.* Academic Press, San Diego, CA.

Morgan G. (1986) *Images of Organisation*. Sage, London.

Pidd M. (1995) Pictures from an exhibition: images of operational research. *European Journal of Operational Research*, **81**, 479–88.

Rowe D. (1983) In J. Adams-Webber and J.C. Mancuso *Applications of Personal Construct Theory*. Academic Press, Toronto.

Schön D.A. (1982) *The Reflective Practitioner. How Professionals think in Action*. Basic Books, New York.

Simon H.A. (1976) From substantive to procedural rationality. In H.A. Simon (1982) *Models of Bounded Rationality: Behavioural Economics and Business Organisation*. MIT Press, Cambridge, Mass.

7
System Dynamics

INTRODUCTION

The first two chapters of Part II have discussed two approaches that are intended to help managers and decision makers to see the consequences of their actions by developing qualitative models. This chapter focuses on system dynamics, an approach which can be used qualitatively or quantitatively. It thus serves as a bridge between Part II and Part III, which deals with quantitative modelling.

Jay Forrester is the prime developer of the ideas now known as system dynamics and these were first published in a book called *Industrial Dynamics* (Forrester, 1961). In this he showed how models of the structure of a human system and the policies used to control it could help to develop understanding of the operation and behaviour of the system. That is, he showed the value of explicit models that combined business process and organisational structure. Forrester developed a set of tools and an approach to simulation which have become known as system dynamics. These tools were based on those used by control engineers to analyse the stability of mechanical and electrical control systems—an idea first suggested by Tustin (1953). Though originally intended for use in the industrial sector, the method has also been applied in other areas such as epidemiology (Roberts and Dangerfield, 1990) and global modelling (Meadows, 1972).

The tools of system dynamics may be used in several ways. The underlying approach provides a way of viewing human systems by stressing the importance of certain structural features, such as feedback control. If human systems are analysed in this way, then Wolstenholme (1990) argues that it is possible to provide useful insights into their operation even without recourse to computer software. The second mode of operation, however, is to use these structural features to develop a simulation model of the systems. This computer-based model can also be used to understand why they behave as they do. Finally, the simulation models can be used to help find better ways of operating the systems by demonstrating their consequences. In all these cases, the idea is to use system dynamics models as tools for thinking, but whereas our mental models are hidden, the system dynamics models are explicit.

Some writers on system dynamics seem to regard its use as fundamental to any systems thinking. For example, the manuals accompanying the Stella II software (Richmond et al, 1994) are explicit in making this case. It should be clear from the earlier chapter here on soft systems methodology (SSM; see Chapter 5), that this book is less sweeping in its claims. The case being made here is that system dynamics is one of the tools available to people wishing to think through the consequences of their possible actions. As with SSM, its core assumption is that the world can be regarded as a set of linked systems whose boundaries depend, in part at least, on the viewpoint of the observer or analyst. Unlike SSM, the idea is to show the likely consequences of such systemic interaction.

FEEDBACK AND DELAYS IN HUMAN SYSTEMS

Feedback Control

One feature of human systems identified in Chapter 5 is that they are self maintaining by the use of feedback control. Sometimes this control may be highly formalised, as in standard costing, statistical process control or performance-related payment systems. On the other hand, it may be rather informal, such as when a decrease in earnings causes a reduction in family expenditure—though optimists may delay the implementation for some time! The basic idea of feedback control is shown in Figure 7.1. This shows that control is exercised by feeding back the output to be compared with the input. Corrective action is then taken to bring the process back within desired limits. This implies that the system has some fairly stable target state (possibly expressed as minimum and maximum performance levels). If the control is based on the difference between the target and the actual output, this is known as control by negative feedback.

Some systems display positive feedback, indeed this is the basis of

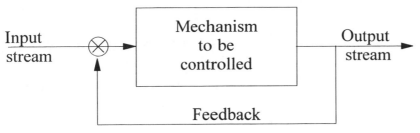

Figure 7.1 *Feedback system*

electronic amplifiers. These devices produce a signal that loops back round to the input side, adding itself to the existing input, thus producing amplification. Properly controlled, this gives us the pleasure of listening to hi-fi systems. Badly controlled, it produces the screeching of audio feedback that occurs in some public address systems when the microphone is placed in front of the loudspeakers. This positive feedback is also found in human systems. As an example, if a company places its spare cash on deposit, then the returns offered may well increase as the amount deposited increases, the idea being to encourage the deposit of larger sums. Indeed, it could be argued that any system of compound interest represents positive feedback, since the interest earned is added on to the original amount deposited.

The presence of feedback loops, whether positive or negative, usually makes the behaviour of human activity systems hard to understand (Dangerfield and Roberts, 1995). In *Industrial Dynamics*, Forrester (1961) called this "counter-intuitive behaviour". It is especially prevalent when several feedback systems are linked in some way or other.

Delays

A further feature, which can make the behaviour of these systems hard to predict, is the delays that occur in transmitting and receiving information. A fundamental principle of control is that the closer to the action that the control is exercised, the more effective it is likely to be. As a simple illustration of this, consider Figure 7.2, which depicts someone standing in a shower attempting to control the water temperature. The graph alongside shows the tap settings and the resulting temperature fluctuations. Imagine that you are the bather. You enter the shower, turn it on and are hit by a blast of cold water—not what you were hoping for. There is a slight increase in

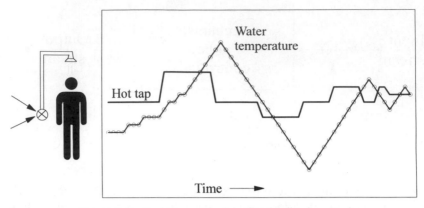

Figure 7.2 *Problems with delays in feedback control*

temperature as the water heats up, but not much. So, you grab the control knob and twist it towards the hot side, but nothing happens immediately, you are still awash in cold water. Thus, you wrench the knob yet further to the hot side. And then? A surge of over-hot water hits you somewhere painful and you wrench the knob back to the cold side ... and the process begins all over again, though eventually you should get the temperature right.

There are two reasons why a simple task such as having a shower can be so hard to control, despite the rapid feedback from water temperature. The first is the delay between turning on the shower and the arrival of any hot water. That is, the system may be full of cold water, unless someone else used the shower just before you. The second is that there is a delay between turning the control valve and the effect reaching the shower head—the water must run through the intervening pipe. Hence your action in twisting the mixer valve turns out to have delayed and unexpected consequences. This scenario can develop even further if, as in many British houses, the same cold water system also fills WC cisterns elsewhere in the house—if someone flushes a toilet while you are trying to get the shower temperature correct, an external instability is introduced which makes your task even harder. We've all heard of road rage—perhaps shower rage will be next?

This simple task is analogous to the problem of managing a large and complex organisation. As another example, a plumber recently installed a new central heating radiator in our house. The radiator is of a special design but nevertheless should be available at 24 hours' notice from local merchants. One week after the plumber first came, no radiator was in sight. "The local merchants are out of stock, they've ordered one." Another week passed, still no radiator. "The manufacturers are out of stock, they're making some more." After a few more days with still no radiator I phoned the manufacturers—a delivery is promised. Meanwhile, the merchant, the plumber and his mate have all also phoned the manufacturer—who now probably believes that there is massive demand for his product. Thus the product of delays (the plumber not ordering in advance, the merchant running out of stock, the manufacturer running out of stock) plus the amplification (four of us phoning the manufacturer independently) might lead to the manufacturer overestimating demand for his product. This is bad enough, but suppose that I, and others like me, grew tired of waiting and found a substitute product. Then, rather than facing normal demand, let alone increased demand, the manufacturer may face a slump in demand. Thus the familiar stop–go cycle of batch manufacturing occurs.

Fundamental to system dynamics is the notion that delays and feedback loops are responsible for much of the behaviour of organised human systems. Thus, if any such system is to be understood, let alone improved, these two features need to be thoroughly accounted for. System dynamics provides a way of doing this via diagramming techniques and a computer-based modelling approach.

BASIC CONCEPTS OF SYSTEM DYNAMICS MODELS

To use system dynamics it is important to understand the basic concepts, which are very simple. They are based on two pairs of ideas: resources and information, levels and rates.

Resources and Information

This is a fundamental distinction in system dynamics modelling. Resources correspond to the "stuff" or "physics" of the system and are the main concerns of the transformation process in which the system engages. Examples of resources might be products in the case of a manufacturing company, patients in the case of a hospital, or money in the case of a finance company. These are the people, objects and other things with which the system is concerned. The resources flow around the system and will change state. Thus materials become products, which become deliveries; patients become people recovering back at home, and cash is collected from customers and lent out to other people. Sometimes the state-change marks a complete change in the resource (as when raw materials are transformed into products) and sometimes it denotes a change in location or in concern (as when patients are discharged).

In the view of Richmond et al (1994), it can also be useful to subdivide the resources into two:

Consumable resources. These are depleted as activity in a system proceeds. For example, a manufacturing process will consume materials of some kind as they are transformed into work in progress or finished products. Similarly, a hospital will use up supplies of drugs and blood in its day-to-day operations.

Catalytic (non-consumable) resources. These are rather less obvious but also need to be considered. They are enabling resources which enable other transformations that involve consumable resources. As an example of this, the rate at which an item is sold may depend on the prices charged by competitors. Price is a catalytic resource in such cases, as the sales rate is dependent on the price and thus, though the physical stocks are consumed by the sales, the prices simply fluctuate.

By contrast, information is the non-physical means by which control of the resource transformations is exercised. The principle is that information about the current state of the resources is used as a basis for making decisions about the use of those resources. Thus a manufacturer may decide to increase production if market research reveals that demand is likely to increase; or a doctor may discharge patients when hospital staff provide information that the patients are fit to return home. Note that there is no need, in a system dynamics model, to assume that the information used in decision making is correct. The information may be delayed in transit, it may be misunderstood and it may be distorted. In the case of the freezing/scalding bather in the shower, one problem was that he thought more hot water was needed, but this was wrong. The amount of hot inflow was fine, he just needed to wait a little longer. In a business system, market research may be wrong or out of date, in a hospital the diagnosis of the doctor may be wrong or may be based on a misinterpretation of laboratory tests. Nevertheless, distorted or not, this information may well be the basis for real decision making. Understanding the effects of such distortions and delays may be the reasons for the modelling exercise.

Levels and Rates

In Forrester's (1961) original development of system dynamics such models of human systems were to be developed out of two basic concepts: levels and rates. Since the appearance in the late 1980s of the Stella and I Think software (High Performance Systems, 1994), some people prefer the term "stock" to level and "flow" to rate. In this chapter, the two terms will be used interchangeably, though the Stella II concept of stock provides some extensions to the basic system dynamics concept of levels.

Levels are accumulations of resources within the system. Sometimes they may literally be physical stocks, say of materials, finished goods or drugs. The same idea can also be used in a more conceptual way to represent notions such as price levels. Rates are the movements of resources which lead to levels rising, falling or remaining constant. For instance, an increase in the rate of patients being referred to a specialist physician will lead to an increase in the waiting list of new patients if the physician has no more time to offer and if the rate of discharge for existing patients does not increase.

Perhaps the easiest way to illustrate this is to consider a simple analogy of a tank into which liquid flows and from which it may flow. This is shown in Figure 7.3. When the inflow rate exceeds the outflow rate then the level in the tank rises; when this relation is reversed, the level falls. The transformations of resources and information are modelled, in system dynamics, as a sequence of linked levels and rates. The rates act to increase or decrease the levels that are interconnected by the flows. In a manufacturing company, raw material flows from raw material stocks (thus decreasing their level) and into finished stocks (thus increasing their level), and this is the transformation process known as "making to stock". Analogous transformations occur in other types of human system.

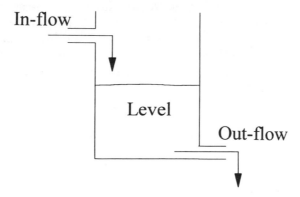

Figure 7.3   *Levels and rates as tanks and flows*

Levels represent the state of the system at any point in time. They continue to exist even if the flow rates all drop to zero in an instant. The analogy from Figure 7.3 should be obvious; if the in-flow and out-flow both drop instantaneously to zero, then the level is frozen at some value. The other use for levels is that they represent stocks or buffers within the system and they thus act to de-couple the flow rates. Most systems include stocks of some kind used for this purpose. This is true even in most just-in-time (JIT) manufacturing systems where deliveries may be received, say, twice per day. The stocks act as buffers which soak up variations in the flows. Of course, if an in-flow and out-flow are persistently different then the system is unbalanced. This provides two tests for thinking about whether a factor should be considered as a level:

- Will it continue to have a value even if all activity ceases for a while?
- Does it act to de-couple flows?

Clearly these both apply to physical stocks of machines and goods, but they also may apply, for example, to the number of people employed in a business or to cash balances. Such factors may, therefore, be regarded as levels.

The activity within a human system is modelled in system dynamics by the rates of flow which connect the levels within a system dynamics model. Unlike levels, rates of flow immediately drop to zero if there is no activity in the system. Thus the purchasing rate for raw materials and the payment rate to creditors may drop to zero if a business goes bankrupt. Similarly, the admission rate to a hospital drops to zero if the hospital is closed. Flows represent rates of change of resources or of information. Information flows are used to link knowledge about the levels to the flow rates. Resource flows deplete and increase the levels through time. If what appears to be a flow rate will persist even if activity ceases, then this factor needs to be represented by a level. An example of this might be a calculation of average sales over a period—this persists even if the sales rate ceases, and is therefore to be modelled as a level.

DIAGRAMMING METHODS

Causal Loop Diagrams

Perhaps the first stage in using system dynamics is to try to understand the feedback loops which are part of the system being studied.

One way of doing this is to use causal loop diagrams, which were first suggested by Maruyama (1963). These diagrams are sometimes known as influence diagrams (Wolstenholme, 1990). They are intended to be of use in understanding the broad structure of a system rather than its detail and they are therefore kept deliberately simple. As an example, consider the following case study.

CASE STUDY: LANCASTER DECOR COMPANY

Lancaster Decor Company (LDC) makes wall coverings that are supplied to customers throughout the world. Its production method is to buy coated paper and to print it in fashionable patterns. These are held in stock for despatch to customers. Ideally it keeps three weeks' finished stock on hand. Orders received from customers are despatched the week after they are received and production is also planned on a weekly basis. Thus, when all is running well, LDC should have an order backlog of one week and it should be possible to meet this from stock. Stock holding is planned by forecasting the order rate for the next period, thus LDC tries to hold three times the forecast of the next period's orders.

A causal loop diagram for LDC is shown in Figure 7.4.

Figure 7.4 reveals a number of the conventions used in these diagrams. The first is that each link is represented by an arrow that carries a sign at its head to indicate the direction of causality of the link. A positive sign indicates that a change in the factor at the tail of

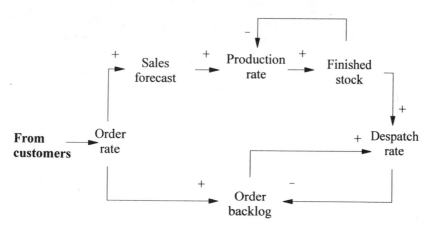

Figure 7.4 *Causal loop for Lancaster Decor Company*

the arrow will tend to lead to the factor at the head of the arrow to change in the same direction, other factors remaining constant. (That is, an increase will lead to an increase and a decrease to a decrease.) A negative sign indicates that the change will be in the opposite direction. Figure 7.4 shows that a increase in the orders received per week will tend to lead to an increase in the sales forecast. Conversely, an increase in the despatch rate to customers should lead to a decrease in the order backlog, other factors remaining constant.

The slight variation of these diagrams presented by Wolstenholme (1990), known as system dynamics influence diagrams, distinguishes between levels and rates as shown in Figure 7.5. In these, a level is shown as a rectangle surrounding the name of the level. Rates are shown as only text with no box. Finished stock, order backlog and sales forecast would remain unchanged and frozen if all activity ceased in LDC, and these are therefore levels. Some people refer to levels that result from such smoothing processes as "implied levels". Use of the terms production rate, despatch rate and order rate indicate that these may be treated as system dynamics flows or rates, as long as they are not averages. Also, brief thought leads to the realisation that these flows drop to zero if all activity ceases. This influence diagram also makes clear one of the points made earlier: information about levels is used to set the rates. This means that levels are not connected directly to one another but only via intervening rates. Hence, if any loop is followed round it should always pass through alternating levels and rates.

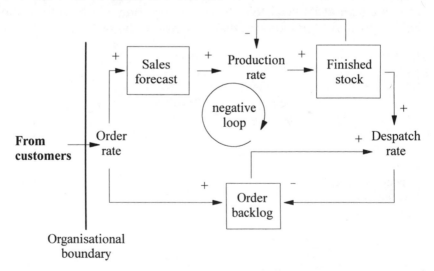

Figure 7.5 *Influence diagram for Lancaster Decor Company*

Despite their simplicity, either of these diagrams, Figures 7.4 or 7.5, can be used to make inferences about the system and its operation. Figure 7.5 shows two feedback loops, both of which are negative. As with cognitive maps (see Chapter 6) the sign of a loop is easily calculated by counting the number of negative signs in the loop. An odd number indicates negative feedback, an even number or zero indicates positive feedback. Effective control relies on negative feedback and this is, thankfully, evident in LDC. It is also clear from the diagram that, apart from the order rate, the other factors in the large control loop are all within the LDC organisation, which means that they have some chance of maintaining control. Whether this control will achieve any desirable end cannot be known just from the diagram. To check this would require the modeller to go further and develop a system dynamics simulation.

System Dynamics Flow Diagrams

Useful though an influence diagram may be, there are times when we wish to go much further. The next stage may therefore be to sketch out a system dynamics flow diagram. The original diagrams are to be found in Forrester (1961). As might be expected, the main point of these diagrams is to represent the relationships between the levels and rates that make up a system dynamics model. The main symbols suggested by Forrester (1961) are shown alongside those used by Stella II (Richmond et al, 1994) in Figure 7.6. Forrester recommended different line styles to represent different types of resource flow—for example, material flow would be shown as a solid line and monetary flows by a solid line interspersed with dollar ($) symbols. Stella II does not require this distinction, insisting only that information flows should be distinguished from resource flows. For Stella II, resource flows are shown as double arrows and information flows (known as connectors) by single line arrows. The basic analogy of system dynamics is with fluid flows and this is emphasised by the diagram symbols which show flows and rates controlled by a tap (spigot in the USA) or valve.

When Forrester first developed the system dynamics approach, the idea was that the modeller would develop the system dynamics diagram and would use this as an aid in writing a set of equations which could be used to simulate the system. The Stella II software automates this drawing process and takes it one step further. Rather than sketching out the diagram on a piece of paper, the idea of Stella II and I Think is that the user sketches out the diagram directly on the

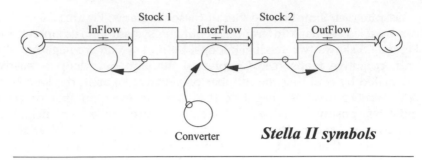

Converter   ***Stella II symbols***

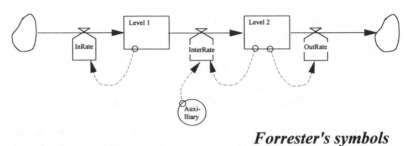

Forrester's symbols

Figure 7.6   *Stella and DYNAMO symbols*

computer screen via a graphical user interface (GUI). The GUI of Stella II is implemented on the Apple Macintosh operating system and on MS Windows for PCs. It presents the user with a palette of icons that include the symbols for stocks, flows and converters shown in the top part of Figure 7.6. The user selects these symbols from the icon palette and draws the diagram on the screen. Stella II then goes one step further in that it automatically generates some of the equations, as will be described later.

The circles are converters (Stella II) or auxiliaries (Forrester). They are used for a number of purposes:

- to combine several flows into one, or to split one into several
- to convert the units in which a level/stock is measured into another, different, unit of measurement
- to simplify the use of complicated algebraic expressions (we will look at this later)
- as part of input or output processes—for example, to set the value of a parameter such as maximum weeks credit allowed to customers
- to model target levels, management goals or ideal values.

CASE STUDY: LANCASTER DECOR COMPANY

SYSTEMS DYNAMICS DIAGRAM

The previous section introduced the Lancaster Decor Company (LDC). Figures 7.4 and 7.5 provide a simple view of its operations by causal loop or influence diagrams. Figure 7.7 shows a system dynamics diagram of LDC's operations, using the Stella symbols. The first point to note is that the diagram shows two resource flows. The top resource flow is the physical transformation of the raw material into stock via a production process and the finished stock is thence despatched to customers. The stock is clearly a level as it serves to de-couple production and despatch, both of which are flow rates that vary over time. The bottom resource flow is catalytic and is used to control the physical flow. It represents the incoming flow of orders, which are held for a time in an order backlog and are then translated into sales. The order backlog is clearly a level as

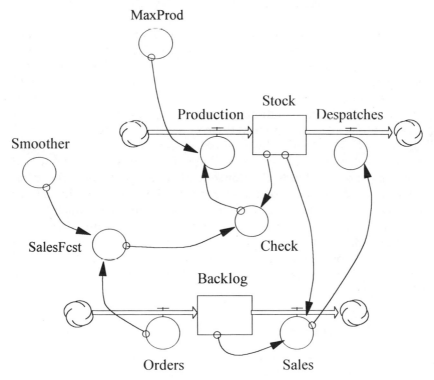

Figure 7.7   *Stella diagram for Lancaster Decor Company*

it serves to de-couple the incoming order rate and the outgoing sales rate.

The diagram also shows the information links between the two flows. Information links represent the instantaneous flow of information unless otherwise indicated. The despatch rate is linked only from the sales rate, the two being, in effect, the same rate; they must, therefore, be kept in step with one another. The sales rate is computed from the order backlog and the actual stock on hand—presumably the lesser of the two will be sold and therefore despatched. The production rate is controlled by taking into account the current stock level, the sales forecast (actually the order forecast) and a maximum limit on the production rate. To simplify the representation, two converters are shown; *Check* is a way of linking the sales forecast and current stock level, *Smoother* is a parameter used to compute the sales forecast. The diagram, drawn by pasting icons on screen from the Stella II icon library, represents the system described earlier and shown as causal loops in Figures 7.4 and 7.5.

BEHIND THE DIAGRAMS

Interesting though it can be to develop the diagrams, they are often just one step on the way to an investigation of the dynamics of the systems being studied—hence the name of the approach. To take this investigation further, the diagrams need to be put into a computable form, as a set of equations, so that a dynamic simulation may be based on them. Two equation formats are in common use for this purpose: Stella (which is used in the computer software Stella II and I Think), and DYNAMO, the original system dynamics simulation system developed by Pugh (1961). The two formats are more or less equivalent. Stella extends the concept of level, preferring the term "stock" instead, and also includes a more modern set of programming concepts which make expression of the equations much more straightforward. Both formats are based on first order difference equations. Both adopt a style that breaks time into equal time increments, known as *DT* in DYNAMO and *dt* in Stella. This chapter will discuss both Stella II and DYNAMO formats and will use the Stella II style in its examples.

Time Handling in System Dynamics

The basic system dynamics simulation approach adopts a simple time slicing approach (Pidd, 1992) and a simple way to understand this is to consider an analogy. Suppose that you wish to record what is happening, say in a car park, over a 24-hour period. Suppose too that you have been given movie film for this purpose, but not enough to record continually, so you will have to sample what is happening. One way to do this would be to take a shot of the car park at regular intervals. When the film is played back, the effect would be to speed up the movement in the car park—this is what TV nature programmes do when they use time-lapse photography to record the growth of a plant. System dynamics simulation works in a similar way, using the time increment *DT* or *dt*. It computes what is happening in the system at regular points of time, each one separated by *DT* or *dt*.

Figure 7.8 shows the basic idea. Imagine that time has just reached a known point at which a sample (actually a computation) is due. In DYNAMO this is known as time *K*, and in Stella as time *t*. Because a fixed time slice (*DT* or *dt*) is being used, we know when the previous computation was done and when the next one is due. In DYNAMO, the previous time point is known as *J* and the next one as *L*. In Stella, the previous one is known as *t-dt* and there is no need to define the next one.

Both systems also have two main types of equations: level or stock equations, and rate or flow equations. As with all such simulation systems, simulated time is moved from point to point and computa-

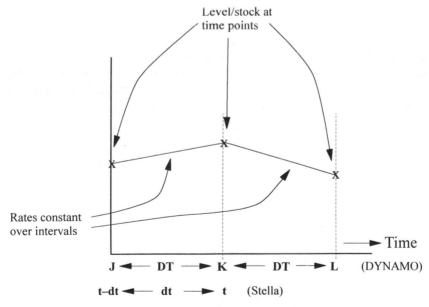

Figure 7.8 *Time handling in system dynamics*

tions are made at each point before moving to the next one. The basic method of handling time and of the resulting computations is as follows:

1. At time K (DYNAMO) or time t (Stella) compute the new values for the levels or stocks, using the level or stock equations. Use the current values of the rates or flows for this purpose. These will have been computed at time J for the interval JK (DYNAMO) or at time t-dt over the same interval (Stella).
2. Now compute the values which the rates or flows will hold over the next time interval (in the case of DYNAMO, this is the interval KL). These may depend on information about the current values of the levels.
3. Move time forward by one increment (DT or dt) and repeat the process.

Thus, levels are computed for the current point of time and then the rates are computed over the next known interval. Rates are assumed to be fixed over that interval once they are computed, they are revised after the next computation of the levels. Figure 7.8 shows that the levels at points J, K and L are connected by straight lines and this is a consequence of the flows being constant over the DT/dt intervals.

Equation Types

As mentioned above, both DYNAMO and Stella employ two main types of equation. Level equations have a simple format which can often be interpreted directly from the system dynamics diagram. Its general form is as follows.

$$\text{Lev(Now)} = \text{Lev(Previous)} + \text{Interval} * (\text{InRate} - \text{OutRate})$$

Thus, at the current time point, the value of the level or stock Lev is simply the previous value of Lev plus the nett inflow or outflow over the interval which has passed since Lev was last calculated. The diagram shows how many such inflows and outflows there are for Lev and therefore the equation often follows automatically. This enables Stella stock equations to be automatically generated by the Stella system from the flow diagram.

Rate equations cannot be inferred from the system diagram. All that can be inferred is which variables affect the rate computation. Thus, in Figure 7.7, the Sales rate is seen to depend on two factors:

Stock and Backlog. How it is affected cannot be determined from the diagram alone as this is an expression of the way in which the information is used to control the system. In Forrester's terms, rate equations capture the policies of the organisation.

The Stella II Style

This assumes that time has now reached time t having previously been at time t-dt—that is, there is a fixed time increment of dt. Using the Stella II style, the standard form of stock equation is as follows:

$$\text{Lev}(t) = \text{Lev}(t\text{-}dt) + (\text{InRate} - \text{OutRate}) * dt$$

assuming that Lev has a single inflow (InRate) and a single outflow (OutRate).

In the case of LDC, the Stella II stock equations are as follows:

$$\text{Backlog}(t) = \text{Backlog}(t\text{-}dt) + (\text{Orders} - \text{Sales}) * dt \quad \text{eqn [S, 1]}$$

$$\text{Stock}(t) = \text{Stock}(t\text{-}dt) + (\text{Production} - \text{Despatches}) * dt \quad \text{eqn [S, 2]}$$

The flow and converter equations might be as follows:

$$\text{Sales} = \text{MIN}(\text{Stock, Backlog}) \qquad \text{eqn [F, 1]}$$

$$\text{Despatches} = \text{Sales} \qquad \text{eqn [F, 2]}$$

$$\text{Smoother} = 10 \qquad \text{eqn [C, 1]}$$

$$\text{Sales\_Fcst} = \text{SMTH1}(\text{Orders, Smoother}) \qquad \text{eqn [F, 3]}$$

$$\text{Check} = 4 * \text{Sales\_Fcst} - \text{Stock} \qquad \text{eqn [C, 2]}$$

$$\text{MaxProd} = 150 \qquad \text{eqn [C, 3]}$$

$$\text{Production} = \text{Min}(\text{IF}(\text{Check} > 0) \text{ THEN Check ELSE } (0), \text{MaxProd})$$
$$\text{eqn [F, 4]}$$

$$\text{Orders} = \text{NORMAL}(100,20) \qquad \text{eqn [F, 5]}$$

The Stella II equations are numbered, with S (for Stock), or C (for Converter) as prefixes. These flow equations imply that LDC's systems work as follows:

[F, 1] Sales will be the minimum of the Stock available or the Backlog.

[F, 2] The physical Despatches are to be the same as the Sales.

[F, 3] The Sales Forecast for the next period will be an exponentially weighted moving average using SMOOTHER = 10, which is equivalent to $\alpha = 0.10$.

[F, 4] The Production rate is set to give three weeks' stock using the sales forecast as the guide. Thus [C, 2] computes four times the forecast, [C, 3] specifies that no more than 150 can be produced, and the rate equation computes the production rate.

[F, 5] This is the main input to the simulation. In this case, the order rate is assumed to follow a normal distribution with a mean of 100 and standard deviation of 20.

The converter equations [C, 1] and [C, 3] are used to give values to the two parameters Smoother and MaxProd. Converter equation [C, 1] is used for intermediate calculation to simplify its expression.

The flow equation [F, 5] is actually the input to the LDC model for it represents the flow of orders from the customers who are external to the model. They are judged to be external since they place orders without any consideration for the internal state of the system. This would not be true, for instance, if a high order backlog led to a lower order rate. In this particular case, LDC has analysed its order pattern and has concluded that their orders per period are random with a mean value of 100 and a standard deviation of 20. This has been represented in the model by samples from a normal distribution— hence the use of the Stella II function, NORMAL().

The DYNAMO Style

This assumes that time has just reached K, having been at J before and expected to be next at L, where J, K and L are DT apart in time. Hence, using the DYNAMO style, the standard form of level equation is as follows:

$$\text{LEV}.K = \text{LEV}.J + (DT)(\text{INRATE}.JK - \text{OUTRATE}.JK)$$

assuming that LEV has a single inflow (INRATE) and a single outflow (OUTRATE).

In the case of LDC, the DYNAMO level equations are as follows:

$$\text{BACKLOG}.K = \text{BACKLOG}.J + (DT)(\text{ORDERS}.JK - \text{SALES}.JK)$$
$$\text{eqn [L, 1]}$$

STOCK.K = STOCK.J + (DT)(PRODUCTION.JK – DESPATCHES.JK)

eqn [L, 2]

As with Stella II, the format of rate equations depends on the make-up of the model.

CASE STUDY: LANCASTER DECOR COMPANY

USING STELLA II TO SIMULATE LDC's OPERATIONS

All that is needed for a Stella II model has now been specified and so the model may be used to show how LDC might be expected to operate. The result of running the LDC model in Stella II for 20 time units is shown in Table 7.1. Notice that this makes clear the starting conditions for the simulation, which were that the initial Stock was set at 300 and the initial backlog was set at 100. The table, as presented by Stella II and as repro-duced here is slightly deceptive. To be properly accurate it should have twice as many rows, with the alternate rows dedicated to the levels/stocks,

Table 7.1 *Results of a Stella simulation for LDC*

Week	Orders	Despatches	Stock	Backlog	Production	Forecast
0	109.26	100.00	300.00	100.00	137.04	109.26
1	96.64	109.26	337.04	109.26	100.00	109.26
2	128.10	96.64	327.78	96.64	104.21	108.00
3	102.40	128.10	335.35	128.10	104.68	110.01
4	101.52	102.40	311.93	102.40	125.06	109.25
5	79.97	101.52	334.59	101.52	99.31	108.47
6	95.01	79.97	332.38	79.97	90.12	105.62
7	101.12	95.01	342.53	95.01	75.72	104.56
8	86.79	101.12	323.24	101.12	93.64	104.22
9	97.66	86.79	315.76	86.79	94.15	102.48
10	103.28	97.66	323.11	97.66	84.86	101.99
11	97.37	103.28	310.32	103.28	98.17	102.12
12	96.57	99.37	305.21	99.37	102.17	101.85
13	108.91	96.57	308.02	96.57	97.25	101.32
14	108.26	108.91	308.71	108.91	99.60	102.08
15	109.74	108.26	299.40	108.26	111.38	102.70
16	81.23	109.74	302.52	109.74	111.08	103.40
17	87.69	81.23	303.86	81.23	100.88	101.18
18	99.33	87.69	323.50	87.69	75.83	99.83
19	136.85	99.33	311.65	99.33	87.49	99.78
20			299.80	136.85		

that is to Stock and to Backlog. If the results were to be displayed in this way, the intermediate would be dedicated to the flows/rates.

For example, the first row should refer to $t = 0$ and should contain just two values: Stock should be 300 and Backlog should be 100. The next row should refer to the time interval (0, 1), assuming that the time increment dt is set to a value of 1. This row should have the values for the rates over that interval, computed as follows using the flow equations defined earlier.

- Orders = 109.26 (sampled from a normal distribution with mean = 100, standard deviation = 20).
- Despatches = 100.00 (this being the value of Sales, which is not shown in the table. Sales is the minimum of the previous Stock and Backlog values, and is thus 100.00).
- Forecast = 109.26 (this being computed as an exponentially smoothed average of Orders. The system assumes that values from before-time-zero are the same as the first value and thus, in this case, that they are all 109.26).
- Production = 137.04 (this being four weeks' sales, using the sales forecast, less the Stock at the start of the week; this being 4 * 109.26 minus 300; that is, 137.04).

The computations proceed through time in this manner. Thus, time is now moved to 1 (if $dt = 1$) and the levels/stocks are computed. Then the flows/rates are computed for the interval (1, 2). Then time is moved to 2, and so on until the simulation is complete.

MODEL BUILDING IN SYSTEM DYNAMICS

Two Approaches: Inside out or Outside in?

So far, this chapter has described the main features of the system dynamics approach, has illustrated the diagrammatic approaches employed and has shown how common computer software builds an equation structure for simulation from the diagrams. However, what has not been covered is any attempt to show how system dynamics models could or should be built. This part of the chapter aims to do just that. It will assume that the user of a system dynamics approach has access to contemporary software such as Stella II or I Think. There seem to be two ways of building models within system dynamics, depending on the reasons for the modelling. This chapter will call the two approaches "inside-out" and "outside-in".

Inside-out modelling assumes that we know a lot about the structure of the system to be modelled, and that we wish to understand how it behaves. This is the way in which many system dynamics models will be built by management scientists who wish to find better ways to operate some system or other. Hence a refinement of this approach is that, having satisfactorily modelled how a system is now, we may wish to modify the model to foresee the consequences of operating the system in new ways.

By contrast, outside-in modelling assumes that much is known about the overall behaviour of a system, but that not enough is known about why this happens. Hence data are available which describe how the system seems to operate ("when we get a short-lived increase in orders it takes us months to get back to normal again, look at this graph of what happened last time") under certain conditions. Thus the aim is to develop a model which provides systemic structures that produce output which mimics the observed behaviour. This type of modelling aims, primarily, to develop some understanding about why things happen.

It is clearly possible to develop a system dynamics model, or indeed other types of management science model, by working simultaneously outside-in and inside-out. Yet, to clarify the issues in the discussion that follows, it may help to distinguish between the two approaches.

Modelling from the Outside-in

This approach is based on the assumption that there are a number of characteristic system structures which enable behaviour of certain types to occur. As mentioned above, the modeller begins with some idea of the type of behaviour that would be expected from the system and its components. For example, it might display exponential growth under certain conditions. These types of behaviour can be related to standard structures that are easily modelled in system dynamics terms. The modeller selects the appropriate structures by thinking through the observed behaviours. The model becomes an assembly of these standard structures. It must be noted that standard structures and process will rarely be used in an unmodified form, but they do provide a useful basis from which to begin the modelling. Richmond et al (1994) use this outside-in approach when presenting a set of generic flow processes which may be employed when modelling in Stella II and I Think. The generic structures presented here are based on those of Richmond et al.

The first, and simplest, structure is one that occurs when a level and a flow are connected in such a way that there is exponential growth or exponential decay in the level. Financial systems based on compound interest will display this form of growth, as might some ecological systems—were there no limits on available food nor predators to kill the system members. This type of decay happens when a proportion of a level is removed during each time interval. An example of this might be a company which is reducing its workforce and has decided to release a proportion in each time period. In the jargon of system dynamics, the proportion applied to the growth or the decay is known as the compounding fraction (shown as CF in Figure 7.9). The compounding fraction itself need not be a constant but could be the result of other factors elsewhere in the model. Figure 7.9 shows Stella diagrams and the resulting output for these simple compound growth and decay systems.

The second type of generic structure occurs in those systems that aim to keep some value at a target level by feedback control. This is sometimes known as a stock-adjustment process. Examples of this abound and might include make-to-stock manufacturing, which aims to keep finished stock levels at a certain value. Other examples might be the number of people employed in a business after allowing for recruitment and labour turnover, or the number of patients on a

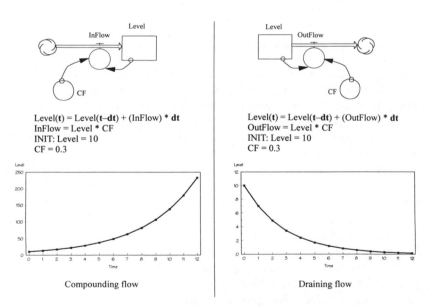

Figure 7.9 *Stella structure for exponential growth or decay*

hospital ward. The basic process is just an extension of the compounding/decay structure, except that a target is introduced as a way of modifying the in and out flows from the level. Figure 7.10 shows the general idea and deploys a bi-directional flow rather than a separate in and out flow. In the figure, the target level is set at 30 with an initial value of 10 for the level, thus the actual level increases quickly at first and then it asymptotically approaches the target level. If the initial level had been higher than the target, the level would quickly have dropped towards the target and then would have approached it asymptotically. Stella II provides built-in functions to model these adjustment processes.

The second structure shown on Figure 7.10 is a production process, this term relating to any process in which the output is controlled by reference to another level. Examples might be a manufacturing company in which each machine can produce a specified number of units or a hospital in which each doctor might be expected to conduct a specified number of outpatient clinics per week. In either case, the capacity of the resource is modelled by the extra level, labelled as Resource in Figure 7.10. The unit productivity of the resource is modelled by CF. Clearly, the value taken by Resource could itself be variable and might be the result of other processes elsewhere in the

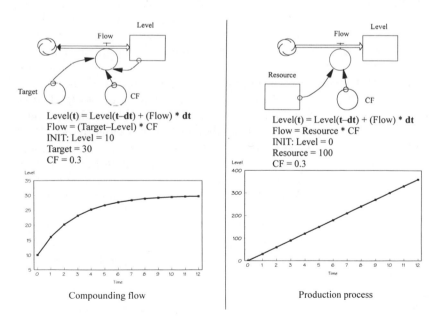

Figure 7.10   Stella structure for a stock adjustment and production process

system. It is also clear that the Flow could be bi-directional, resulting in a combined stock adjustment and production process.

Modelling from the Inside-out

The earlier example of LDC was an illustration of this approach, and a second example will be developed here, this time one related to the delivery of health care. The example is simplified, but it serves to illustrate how system dynamics models may be developed and used in inside-out mode.

CASE STUDY: LANCASTER DISTRICT HOSPITAL

Suppose the Lancaster District Hospital (LDH) includes a surgical ward into which two types of patient are admitted: emergencies and routine patients—the latter coming from a waiting list that is operated on a first-come-first-served basis. The hospital is required to admit all appropriate emergencies and any empty beds are taken by routine admissions from the waiting list. To keep the model manageable, it can be assumed that any overflow emergency admissions can be accepted at another hospital, though the board of LDH will have to pay a large financial penalty whenever this happens.

The surgeons who work in the ward have a predictable demand from routine patients and analysis of their referrals shows that, in total, they add 20 patients per week to the waiting list. The ward is notified of these patients once a week, on a Monday, though they can be admitted to the ward on any day. Demand from emergency patients is much more variable. An analysis of the past two years shows that, on any day, the number of emergency cases that need admission can be represented by a normal distribution with a mean value of 4 and a standard deviation of 2.

Though the length of stay (the time that a patient spends on the ward) is slightly variable, it seems reasonable to assume that emergency patients spend five days on the ward. At the end of this period they may be transferred to a nursing home if they need further care. Routine patients tend to spend three days on the ward.

The admissions policy is that all emergencies must be admitted to the ward and any spare beds are used for routine patients. How many beds will be needed in the ward?

FIRST STAGE OF MODELLING LDH USING STELLA

In any modelling of systems that involve probabilistic variation, the first stage of any modelling is to work with average values so as to get some ideas of the size of the system that is needed. The expected (i.e. average) demand from emergencies is four per day and they occupy a bed for five days, making a total of 20 bed days per admitting day. Similarly, each admitting day for routine patients must cope with about three patients for three days—making a total of nine bed days. Thus, the use of average values suggests that the ward may need about 29 or 30 beds if it is to cope with the demand.

Note that the term "cope with the demand" is rather vague at this stage. What does it mean? Perhaps an initial view might be that all emergencies should be admitted on the day that they arise and that no routine patient should wait more than three weeks for admission after having been placed on the waiting list. The basic Stella flow diagram for this system is shown in Figure 7.11. It assumes that *dt*, the time slice, is equal to one day.

THE STELLA FLOW DIAGRAM FOR LDH

The model shown in Figure 7.11 has three stocks and associated flows, but it may not be obvious why the system has been modelled in this way.

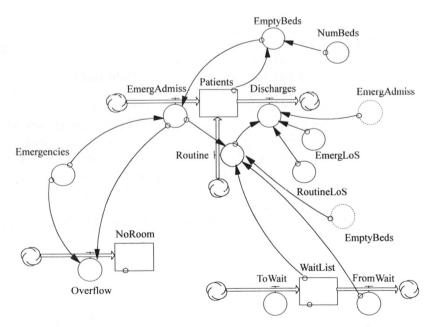

Figure 7.11 *Stella diagram for Lancaster District Hospital*

Consider, first, the physical flow of patients into the ward and their subsequent discharge. This is modelled by a stock/level known as Patients, with two input flows: Routine (which represents the daily admission rate for patients from the waiting list) and EmergAdmiss (the daily rate at which emergencies are admitted). The corresponding outflow is modelled by Discharges, which represents the total number of patients of both types that are discharged each day. Hence, this sector of the diagram handles the "physics" of the system.

The other two stocks/levels and associated flows are used to model the unmet demands from emergencies for direct admissions and the addition of routine patients from the waiting list. The actual number of emergencies arising on any day is handled by the Stella converter labelled as Emergencies and which will take samples from a normal distribution. Ideally, all such emergencies will be admitted immediately. However, there may be occasions when this cannot happen because there are not enough beds free. Hence the actual number of emergency admissions (EmergAdmiss) on any day is modelled by comparing the number of free beds at the start of the day (shown by the EmptyBeds converter) and the number of Emergencies that arise. Should there be a bed shortage, then excess emergencies must be treated elsewhere. The number so treated on each day is modelled by the flow rate Overflow and the total to date is accumulated in the stock/level labelled as NoRoom. Thus, the number of EmergAdmiss on any day will be the minimum of the EmptyBeds and the actual Emergencies on that day.

The waiting list and the resulting demand from routine patients is modelled by the third stock/level known as WaitList. Patients are added to this by the flow rate labelled as ToWait and the depletion rate of the list is modelled by the flow rate labelled as FromWait. Note that the latter is a direct reflection of the input rate of routine patients (Routine) to the Patients stock/level.

Patients are admitted to the ward from two sources. Emergencies will always be admitted unless there is a bed shortage, in which case they are diverted elsewhere, as discussed above. Routine admissions, modelled by the flow rate Routine are computed by taking up any slack in the ward after emergencies are admitted. Thus the diagram shows that the Routine flow rate stems from the size of waiting list, the number of empty beds and the number of emergencies admitted. These links are indicated by the in-going information arrows to the Routine flow.

THE STELLA EQUATIONS FOR LDH

As was stated earlier when introducing Stella/I Think, the software can generate the stock equations from the links that are painted on the flow diagram. It may sometimes be necessary to modify the stock equations produced by the system, but not in this case. The flow equations, however, have to be input by the modeller. Stella/I Think organises its equations into groups around the main stocks; these are as follows in this case.

The overflow of emergencies that cannot be handled at LDH is modelled by the NoRoom stock from the Overflow inflow. The stock and flow equations are as follows:

$$
\begin{aligned}
&\text{NoRoom}(t) = \text{NoRoom}(t\text{-}dt) + (\text{OverFlow}) * dt \\
&\text{INIT NoRoom} = 0 \\
&\text{INFLOWS:} \\
&\text{OverFlow} = \text{Emergencies} - \text{EmergAdmiss}
\end{aligned}
$$

The NoRoom stock has no outflow and this is reflected in the stock equation produced by Stella from the flow diagram. The initial value for NoRoom had to be provided, as did the formula to be used in the computation of Overflow. The latter is a statement of the obvious, that the number of overflowed emergencies is the difference between the actual number of such emergencies and the actual number that are admitted to the ward.

The number of patients in the ward is modelled by the Patients stock, this having inflows from EmergAdmiss and Routine, and an outflow of Discharges. Thus the stock and flow equations are as follows:

$$
\begin{aligned}
&\text{Patients}(t) = \text{Patients}(t\text{-}dt) + (\text{Routine} + \text{EmergAdmiss} - \text{Discharges}) * dt \\
&\text{INIT Patients} = 0 \\
&\text{INFLOWS:} \\
&\text{Routine} = \text{MIN}(\text{WaitList} (\text{EmptyBeds} - \text{EmergAdmiss})) \\
&\text{EmergAdmiss} = \text{MIN}(\text{Emergencies}, \text{EmptyBeds}) \\
&\text{OUTFLOWS:} \\
&\text{Discharges} = \text{DELAY}(\text{EmergAdmiss}, \text{EmergLoS}, 0) + \text{DELAY}(\text{Routine}, \\
&\qquad\qquad\qquad\qquad\qquad\qquad\qquad\qquad\qquad\qquad\qquad \text{RoutineLoS}, 0)
\end{aligned}
$$

where EmergLoS and RoutineLoS represent the emergency and routine lengths of stay for patients.

As in the case of the NoRoom stock, the Patient stock equation is derived by the Stella system, but equations for the flows have to be provided, along with an initial value for Patients. As discussed earlier, the EmergAdmiss rate is the minimum of Emergencies and EmptyBeds. Thus, given that routine admissions are made once the number of emergencies is known, the Routine flow is the minimum of WaitList and the current difference between EmptyBeds and EmergAdmiss. Finally, as is clear from the flow diagram in Figure 7.11, the number of patients discharged in a day is a function of the Routine and EmergAdmiss flows. The equation shows that the two inflows, delayed, lead to the outflow. Emergency admissions occupy a bed for five days (modelled by EmergLoS) and the length of stay for routine patients (RoutineLoS) is three days. Thus these delays are applied to the patient inflows to give the patient outflows from the ward.

The waiting list is modelled by the WaitList stock, the equations of which are shown below. As with the other two stocks, the stock equation for WaitList is generated by the Stella system from the links drawn on the screen. Thus, the stock and flow equations are as follows:

> WaitList(t) = WaitList(t-dt) + (ToWait − FromWait) * dt
> INIT WaitList = 0
> INFLOWS:
> ToWait = IF(MOD(TIME,7) = 1) THEN 20 ELSE 0
> OUTFLOWS:
> FromWait = Routine

WaitList is given an initial value of 0 and the outflow, FromWait is a direct copy of the current value of Routine, the number of routine admissions. ToWait is slightly more subtle since patients are only admitted to the waiting list, as known in the ward, once a week. Hence the MOD function of Stella is used with the built-in TIME function. TIME returns the current simulation time (in days in this case). MOD(TIME,7) means divide the current value of TIME by 7. If the result is zero (which will be the case once each week), then ToWait takes the value of 20, otherwise it is zero. Thus a once a week figure of 20 will be added to the waiting list.

Finally, the diagram contains a number of converters, used for a variety of purposes, mostly for input data. The number of actual emergencies per day is computed by a sample form a normal distribution with a mean of 4 and a standard deviation of 2. Since a normal distribution can produce negative values, this must be prevented. Hence Emergencies is the maximum of the sample or zero. The number of empty beds is just the difference between the number of beds on the ward and the number of patients. NumBeds, EmergLoS and RoutineLoS are input values.

> Emergencies = MAX(ROUND(NORMAL(4, 2, 1)),0)
> EmergLoS = 5
> EmptyBeds = NumBeds − Patients
> NumBeds = 30
> RoutineLoS = 3

Running the LDH Model

Though the focus of this chapter is on qualitative system dynamics, one advantage of using the Stella/I Think system is that a simulation can be performed using the above equations. These can be used to give some indication of the suitability of the policies intended for use in this ward of LDH. Because the initial values given to the various stocks was zero, it is important to run such a simulation over a long enough time period for the effect of these zero values to be lost. This period, the run-in period, needs to be excluded from the analysis of the results—unless the aim of the modelling is to understand what might happen in the ward on the first few days after it is opened with all beds empty and no waiting list.

Figure 7.12 is a graph of Patients and Overflow for a 200-day simulation of LDH using the above equations. Two things are obvious. The first is that, even when the first few days of this simulation are ignored, there is considerable oscillation in the number of patients occupying beds on the ward. This suggests that a different admissions policy might be considered—for example, some attempt might be made to forecast the number of patients to leave on a day *before* deciding how many empty beds will be available on that day. The second obvious feature is that Overflow is non-zero on quite a number of days—that is, LDH is unable to meet the demands for emergency beds on all occasions.

If the first 10 days of the simulation are ignored, for the reasons

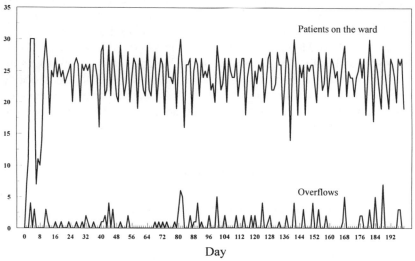

Figure 7.12 *Simulation results for Lancaster District Hospital*

Table 7.2 *Patients and Overflow for LDH simulation*

	Patients	Overflow
Mean	24.2	0.6
Standard deviation	3.1	1.3
Maximum	30	7
Minimum	14	0

discussed above, a simple analysis of the two flows Patients and Overflow reveals figures shown in Table 7.2. Thus, this system appears not to make good use of the available beds, the evidence being that the average number of patients on the ward is only 24. In addition, up to seven emergencies on any day had to be diverted to other hospitals—not good. It would now be possible to use this Stella model to conduct experiments with different admissions policies so as to find some better way to operate this ward of the hospital. However, that is beyond the scope of this chapter.

One thing that should be noted, however, is apparent in Figure 7.12— it contains quite a number of exogenous factors, i.e. things determined outside the system. These can be regarded in one of two ways in any further modelling of LDH. The first is that they are parameters whose values can be varied to see what effects this might have on the perfor- mance of the system—what, for example, is the effect of reducing length of stay? The other view of these factors, which are shown by circular converters in Figure 7.11, is that they are simplifications of what actually happens. There will, for example, be a reason why the length of stay takes the values that it does, and these may be related to other factors in the diagram. Would length of stay remain the same if the number of beds were increased but staffing levels were unchanged? If this were to be an important question, then this relationship would need to be properly modelled in Stella, rather than simplifying it into a converter. This type of thinking about apparently exogenous factors should characterise system dynamics modelling.

SUMMARY

This chapter has explained how, in many human systems, control is exercised by feedback processes that use information as the basis for action. This information is often delayed and may be distorted, and these factors need to be taken into account when considering how human systems might be managed. System dynamics, as proposed by

Forrester, provides a way of modelling such human systems with their feedback, delays and distortions. This relies on a simple analogy between human systems and mechanical or hydraulic systems in which activity is represented by rates or flows and accumulations by levels or stocks. These ideas are embodied in simple to use software, of which the best known example, at this time, is Stella/I Think. Even without using such software, a system dynamics approach may be used via diagramming methods to try to gain some understanding of how a proposed system may operate. Using the software enables a modeller to gain both qualitative and quantitative insight into the proposed system's operations.

It must be recognised that, compared to SSM and cognitive mapping, system dynamics could be a rather mechanistic approach. Certainly, its roots in control theory mean that there is this danger. However, it is very easy, and perhaps best, to use system dynamics in an interpretive mode to try to understand different views of a system and its possible operation.

REFERENCES

Dangerfield B.C. and Roberts C. (1995) Projecting dynamic behaviour in the absence of a model: an experiment. *System Dynamics Review*, **11**, 2, 157–72.

Forrester J.W. (1961) *Industrial Dynamics*. MIT Press, Cambridge, Mass.

High Performance Systems (1994) Stella II Technical documentation. High Performance Systems Inc, Hanover NH.

Maruyama M. (1963) The second cybernetics: deviation amplifying mutual causal processes. *American Scientist*, **51**, 2, 164–79.

Meadows D.H. (1972) *The Limits to Growth*. Universe Books, New York.

Pidd M. (1992) *Computer Simulation in Management Science*. (Third edition.) John Wiley, Chichester.

Pugh A.L. III (1961) *DYNAMO User's Manual*. MIT Press, Cambridge, Mass.

Richmond B. and Petersen S. et al (1994) *Stella II. An Introduction to Systems Thinking*. High Performance Systems Inc., Hanover, NH.

Roberts C. and Dangerfield B.C. (1990) Modeling the epidemiologic consequences of HIV-infection and AIDS—a contribution from operational-research. *Journal of the Operational Research Society*, **41**, 4, 273–89.

Tustin E. (1953) *The Mechanism of Economic Systems*. Harvard University Press, Cambridge, Mass.

Wolstenholme E.F. (1990) *System Enquiry. A System Dynamics Approach*. John Wiley, Chichester.

PART III

Mathematical and Logical Modelling

Introduction

The next three chapters typify what many readers might expect to find in a management science book. Each chapter describes an approach to developing mathematical, statistical and logical models. The aims in so doing are twofold. The first is to provide the reader with enough working knowledge of these approaches and techniques so as to be able to make a start on their use in real situations. Clearly there is a limit to what can be covered about each in a single chapter, nevertheless it should be possible to do something useful with the ideas presented here and interested readers should follow up the references if they wish to deepen their knowledge.

The second reason is to contrast these approaches with the interpretive methods discussed in Part II. Though it is possible to use "hard" methods in a partially interpretive mode, this does not come as naturally as is the case with the "soft" approaches. Indeed, as was argued in the introduction to Part II, there are some major differences between the hard and soft approaches.

The three chapters introduce the following:

- Mathematical programming methods: These are often strongly associated with management science in people's minds and they are part of the routine toolkit of "hard" management science. They exemplify the way in which models may be used in an optimising mode and that is why they are included here.
- Simulation approaches: These are used for situations in which changes through time loom large and in which entities interact with one another in complicated ways. Computer simulation methods have led to an approach now known as visual interactive modelling, and its for this reason that they are included here.

- Heuristic approaches: These are methods that aim to find ways of tackling problems that are very close to the ideas of satisficing as developed by Simon (see Chapter 2). Though there are some general principles that may be employed in the development of these heuristics, each application is to a great degree rather unique. They are included here because they illustrate the creative way in which some of the limitations of optimisation approaches are overcome and also because the methods take management science to the edge of artificial intelligence approaches.

8
Optimisation Modelling— Linear Programming

BACKGROUND

In many people's eyes, management science is synonymous with the use of optimisation techniques. One view of management science, common some years ago, was that it was about "how to get a quart out of a pint pot". The idea being that we live in a world of increasingly scarce resources and it therefore makes sense to use these resources as efficiently and as effectively as possible. In general terms, this is the aim of using optimisation methods in management science. There are many different optimisation approaches available to management scientists, but this chapter will concentrate on just one of these, linear programming. It is intended to illustrate how such modelling approaches can be of great value when used properly. There are many excellent books on linear and mathematical programming and I recommend in particular two books by Paul Williams (1990, 1993).

Basic Ideas

Linear programming is a subset of mathematical programming, which is itself a subset of constrained optimisation. The idea of the latter is that some measure of performance should be optimised (which usually means minimised or maximised) subject to some known constraints. It is very common for this measure of performance to be expressed in monetary terms, but this need not be the case. A simple example, expressed in monetary terms, might be the common one of needing to blend a set of ingredients so as to achieve some required quality of mix, while minimising the total cost of this blend. This might, for instance, be a way of planning the diet of livestock: the constraints being the vitamin and other requirements needed to keep the animals in a healthy condition. These requirements might be available in a wide range of foodstuffs, which could be blended to form some minimum cost diet that satisfies the dietary constraints. Hence, in constrained optimisation, there is a measure of performance, often known as an objective function, that must be optimised subject to a set of constraints. The constraints define the solution space for the optimisation—that is, any acceptable solution must satisfy the constraints that act as bounds on the solution space.

As an approach, mathematical programming has enjoyed many successful applications since its development in the 1950s. As well as its use in blending and mixing problems, other recent applications include the following:

- production scheduling (Hendry et al, 1996)
- planning telecommunications networks (Cox et al, 1993)
- global supply chain management (Arntzen et al, 1995)
- financial services products (Litty, 1994)
- balancing workloads in large organisations (Grandzol and Traaen, 1995).

The journal *Interfaces* is a good source for keeping up to date with applications.

The ideas that underpinned linear programming first appeared in economics and its pioneer is generally agreed to be George Dantzig (discussed in Dantzig, 1963), who was the first to suggest how what is known as the simplex method might be used to tackle this type of constrained optimisation. Methods of tackling the special type of linear programme, called a transportation problem, were suggested by Kantorovitch (1942). Since then, there have been many developments in solution methods for linear programming, most of which have been dependent on the increasing power of computers for their successful implementation.

Computer Software

Linear programming really comes into its own for large and medium-scale problems in which there are many variables and many constraints to be considered. Therefore the development of efficient and accurate computer algorithms has been a major preoccupation among researchers. Suitable programs exist for virtually every commercial computer system that has been developed in the last 20 years. Very large-scale problems require large-scale and powerful computer systems and thus parallel and hyper-cube systems have been used in recent years (for a discussion of these issues see Zenios, 1994). However, useful work can be done on single-user personal computers and packaged software is widely available for these, for example XPress-MP (Dash Associates, 1995), LINDO (LINDO Systems, 1995a) and MINOS (Stanford Business Systems, 1995).

For problems of medium scale, the use of add-ons for common spreadsheets has much to commend it. Examples of these include "What's Best?" (LINDO Systems, 1995b) for Lotus 1-2-3, Microsoft Excel and Borland Quattro, and The Solver (Microsoft, 1993) for Microsoft Excel. Both of these are well written and are rather powerful, despite their simple appearance. The Excel Solver will be used in some examples later in this chapter. An extended version of the Excel Solver (Premium Solver) is also available from Frontline Systems (Frontline Systems, 1995). The Institute for Operations Research and the Management Sciences (INFORMS) publishes an occasional survey of mathematical programming software in its *OR/ MS Today* magazine. The 1995 report (Sharda, 1995) covers software that runs on personal computers and highlights software able to cope with large-scale problems as well as simple spreadsheet extensions.

Linear Programming and Rational Choice

As will become clear later, linear programming is an example of a modelling and solution approach that corresponds very closely to the approach to rational choice discussed in Chapter 2 and shown in Figure 2.1. At its core is a set of assumptions that fit those listed in Chapter 2. These were as follows:

1. A set of alternative courses of action.
2. Knowledge and information that permit the prediction of the consequences of choosing any alternative.
3. A criterion for determining which set of consequences is pre-ferred.

The number of alternative courses of action may be, as will become clear later, very large, possibly infinite, but known. The knowledge and necessary information is captured in the constraints and in the objective function. The criterion of choice is usually one of minimis-ation or maximisation.

However, it should not be imagined that linear programming must be used in a simple-minded manner in which the only goal is to find some optimum solution. In many cases, there are much broader aims than this. Though the search for the optimum is important, it may be even more important to know how sensitive this optimum is to changes in the assumptions that underpin a model. It may sometimes be better to base action on a position that is slightly less than the theoretical optimum if that position is less vulnerable to changes in the environment. Thus, linear programming, like all the other modelling approaches in this book, may be used in an exploratory mode to investigate preferred courses of action. How this may be done will be illustrated later.

A SIMPLE EXAMPLE

As was mentioned earlier, the real power of linear programming becomes apparent when it is applied to problems with many variables and constraints. However, large-scale problems tend to be somewhat confusing to people who are investigating the method for the first time. Hence, it seems sensible to start with a simple example, one that is far too simple to be of any practical value, but which will illustrate the basic ideas of the approach.

CASE STUDY: THE LANCASTER DECOR COMPANY

The Lancaster Decor Company (LDC) makes wallpaper that is sold throughout Europe. One of its factories makes two types of wallpaper, pasted and unpasted. Both types of wallpaper are printed by a high-quality gravure process and both are packed on the same packing plant. The difference is that the pasted wallpaper must pass through a pasting process before it is packed. Though LDC makes many different patterns within these two wallpaper types, for its medium-term plans it need only think in terms of the two categories. The production planner wishes to know how many of each to produce next week so as to maximise the expected gross profit. In the case of pasted, this is £0.090 per metre and is £0.075 per metre for unpasted.

There are constraints on the production facilities which will limit the planner's freedom of action. The factory has the gravure print capacity to produce 50 metres per minute of either type of wallpaper and the gravure printer is available for 40 hours during the week. The capacity of the packing plant is measured in "packing units", of which there are

30 000 available. A packing unit is the length in metres of so-called standard wallpaper (which is no longer made by LDC). Pasted wallpaper is three times as thick as standard and unpasted is twice as thick as standard, the adhesive accounting for the difference. The pasting plant has a capacity of 10 000 metres per week.

The LDC Marketing Department insists that the factory must produce at least 3000 metres of each type of wallpaper. How many metres of each type of wallpaper should be planned so as to maximise the expected gross profit?

Though this example is very simple, it will provide a useful basis for illustrating some of the important concepts within linear programming.

Problem Formulation

The first stage in developing a linear programming model is to try to formulate the problem in appropriate terms. This means that a set of equations need to be constructed so as to capture the objective function and the constraints. The first stage in doing this is to decide on some suitable variables. It seems clear that the planner's aim is to decide how many metres of each type of paper to produce, and there are two types of paper—pasted and unpasted—so it will be convenient to label the decision variables as P and U, where,

P = metres of pasted wallpaper to be produced next week
U = metres of unpasted wallpaper to be produced next week.

Hence, it is possible to write a simple algebraic expression that represents the planner's objective, and this is known as the objective function. This is

$$0.09P + 0.075U$$

and the planner wishes to maximise this function.

In a similar manner, it is possible to use simple algebra to capture the constraints that inhibit the planner from simply making infinite amounts of each type of wallpaper. Consider, first, the constrained gravure printing capacity, of which 40 hours is available and which produces 50 metres per minute of either type of wallpaper. There are 40×60 minutes in 40 hours, and if the print rate is 50 metres per minute, then the gravure print capacity is $(40 \times 60 \times 50)$ metres/week. That is, the maximum total gravure print output is 12 000 metres per week. It seems reasonable to assume that any combination of pasted and unpasted can be accommodated within this limit and thus this first constraint can be captured in the following inequality:

$$P + U \leqslant 12\ 000 \text{ metres}$$

This is an inequality, because $(P + U)$ must be less than or equal to the 12 000 metres of capacity that is available. In this inequality, the symbol $\leqslant$ represents less than or equal to.

The second constraint is that of the packing plant. This can cope with 30 000 metres of standard wallpaper, and pasted wallpaper is three times as thick as the standard and unpasted is twice as thick as the standard. Hence the packing constraint becomes:

$$3P + 2U \leqslant 30\ 000$$

The remaining three constraints are much easier to handle. The constraint on pasting only affects the pasted wallpaper and limits its production to 10 000 metres per week. Expressed algebraically, this becomes:

$$P \leqslant 10\ 000$$

The marketing constraints are also simple, each requiring the minimum production of the wallpapers to be 3000 metres. Hence these two constraints are:

$$P \geqslant 3000$$
$$U \geqslant 3000$$

Where the $\geqslant$ symbol represents greater than or equal to.

The final formulation of the problem can be summarised as follows:

		Constraint number
Objective function	Maximise $(0.09P + 0.075U)$	
Gravure constraint	$P + U \leqslant 12\ 000$	(1)
Packing constraint	$3P + 2U \leqslant 30\ 000$	(2)
Pasting constraint	$P \leqslant 10\ 000$	(3)
Minimum pasted	$P \geqslant 3000$	(4)
Minimum unpasted	$U \geqslant 3000$	(5)

Thus, the problem as posed has been formulated as a two-variable linear programme, which is the simplest type of formulation possible. As it is so simple, this formulation can be solved using a graphical approach. Drawing graphs with more than two variables is tricky and so the graphical approach is useful for illustrating the principles of linear programming, but no more. Anything above two variables requires a mathematical approach, preferably using a computer program. The next section will show how this simple problem may be solved graphically and the section after that will show the application of the Excel Solver, a powerful spreadsheet extension.

GRAPHICAL SOLUTION

The key to this approach is the representation of the constraints on a simple graph, but it may not be obvious how a set of inequalities can be so represented. As an example, consider the packing constraint, which is:

$$3P + 2U \leqslant 30\ 000$$

Figure 8.1 shows this constraint drawn on a graph, of which the

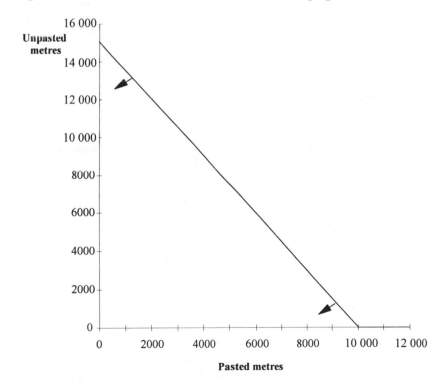

Figure 8.1 *Lancaster Decor Company—the packing constraint*

vertical axis represents U, the number of metres of unpasted wallpaper produced, and the horizontal axis represents P, the metres of pasted wallpaper produced. The sloping line on the graph represents the constraint. It is drawn by considering the maximum values that the variables P and U may take. These values may be found by putting the other variable in the inequality to zero and by treating the inequality as if it were an equation.

Thus, if $U = 0$, then
$3P \leqslant 30\ 000$, or $P \leqslant 10\ 000$. That is, the maximum value of P is 10 000.

If $P = 0$, then
$2U \leqslant 30\ 000$, or $U \leqslant 15\ 000$. That is, the maximum value of U is 15 000.

Hence the line crosses the P axis at 10 000 and crosses the U axis at 15 000. Since this was a less-than-or-equal-to constraint, then any acceptable solution must lie to the left of the line as shown by the arrows on the diagram.

Figure 8.2 shows the effect of drawing all of the constraints on the graph in the same way. The first three constraints are all less-than-or-equal-to, but the final two are greater-than-or-equal-to. The combination of these constraints produces a solution space, usually known as the feasible region, which is shown as the cross-hatched area in Figure 8.2. Any combination of P and U must lie in this feasible region if it is to satisfy this set of constraints.

There are two ways to find the combination of P and U that maximises the objective function, and therefore the expected gross profit. The first, and preferred way, is use standard algebra on the objective function. In this, the gross profit G is:

$$G = 0.090P + 0.075U$$
$$\therefore \quad 0.075U = G - 0.090P$$

$$\therefore \quad U = -\frac{0.090}{0.075}.P + \frac{G}{0.075}$$

$$\therefore \quad U = -1.2.P + \frac{G}{0.075}$$

Which, with U as the vertical axis and P as the horizontal axis, is the equation for a straight line with a slope of -1.2. This value, -1.2 in this case, is known as the iso-profit slope and it reflects the objective function. Thus, any values of P and U which satisfy the objective

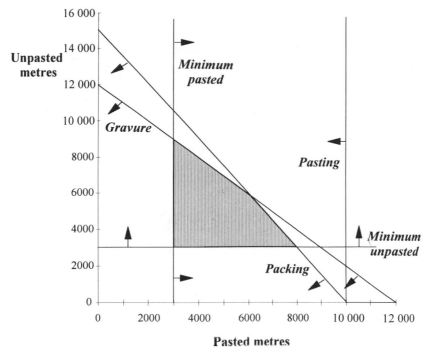

Figure 8.2 *Lancaster Decor Company—the feasible region*

function will lie on a line with this slope. That is, the values of P and U can be in any combination which fits this equation. The problem is to find the values of P and U that maximise G.

It can be shown mathematically that the values of P and U that lead to a maximum profit will lie on one of the corners (usually known as vertices) of the feasible region, which is the hatched area of the graph. The profit will be highest when P and U are as high as possible and when they are in the combination allowed by the line of iso-profit slope. Thus, to find the solution, imagine a series of parallel lines, each with a slope equal to the iso-profit slope (-1.2 in this case), moving out from the origin of the graph until the lines hit the extreme point of the feasible region. This is shown in Figure 8.3, which demonstrates that this will occur when $P = 6000$ and $U = 6000$. In this case, the profit will be £990. This occurs at the intersection of the packing and gravure constraints. These are known as binding constraints.

The way in which the iso-profit slope approaches the optimum vertex can also give some idea of the sensitivity of the solution to changes in the values taken by the coefficients of the constraints and

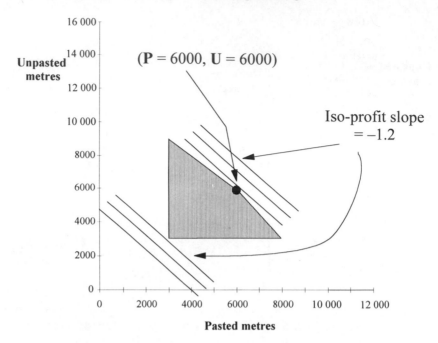

Figure 8.3 *Lancaster Decor Company—finding a solution*

of the objective function. The coefficients of the objective function determine the angle at which the iso-profit slope approaches the edges of the feasible region. The coefficients of the constraints determine the slopes of the sides of the feasible region and thus determine where the vertices lie. Hence, if the slope of one or more of the constraints changes, then so will the angles between two or more of the constraints. Therefore, alterations to the coefficients will change the shape of the feasible region and/or the angle of the iso-profit line. If small changes in the coefficients result in relatively large changes to the iso-profit line or to the binding constraints, then this suggests that the solution may be very sensitive to the values included in the model. As will be clear later, the sensitivity analysis of an optimum solution is one of the benefits conferred by the use of properly designed computer software for linear programming.

The other way of reaching this solution, which is rather clumsy, is to compute the co-ordinates of each vertex of the feasible region. Each vertex consists of two equations, and thus, for example, the vertex that we already know contains the solution occurs at the intersection of constraints (1) and (2). Hence these two equations may be solved as follows:

$$P + U = 12\ 000 \qquad (1)$$
$$3P + 2U = 30\ 000 \qquad (2)$$

Multiply (1) by 3, gives $\qquad 3P + 3U = 36\ 000 \qquad (3)$

Subtract (2) from (3), gives $\qquad\qquad U = 6000$

Thus, $\qquad\qquad\qquad\qquad\qquad P = 6000$

For which the gross profit = £990. Similar computations for all the other vertices will show that this is indeed the maximum profit.

USING THE EXCEL SOLVER

As was mentioned earlier, the application of linear programming need no longer be restricted by the need for specialist software. Spreadsheet packages often contain add-ons which can be used to tackle problems of non-trivial size. Perhaps the two most widely used spreadsheets are Microsoft Excel, which has an add-on known as The Solver, and Lotus 1-2-3 which has What's Best? Both of these systems are very easy to use and, though somewhat slower than specialist software, may be used to tackle problems of a reasonable size. There is, of course, some danger in their ease of use, as there are pitfalls to be avoided in building and running linear programming models that may be glossed over in this friendly software. Nevertheless, the availability of this software is something to be applauded. The current discussion is based on Microsoft Excel v5. Later or earlier versions of the software may have slightly different menu structures, but the basic ideas are the same.

Formulation for The Solver

At the core of any linear programming model is a set of constraints within which some objective function is to be optimised. The simple production planning example of LDC was formulated earlier in this chapter by using conventional algebra as follows:

Maximise $(0.09P + 0.075U)$ Objective function
Subject to:
$P + U \leqslant 12\ 000$ Gravure constraint
$3P + 2U \leqslant 30\ 000$ Packing constraint
$P \leqslant 10\ 000$ Pasting constraint
$P \geqslant 3000$ Minimum pasted constraint
$U \geqslant 3000$ Minimum unpasted constraint

This algebra could be replaced by a different form of expression that relies upon tables (or matrices) for its presentation. This might look as follows:

	P = Pasted metres	U = Unpasted metres		
Maximise	0.09	0.075		
Subject to:				Limit
	1	1	⩽	12 000
	3	2	⩽	30 000
	1	0	⩽	10 000
	1	0	⩾	3000
	0	1	⩾	3000
				Gross profit
Solution	0	0		0

Apart from the bottom line, this is self-explanatory. The bottom line represents the values assigned to P (metres of pasted) and U (metres of unpasted) before any optimisation. In this state, both U and P are set to zero, which results in a gross profit of zero.

The first stage of using The Solver is to set up these matrices on the spreadsheet, and this is shown in Figure 8.4. As in all spreadsheet usage it is crucial to understand that some cells contain values (constants that do not change), but others contain formulae which lead to values being displayed in those cells. In this example, cells D4, D5, D6, D7, D8 and E10 contain formulae. The rest are used for text, to make the example clearer, or for values.

An explanation of Figure 8.4 is given below.

- In this example, columns B and C are used to set up the values contained in the expressions used in the algebraic formulation and in the above tables.

  - Row 2 contains the values of the coefficients of the objective function (0.09 and 0.075).
  - Rows 4 to 8 contain the values that represent the coefficients of the constraints.

- Row 10 contains the initial values given to P and U before any optimisation.

- Column D contains zeroes, but these are computed values which represent the usage of the five constraints. Thus cell D4 contains the formula:

$$=\$B\$10^*\$B4+\$C\$10^*\$C4$$

which is the sum of two products. The first product represents the gravure usage from P metres of pasted wallpaper and the second product represents the gravure usage from U metres of unpasted wallpaper. Note that the references to cells B10 and C10 are both absolute. Thus the formulae underlying cells D4 to D8 are as follows:

- D4 $=\$B\$10^*\$B4+\$C\$10^*\$C4$
- D5 $=\$B\$10^*\$B5+\$C\$10^*\$C5$
- D6 $=\$B\$10^*\$B6+\$C\$10^*\$C6$
- D7 $=\$B\$10^*\$B7+\$C\$10^*\$C7$
- D8 $=\$B\$10^*\$B8+\$C\$10^*\$C8$

- Column E has been used to set up the limits on the constraints, often known as right-hand-sides (abbreviated to RHS by many people). Thus there is a limit of 12 000 on gravure usage, of 30 000 on packing and so on. Column D, as mentioned above, is used to

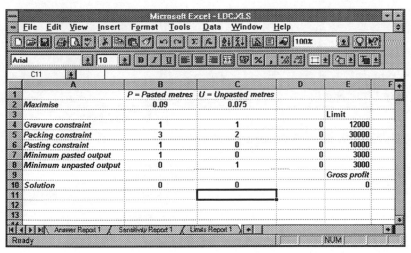

Figure 8.4 *MS Excel™—basic problem formulation*

store the actual usage of these resources. Thus, cell D4 represents the amount of gravure that has been used and this is zero since cells B10 and C10 contain zero values before any optimisation.

- Finally, a spreadsheet cell needs to be used to show the result of the optimisation (the gross profit, in this case) and this will be placed in cell E10.

The Solver Parameters Window

Using normal mouse clicks or key strokes, The Solver may be selected from the Tools menu of Microsoft Excel. This results in the window of Figure 8.5 appearing on the screen. This Solver Parameters window is used to provide the information needed by The Solver to carry out the required optimisation. To optimise the above LDC problem, The Solver needs to know the following:

- Where will the objective function value be placed? This is the result of the optimisation and is the effect of computing the function using whatever values of P and U are found by the optimisation. In this case, the result will be placed in cell E10. This means that cell E10 must contain the appropriate formula, and in this case, this will be: =$B$2*$B$10+$C$2*$C$10. Note that the cell references are absolute—this is advisable, though not absolutely necessary.
- What are the constraints and what form do they take? To set these up, click on the Add button of the constraint subwindow of The

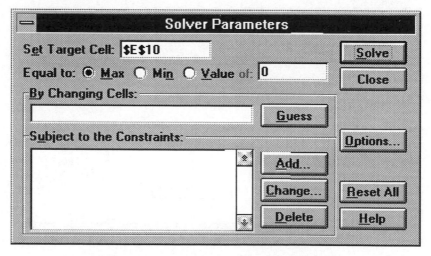

Figure 8.5 *The Solver—parameters window*

Solver parameters window. This produces the dialogue box shown in Figure 8.6. In this, the dialogue relates to the first, gravure constraint whose coefficients are in cells B4 and C4 and whose expression is in the formula of cell D4. Thus, $D$4 must be entered in the cell reference box, since this contains the constraint expression. This constraint is a less-than-or-equal-to and thus this is selected from the middle, drop-down list. Finally, the actual value of the constraint is to be found in cell $E$4 and this is entered in the constraint box. Pressing the OK button returns control back to The Solver parameters window. Each of the constraints must be added in this way—noting that two of them are greater-than-or-equal-to and that therefore the correct symbol must be selected in the constraint dialogue box.

- Which cells will contain the values of P and U that are to be varied so as to optimise the objective function, and what type of optimisation should be attempted? This information is provided by the user via The Solver parameters window. The cells whose values will be varied are B10 and C10 and thus, as shown in Figure 8.7, these are entered as absolute cell references in the By Changing Cells box. This is a maximisation and thus the Max option is selected.

Before performing the optimisation it is a good idea to inform The Solver that all constraints are linear expressions, as is the objective function. That is, that this is a linear programming problem. This is done by clicking the Options button of The Solver parameters window. This opens a subsidiary window within which the Assume linear model option should be selected. This will increase the speed of the optimisation computation and also leads to reports (see below) tailored to linear programming problems.

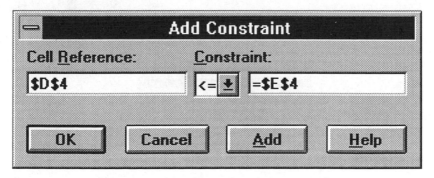

Figure 8.6 *The Solver—the constraints window*

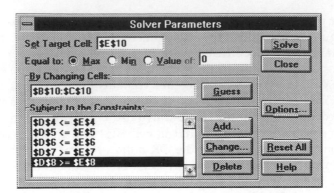

Figure 8.7 *The Solver—by changing cells window*

To perform the optimisation, return to The Solver parameters window and press the Solve button of this window. This results in the output shown in Figure 8.8, which indicates that producing 6000 metres of unpasted wallpaper and 6000 metres of pasted wallpaper will result in a gross profit of £990 and that this is the maximum, given the problem as it was formulated.

It is important to realise that much more information can be gained

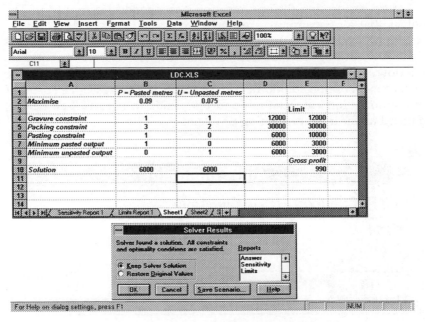

Figure 8.8 *The Solver—solution to the LDC problem*

from the solution to a linear programming problem than just the optimum values of the decision variables. A good computer package such as The Solver provides reports that help the user to understand much more about the solution than this. The Solver provides three standard reports and it is also possible to export the solution to other computer packages should further analysis be needed.

The Solver's Answer Report

This summarises the results from the worksheet screen and also provides a little more information. This extra information could be calculated by the user, but it is useful to have this in one place. The answer report for the LDC problem is shown in Figure 8.9 and it has three parts, one after the other:

- Target Cell (Max) shows the maximum profit obtained by The Solver. If this were a minimisation problem this section would contain the minimum value.
- Adjustable Cells shows each of the input variables, the values that they take in the optimum solution and their initial values (zero in this case).
- Constraints indicates the usage of each of the constraints in the problem. The Status column labels each constraint as Binding or Not Binding, the latter being ones that have some unused resource—indicated by a non-zero value in the Slack column. As with the graphical solution presented earlier, only two constraints are binding, those for gravure and packing.

The other two reports provide more information about the sensitivity of the optimum solution and this can be very important for a number of reasons. First, it is rarely the case that all the coefficients or values in any type of management science model are known with complete certainty. Some will be certain but many will be approximations, estimates or even best guesses. What if these values turn out to be wrong? What would be the effect of such errors in the solution? An optimum solution that turns out to be highly sensitive to the values assigned to the coefficients may be worse that another solution that is a little less than optimum. The second reason for the importance of sensitivity analysis is that the world is dynamic and, therefore, things are constantly changing. For example, it may be true this week that a raw material has a certain cost/tonne, but in a month's time, this may have changed. Thus it is important to know what effect changes in the coefficients may have on the optimum solution.

Microsoft Excel 5.0 Answer Report
Worksheet: [Book 2]Sheet 1
Report created: 27/2/96 15:41

Target cell (max)

Cell	Name	Original value	Final value
$E$10	Solution Gross profit	0	990

Adjustable cells

Cell	Name	Original value	Final value
$B$10	Solution P = Pasted metres	0	6000
$C$10	Solution U = Unpasted metres	0	6000

Constraints

Cell	Name	Cell value	Formula	Status	Slack
$D$4	Gravure constraint	12000	$D$4<=$E$4	Binding	0
$D$5	Packing constraint	30000	$D$5<=$E$5	Binding	0
$D$6	Pasting constraint	6000	$D$6<=$E$6	Not Binding	4000
$D$7	Minimum pasted output	6000	$D$7>=$E$7	Not Binding	3000
$D$8	Minimum unpasted output	6000	$D$8>=$E$8	Not Binding	3000

Figure 8.9   *The Solver—answer report for the LDC problem*

The Solver Sensitivity Report

The first report that provides information about sensitivity is known as The Sensitivity Report—shown, in Figure 8.10, for the LDC problem. The report comes in two parts, shown in the figure, and these are to be understood as follows.

The first part is headed Changing Cells and refers to an analysis usually known as Objective Ranging in the linear programming literature. It gets this name because it shows the range across which each coefficient in the objective function may individually change without altering the values taken by the variables in the optimum solution. Consider, for example, the variable P, which represents the number of metres of pasted wallpaper to be made. In the optimum solution this takes a value of 6000 metres. Its coefficient in the objective function is 0.09 and the Allowable Increase and Allowable Decrease columns show by how much this coefficient may change without altering the recommendation that 6000 metres should be made. The values for the objective function coefficient of U cover the range $(0.09 + 0.0225$ to $0.09 - 0.015)$, that is, from 0.1125 to 0.075. If the coefficient of P stays within these values then its optimum value remains unchanged. Similarly, the optimum value for U is 6000 if its objective function coefficient stays with the range of $(0.075 + 0.015$ to $0.075 - 0.015)$, that is, from 0.09 to 0.06. Note that this objective ranging only applies to each of the variables independently—if more than one variable changes, then the situation is much more complicated.

Referring back to the graphical solution in which an iso-profit slope was used, objective ranging is equivalent to tilting the iso-profit slope

Microsoft Excel 5.0 Sensitivity Report
Worksheet: [Book 2]Sheet 1
Report created: 27/2/96 15:41

Changing cells

Cell	Name	Final value	Reduced cost	Objective coefficient	Allowable increase	Allowable decrease
$B$10	Solution P = Pasted metres	6000	0	0.09	0.0225	0.015
$C$10	Solution U = Unpasted metres	6000	0	0.075	0.015	0.015

Constraints

Cell	Name	Final value	Shadow price	Constraint R.H. side	Allowable increase	Allowable decrease
$D$4	Gravure constraint	12000	0.045	12000	1500	1000
$D$5	Packing constraint	30000	0.015	30000	3000	3000
$D$6	Pasting constraint	6000	0	10000	1E+30	4000
$D$7	Minimum pasted output	6000	0	3000	3000	1E+30
$D$8	Minimum unpasted output	6000	0	3000	3000	1E+30

Figure 8.10   *The Solver—sensitivity report*

at different angles to see what difference this will make. If the iso-profit slope of the objective function were to vary, eventually it would cease to cross the feasible region at the current optimum solution and would cross at another vertex. Thus, the limits on the ranges relate to the slopes which the iso-profit line would cease to cross the feasible region at the optimum vertex and would instead cross at another vertex. In the case of LDC, if the gross profit for pasted wallpaper were to rise above £0.1175 per metre then it would presumably be better to devote more capacity to make unpasted than to making pasted wallpaper. The reverse would apply if its gross profit were to fall below £0.075 per metre.

The second part of The Solver's sensitivity report is headed Constraints and it reports on what are often termed Shadow Prices and RHS Ranging, where RHS is an abbreviation for right-hand-side, referring to the limits on the constraints. This is presented as a table with a row devoted to each constraint within the constraint set. The columns should be interpreted as follows:

Final Value. This is the total usage of the constraint in question. In the case of gravure printing, this is shown as 12 000, this being the actual amount of time available as specified by the limit of the constraint. Time for packing is also used up and thus its final value is 30 000. None of the other constrained resources is fully utilised.

Shadow Price. This is the value of providing a single extra unit of a fully constrained resource. In this solution there are two such fully constrained resources, the time available for gravure printing and for packing. In the case of LDC, this indicates that an extra unit of gravure time is worth £0.045 and an extra unit of packing time is worth £0.015, both expressed in terms of gross profit. It might, thus, be worth LDC paying up to these amounts in order to gain an extra unit of the resource. Note that this is a marginal analysis which applies only within a certain range, and therefore that subsequent units outside of these ranges will have different shadow prices. The ranges are shown by the values in the last two columns of the table. Note also that, as with objective ranging, these shadow prices apply only to each constraint taken individually. Combined changes require a more complicated analysis.

Constraint R.H. Side. The limits placed on the constraints in the problem formulation.

Allowable Increase and *Allowable Decrease.* These show the range across which the shadow prices are applicable and, clearly, these have no meaning unless the resource is fully utilised. Thus, the shadow price of £0.045 for extra gravure capacity applies within a range of values

Microsoft Excel 5.0 Limits Report
Worksheet: [Book 2]Sheet 1
Report Created: 27/2/96 15:41

Cell	Target name	Value
$E$10	Solution gross profit	990

Cell	Adjustable name	Value	Lower limit	Target result	Upper limit	Target result
$B$10	Solution P = Pasted metres	6000	3000	720	6000	990
$C$10	Solution U = Unpasted metres	6000	3000	765	6000	990

Figure 8.11   *The Solver—limits report for LDC*

from (12 000 + 1500 to 12 000 – 1000), that is, from 12 500 to 11 000. When the RHS values are changed within the allowable limits, the optimum values of P and U may change, unlike in objective ranging. In graphical terms, this is equivalent to moving a constraint line without altering its slope.

The Solver Limits Report

The second sensitivity report provided by Excel is known as the Limits Report. The report produced for LDC is shown in Figure 8.11. As this is a maximisation problem, the column labelled Upper Limit shows the optimum values for P and for U, with the corresponding profits in the Target Result column. The Lower Limit column shows the minimum value that each variable could take without breaking the constraints. In the LDC problem, both variables have lower bounds of 3000 metres (the marketing constraints). The Target Result alongside the Lower Limit shows the gross profit that would result if each variable were reduced to its lower bound.

SOME MATHEMATICAL IDEAS

In order to make more progress with linear programming, it is important to define and develop a few mathematical ideas, of which the first is the concept of linearity. Linear programming applies to systems in which the objective function and the constraint are all linear expressions. What this means is that each of the variables that appears in the formulation does so in the form

<constant> multiplied by <variable>

Thus, there are no terms such as

$$x^2, e^x, 1/x \text{ or } x.y$$

where x and y are variables.

This idea is known as linearity because, when there are only two variables in a linear equation, this equation is a straight line when plotted on a graph. For example, the equation:

$$x_2 = A.x_1 + B$$

represents a straight line in which x_2 is plotted on the vertical axis, x_1 is plotted on the horizontal axis and in which the slope of the line is A and the line crosses the x_2 axis at B.

If the objective function were non-linear then it could not be represented by a straight line and therefore it might cross the feasible region at more than one point. For example, it might form a tight curve that crosses the feasible region at one point, leaves it and then crosses it again elsewhere. If the constraints were non-linear, the edges of the feasible region would not be straight and there could be no assurance that the objective function would touch it at a vertex. For example, if they were concave, the extreme point at which the iso-profit line touches might not be a vertex since it might, instead, form a tangent to the curve.

A second mathematical idea useful in linear programming is the summation notation. This uses the Greek capital letter sigma, Σ, chosen because it is equivalent to the letter S, an abbreviation for "Sum of". It can be very tedious to write down an expression such as:

$$a_1 x_1 + a_2 x_2 + a_3 x_3 + a_4 x_4 + a_5 x_5$$

Instead, we can abbreviate this to the following form:

$$\sum_{j=1}^{5} a_j x_i$$

This enables us to write down general forms of constraints or of objective functions in a much more economical way. In general, this notation may be used to formulate a maximisation linear programme as follows.

$$\text{Maximise } \sum_{j=1}^{m} c_j x_j$$

$$\text{Subject to } \sum_{j=1}^{m} a_{1,j} x_j = b_1$$

$$\sum_{j=1}^{m} a_{2,j} x_j \leq b_2$$

$$\sum_{j=1}^{m} a_{3,j} x_j \leq b_3$$

$$\ldots\ldots$$

$$\sum_{j=1}^{m} a_{i,j} x_j \leq b_j$$

$$\ldots\ldots$$

$$\sum_{j=1}^{m} a_{n,j} x_i \leq b_m$$

where there are m input or decision variables and n constraints. The $\{a\}$ values are the coefficients of the constraints and each of these has a subscript $\{i, j\}$. Thus $a_{i,j}$ refers to the coefficient of the jth variable in the ith constraint. The RHS values are represented by the bs, whose subscripts indicate their constraint.

In the case of minimisation problems, the objective function becomes:

$$\text{Minimise } \sum_{j=1}^{m} c_j x_j$$

and the constraint set is represented by a set of greater-than-or-equal-to expressions of the following general form:

$$\sum_{j=1}^{m} a_{i,j} x_j \geq b_j, \text{ where } i = 1 \ldots n \text{ and } j = 1 \ldots m$$

There is, of course, no particular reason why minimisation and maximisation problems cannot contain constraints that are less-than-or-equal-to, greater-than-or-equal-to or are equalities.

Other Types of Mathematical Programming Models

In some circumstances, simplified approaches to linear programming are possible. Two examples of this are what are known as transportation and assignment problems. A transportation problem occurs when material must be distributed to several destinations from a number of sources. As an example of this, consider the problem faced by LDC in distributing its pasted wallpaper from its two factories to five customers. This could be represented as in Table 8.1.

The table shows that the requirements of customers 1 to 5 are for 1500, 3500, 2000, 2500 and 2500 metres respectively, and there are 6000 metres of pasted wallpaper available from each factory. The other numbers in the matrix represent the costs of delivering the wallpaper to the different customers. Thus, it cost 1.0p per metre to deliver pasted wallpaper from factory 1 to customer 1, 1.1p to deliver it to customer 2, and so on.Though this could be form-ulated as a linear programme in the normal way, it is simpler and usually faster to solve it by using a method known as the transportation algorithm. Most books on the techniques of OR/MS give full details of how to tackle such problems—see for example Wagner (1975).

The assignment problem is a simplified version of the transportation problem. It occurs, for example, when there are a number of tasks to be performed by the same number of people, and each person may only perform any one task. Thus, the tasks must be assigned to people, one person per task. As with the transportation problem this could be formulated as a standard linear programme, but instead it is normal to use a more efficient method, known as the linear assignment algorithm. See any standard text on OR/MS techniques for details of this.

Table 8.1 LDC distribution

	Customer 1	Customer 2	Customer 3	Customer 4	Customer 5	Total supply
Factory 1	1.0	1.1	2.1	1.7	1.5	6 000
Factory 2	1.5	0.9	1.5	2.1	1.2	6 000
Total demand	1500	3500	2000	2500	2500	12 000

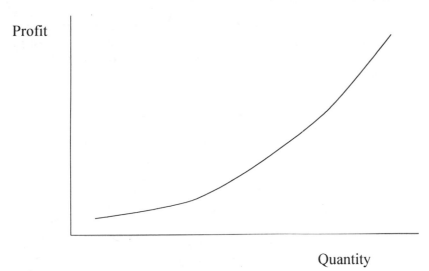

Profit

Quantity

Figure 8.12 *Non-linear function*

Though linear programming is limited to systems in which the objective function and constraints arc all linear expressions, extensions to the approach have been devised to cope with other types of equations. Sometimes the expressions are linear but, in addition, the variables must take integer values—this might be true, for example, in applications for manpower planning where people cannot be subdivided. In these cases integer linear programming (ILP) methods can be used. The extended versions of The Solver and What's Best? provide algorithms to cope with these types of problem. However, it is important to realise that the formulation and solution of integer linear programs is a complicated matter. Friendly software is a great help, but it would be best for novices to seek expert help before tackling such problems.

Further complications occur when the expressions are non-linear, which might happen when the objective function displays increasing or decreasing returns to scale. Figure 8.12 shows a graph of a function in which there are increasing returns to scale. In these non-linear cases, other algorithms must be employed—though, sometimes, linear approximations may be good enough.

COMMON TYPES OF CONSTRAINT

In his detailed discussion of model building in mathematical programming, Williams (1993) examines a number of common types of constraint that are encountered when building mathematical programming models. Some of these will be discussed here in an attempt to shed light on some issues that have to be faced when developing such models.

Productive Capacity Constraints

This type of constraint was encountered in the LDC problem discussed earlier in this chapter. They occur when some necessary resource is available in a limited supply, of which the best use must be made. LDC was short of capacity for gravure printing and for packing. Thus, these constraints were as follows for LDC.

$$P + U \leqslant 12\ 000$$
$$3P + 2U \leqslant 30\ 000$$

Hence, any optimisation had to be conducted within those constraints. Other common examples of these constraints include available labour, or time for a particular set of operations.

Raw Material Availabilities

These are very similar to productive capacity constraints and they occur when limited raw material supplies are available for use across a range of finished products. A similar situation would occur when facing investment decisions for which a limited amount of cash might be available for investment across a range of possible projects.

Marketing Demands and other Limitations—Simple Bounds

There are sometimes rather simple bounds on the values that may be taken by the decision variables and these occur in two ways. First, when the demand for a particular item requires that at least a minimum amount must be produced. For instance, two such constraints occurred in the LDC example, when at least 3000 metres of pasted and unpasted output was required. In this case, the constraints were:

$$P \geqslant 3000$$
$$U \geqslant 3000$$

Thus, 3000 metres is a lower bound on the amount of pasted and unpasted wallpaper to be produced. It might occur because of contracts with customers which specify the minimum amounts.

The second, and opposite, case occurs when there is a direct maximum limitation on the amount that is to be produced. This might occur, for example, when a business reckons that there is a limit to the amount that can be sold to its customers. These upper bounds resemble the lower bounds, except they are less-than-or-equal-to.

It is useful to identify this type of constraint for two reasons. The first, connected with the solution algorithms used in most computer software, is that the solution may be reached much more quickly when some constraints are identified as simple bounds. In essence they reduce the amount of searching that the algorithm must do. Some software identifies these automatically, other packages may need a little help. The second reason is more to do with the sensitivity analysis that follows the solution. Marketing constraints are, for example, of a different order to productive capacity constraints. Though the productive capacity may be within the control of the business, the same may not be true of the market for the product.

Material Balance Constraints

These are less obvious than the previous types of constraint. They represent the simple fact that all the items that go into some process must be present in the outputs from the process—whether as losses or as planned output. This is a typical feature of blending problems in which a number of ingredients are mixed together to form some finished product.

As an example, suppose that feedstuff for animals must be blended from a number of ingredients and that the feedstuff blender wishes to maximise his profit, subject to a number of constraints such as the nutritional quality of the blend. Suppose that four raw materials make up the blend, then the objective function might be:

$$\text{Maximise } (-c_1 x_1 - c_2 x_2 - c_3 x_3 - c_4 x_4 - py)$$

where:

c_i represents the cost of one tonne of raw material i
p is the gross income received from selling one tonne of the blended foodstuff

x_i is the number of tonnes of raw material i in the final blend, and y is the number of tonnes of the blend produced.

Thus, the objective is to maximise the profit, this being the gross income from sales, less the cost of the raw materials that have been blended.

Given this objective function, the constraints *must* include the following—plus, of course, all of the others as required by the circumstances:

$$x_1 + x_2 + x_3 + x_4 - y = 0$$

This ensures that the material will balance. Thus, in problems of this type, the objective function will include something like the following:

$$\text{Maximise} \sum_{i=1}^{n} - c_i x_i - py$$

and the constraints will include the following:

$$\sum_{i=1}^{n} x_i - y = 0$$

CASE STUDY: GARDENING DEPARTMENT

THE PROBLEM POSED

Suppose that the gardening department of a local authority uses large quantities of compost to grow the plants that it displays at official functions during the year. An external consultant has recommended that they mix their own compost from the four normal materials, known as RS1, RS2, SA1 and SA2. These materials are available at costs of £10, £9, £8 and £5 per tonne. No other material is part of the compost. They would like to produce 20 tonnes of the compost and would like to do so at minimum cost. The compost itself must contain certain quantities of two important organic nutrients, as shown in Table 8.2.

The four materials come from two different sources. RS1 and RS2 come from Robin Smith quarries and this company is prepared to deliver up to 10 tonnes in total of these two materials in any proportion. SA1 and

Table 8.2 *Compost production*

	Amount in each tonne of each of the four materials				Minimum amount needed in total
	RS1	RS2	SA1	SA2	
Nutrient 1	0.10	0.11	0.12	0.12	2
Nutrient 2	0.50	0.40	0.40	0.20	8

SA2 come from Southern Aggregates who are willing to deliver up to 15 tonnes, again in any proportions. The "feel" of the compost is also important, and for that reason they wish to ensure that the 20 tonne batch contains at least 3 tonnes of RS2 and 3 tonnes of SA2.

A LINEAR PROGRAMMING FORMULATION

As before, the first stage is to define some suitable variables. Suppose that

r_1 represents the tonnes of RS1 to be used
r_2 represents the tonnes of RS2 to be used
r_3 represents the tonnes of SA1 to be used
r_4 represents the tonnes of SA2 to be used

Hence, the objective function is:

$$\text{Minimise } 10r_1 + 9r_2 + 8r_3 + 5r_4$$

The constraints are as follows.

1. Minimum quantities of nutrient 1:

$$0.10r_1 + 0.11r_2 + 0.12r_3 + 0.12r_4 \geqslant 2$$

2. Minimum quantities of nutrient 2:

$$0.50r_1 + 0.40r_2 + 0.40r_3 + 0.20r_4 \geqslant 8$$

3. Quantity of compost needed:

$$r_1 + r_2 + r_3 + r_4 = 20$$

4. Maximum delivery from Robin Smith:

$$r_1 + r_2 \leqslant 10$$

5. Maximum delivery from Southern Aggregates:

$$r_3 + r_4 \leqslant 15$$

6. Lower bounds on all four materials:

$$r_1 \geqslant 0$$
$$r_2 \geqslant 3$$
$$r_3 \geqslant 0$$
$$r_4 \geqslant 3$$

The formulation is now complete, and the solution that emerges from the Excel Solver is shown in Table 8.3. This is achieved at a cost of £166. This means that constraints are non-binding and have slack or surpluses available, as shown in Table 8.4.

The sensitivity report reveals that the shadow prices of binding constraints are as shown in Table 8.5. Thus, each unit of nutrient 1 that is required is costing £20, and the requirement to use at least 1 tonne each of RS2 and SA2 adds a extra £1 per tonne to the final compost.

Table 8.3 *The solution from the Excel Solver*

Material	RS1	RS2	SA1	SA2
Tonnage	6	3	8	3

Table 8.4 *Slack or surpluses available*

Constraint	Usage	Slack or surplus
Minimum quantity of nutrient 1	2.25	2.25
Maximum delivery from Robin Smith	9	1
Maximum delivery from Southern Aggregates	11	4
Lower bound on RS1	6	6
Lower bound on SA1	8	8

Table 8.5 *Shadow prices of binding constraints*

Constraint	Shadow price	Range
Minimum quantity of nutrient 2	20	7.9 to 8.4
Lower bound on RS2	1	0 to 2
Lower bound on SA2	1	0 to 2

SUMMARY

This chapter has provided an introduction to the ideas of linear programming as an example of optimisation modelling. It has illustrated this with two simple examples, one of which was solved by graphical means and both of which were used to illustrate the use of computer software usable by anyone familiar with spreadsheets. The purpose of the chapter was to show how situations might be modelled in which there is a need to make the best of use of some limited resources. It also shows that, in many cases, the model is used as a vehicle to explore the solution space in such a way as to understand how sensitive it is to changes in the parameters of the model.

In this way, even mathematical programming models may be used in an investigative mode. It would perhaps be stretching the meaning of the word "interpretive" too far to regard mathematical programming as an interpretive approach; nevertheless there seems no particular reason why the techniques cannot be employed in a complementary way with some of the softer modelling approaches discussed in Part II.

REFERENCES

Arntzen B.C., Brown G.B., Harrison T.P and Trafton L.L. (1995) Global supply chain management at Digital Equipment Corporation. *Interfaces*, **25**, 1, 69–93.

Cox L.A. (Jnr), Kuehner W.E., Parrish S.H. and Qiu Y. (1993) Optimal expansion of fiber-optic telecommunications networks in metropolitan areas. *Interfaces*, **23**, 2, 35–48.

Dantzig G. (1963) *Linear Programming and Extensions*. Princeton University Press, Princeton, NJ.

Dash Associates (1995) *The XPRESS-MP System*. Dash Associates, Blisworth, Northants.

Frontline Systems (1995) *The Premium Solver for Excel System Manuals*. Frontline Systems Inc., PO Box 4288, Incline Village, NV 89450, USA.

Grandzol J.R. and Traaen T. (1995) Using mathematical programming to help supervisors balance workloads. *Interfaces*, **25**, 4, 92–103.

Hendry L.C., Fok K.K. and Shek K.W. (1996) A cutting stock and scheduling problem in the copper industry. *Journal of the Operational Research Society*, **47**, 1, 38–47.

Kantorovich L.V. (1942) On the translocation of masses. *C.R. Acad. Sci. URSS*, **37**, 199–201.

LINDO Systems (1995a) *The LINDO System*. Lindo Systems Inc, 1415 N. Dayton St, Chicago, IL 60622, USA.

LINDO Systems (1995b) *What's Best? System Manuals*. Lindo Systems Inc., 1415 N. Dayton St, Chicago, IL 60622, USA.

Litty C.J. (1994) Optimal leasing structuring at GE Capital. *Interfaces*, **24**, 3, 34–45.

Microsoft (1993) *Microsoft Excel User's Guide*. Microsoft Corp. Inc., Seattle.

Sharda R. (1995) Linear programming solver software for personal computers: 1995 report. *OR/MS Today*, **22**, 5, 64–57.

Stanford Business Systems (1995) *The MINOS System*. Stanford Business Systems, Mountain View, CA.

Wagner H. (1975) *Principles of Operations Research with Applications to Managerial Decisions*. Prentice-Hall International, London.

Williams H.P. (1990) *Model Building in Mathematical Programming*. (Third edition.) John Wiley, Chichester.

Williams H.P. (1993) *Model Solving in Mathematical Programming*. John Wiley, Chichester.

Zenios S.A. (1994) Parallel and supercomputing in the practice of management science. *Interfaces*, **24**, 5, 122–40.

9

Visual Interactive Modelling—Discrete Event Computer Simulation

COMPUTER SIMULATION DEFINED

The basic idea of computer simulation in shown in Figure 9.1. Strictly speaking, computer simulation is the *use* of a model as a basis for exploration and experimentation. Like all modelling approaches, simulation is used because it may be cheaper, safer, quicker and more secure than using the real system itself. The idea is that the model becomes a vehicle for asking "what if...?" questions. That is, the simulation model is subject to known inputs and the effects of these inputs on the outputs is noted. Statisticians would recognise that the inputs may be considered as factors at different levels and that the outputs may be considered as a response surface.

As the term is used in this chapter, such simulations are dynamic. That is, they make use of a model whose behaviour may be unfolded through time. Rather like a video film, the dynamics of the unfolding scene may be slowed down, or sped up and different levels of detail may be incorporated.

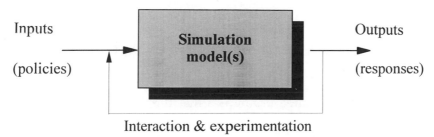

Interaction & experimentation

Figure 9.1 *Simulation as computer-based experimentation*

Given enough time, money, expertise and computer power almost any system can be simulated on a computer, but this may not be sensible. Hence the first question to face is, to what type of systems are modern computer simulation methods best suited? The following features tend to characterise the systems best suited to computer simulation:

- They are *dynamic*—that is, they display distinctive behaviour that is known to vary through time. This variation might be due to factors that are not well understood but which may still be amenable to statistical analysis—for example, the apparently random failures of equipment. Or they might be due to well-understood relationships that can be captured in equations—for example, the flight of a missile through a non-turbulent atmosphere.
- They are *interactive*—that is, the system consists of a number of components that interact with one another and this interaction produces the distinctive behaviour of the system. For example, the observed behaviour of aircraft under air traffic control will be due to factors such as the performance characteristics of the individual aircraft, the intervention of the air traffic controllers, the weather and any local problems due to political action on the ground. This mix of factors will be varying all the time, and their interaction will produce the observed behaviour of the air traffic.
- They are *complicated*—that is, there are many objects which interact in the system of interest, and their individual dynamics need careful consideration and analysis.

In short, computer simulation modelling is best suited to systems that are dynamic and interactive as well as complicated. As a technique, it has been in use in management science since the early 1950s and its methods have gradually evolved alongside general developments in computing since then.

SOME SIMULATION APPLICATIONS

In surveys of management scientists, computer simulation usually figures in the top three techniques that they employ in their work. There are thousands of applications across many areas of work in management science. This section of the chapter will briefly discuss some of those applications.

Manufacturing

As markets for manufactured goods have become globalised, manufacturers have increasingly attempted to mass customise their products. That is, they have sought economies of scale by developing products that will have global appeal and should sell in many countries. At the same time they have had to ensure that the products themselves are suited to local preferences, which means they have had to produce local variants of the global designs. This mass customisation, sometimes known as glocalisation, has placed great pressure on manufacturers to develop and install manufacturing systems that can deliver high volume, high-quality goods at low cost to meet local needs. This has led to huge investments in manufacturing plant and their control systems. It is important to ensure that such systems operate as intended, and therefore computer simulation methods have found an important place in the process of designing and implementing these manufacturing plant and systems.

Examples of this use of computer simulation occur across most manufacturing sectors and include the food industry (Pidd, 1987), semi-conductor wafer fabrication (Miller, 1994), beverages (Harrell, 1993), pharmaceuticals (Park and Getz, 1992), automobile manufacture (Beadle, 1986), aerospace (Bier and Tjelle, 1994). Simulation is employed because it allows alternative designs and control policies to be tried out on the model before starting to build the physical plant. It helps to reduce the cost and risk of large-scale errors. Simulation approaches are also used on existing plant to find better ways to operate, and these studies might be once-off exercises or may be part of a periodic check on the running of the system.

Health Care

As with manufacturing, there is also a need to make effective use of limited resources when providing and delivering health care. Thus, simulation approaches have found widespread application in health care systems around the world. Wears and Winton (1993) report on its use to examine options, particularly those of triage, in pre-hospital trauma care. Ceric (1990) describes how the methods were used to plan a system to move goods and equipment around a large new hospital in an effective and efficient manner. McGuire (1994) reports on the use of simulation for the planning of effective emergency departments. In all these simulations and in others, the idea was to test different policies without putting patients to inconvenience or placing them at risk. In a different context, Brailsford et al (1992) describe how the approach has been used to investigate different policies for handling the AIDS epidemic.

Business Process Re-engineering

Recent years have seen an increasing concern by businesses to ensure that their core processes are operated effectively and efficiently, and this has been the aim of business process re-engineering (BPR). In BPR the idea is to take a fundamental look at the basic processes without which the business could not function and which contribute in a major way to both profit and cost. In some ways, the stress on BPR mirrors the shift in manufacturing from batch production towards flow-line manufacturing. An example of a BPR exercise might be an investigation of the various operations and activities involved in delivering goods to a customer, and in invoicing that customer and in receiving payment. In a traditional system, the paperwork and computer-based documentation might need to pass through several different departments. Taking a radical look at such processes might lead to great simplification and thus to reduced costs and to better service. The aim of BPR is to take an integrated view of such activities and to find ways to provide a better service at lower cost by more effective organisation.

Bhaskar et al (1994) identify computer simulation as one of the key approaches to understanding how business processes might be re-engineered to improve performance. Davies (1994) describes how simulation has been used in BPR in the UK financial services industry. Companies providing these financial services in the UK must meet legal time limits for their responses to customers and must also carry out a series of checks required by law—in addition to their own internal monitoring. Davies (1994) developed a simulation model known as SCOPE to enable organisations to organise their office processes so as to achieve target performance levels. SCOPE works by simulating the flow of documents through the organisation.

Transport Systems

Computer simulation is also used in a wide range of transportation systems. As with other applications, the idea is to ensure that the system operates as efficiently and as effectively as possible. In the aviation sector, simulation methods have, for example, been used to help plan large passenger terminals. Airport terminals include systems for moving baggage and for ensuring that passengers can get to the departure gates in time for their planes, and a number of simulations have been used to assess their performance. Also in the aviation sector, air traffic control systems are used to ensure that air space is used efficiently and safely. As part of this, the air traffic controllers must ensure that the movement of aircraft is planned in advance and then managed in real-time. Simulation approaches have made a great contribution to safer and more cost-effective air traffic control.

The shipping sector has also been a long-term user of computer simulation methods. Indeed, one of the computer simulation programming languages (CSL; Buxton and Laski, 1962) was first developed by Esso (predecessor of Exxon) to support simulations of the movement of crude and refined oil around the world. Shipping applications continue to this day and an example is given in Heath (1993).

Salt (1991) reported how simulation methods were used to help plan the movement of traffic in the Channel Tunnel that links the UK and France. Though the introduction of this service was controversial, it is clear that one key to its future success is the reliability of the service that it offers. Unlike the ferries which also ply the route, bad weather should not prevent the operation of the tunnel service. It was therefore crucial that its operations were properly planned and managed. Salt (1991) gives interesting examples of how this was supported by computer simulation approaches.

The road transport sector is also a major user of computer simulation methods both to plan individual companies' operations and to investigate road traffic systems in general. Traffic simulators are now a standard part of the armoury of road traffic planners (Pidd, 1995; Rathi and Santiago, 1990; Young et al, 1989) since they permit possible road configurations and traffic management schemes to be refined before their physical implementation.

Defence

The defence sector is also a major user of simulation methods and the *Proceedings of the Winter Simulation Conference* usually include a range of papers discussing work in this area (see Evans et al, 1993, for example). Applications range from studies of logistics operations through to battle simulations, which investigate possible strategies and tactics to be used in defence or attack. Their appeal here is obvious; no battle commander wishes to be defeated and the chance to develop tactics beforehand and to prepare counter-measures is of some importance. Not surprisingly, the majority of defence simulations are not reported in the public literature.

DISCRETE EVENT SIMULATIONS DEFINED

Whatever the simulation modelling approach adopted, a simulation model must be able to mimic the changes that occur, through time, in the real system. In management science it is usual to distinguish between three different approaches to simulation modelling. These are known as discrete event simulation, continuous simulation and mixed discrete/continuous simulation. The majority of applications of dynamic simulation methods in management science seem to use discrete event models and thus this chapter will concentrate on these. System dynamics (see Chapter 7) includes a simulation approach which is a simple version of continuous simulation. Stella (also described in Chapter 7) extends this to allow for the limited inclusion of some discrete elements.

Discrete Event Simulation

This approach gets its name from its main features. Systems to be simulated in this way are considered to consist of discrete entities which occupy discrete states that will change over time. Thus, a hospital will include individual patients whose states may include "being admitted", "on emergency ward 10", "in surgery", and so on. Similarly, the staff who treat the patients may themselves be regarded as entities that change state. For example, doctors may be "examining a patient", "writing case notes", "operating on a patient", and so on. Many of these states require the co-operation of two or more classes of entity—for example "examining a patient" (the doctor's perspective) is the same as "being examined by a doctor" from a patient's perspective. Thus, the essence of discrete event modelling is an attempt to capture the important features of the system in terms of entities and states.

The bulk of a discrete event simulation model consists of a set of logical statements, expressed in some computable form, which describe how the entities change state. Thus there might be statements of the following type:

```
If (ThisDoctor=Free) and (PatientsWaiting>0) then
{
  Take ThisPatient from PatientsWaiting;
  Engage ThisDoctor to ThisPatient;
  Compute ConsultationTime;
  Release ThisDoctor and ThisPatient after
  ConsultationTime.
}
```

This set of statements, which are not written in any particular programming language, describe what must happen for a consultation to begin. The conditions governing the start of this are that ThisDoctor must be Free and there must be PatientsWaiting. If those conditions hold, then a waiting patient and ThisDoctor are placed in an engaged state in which they will remain until the Consultation-Time is over. This example also illustrates another feature of a discrete simulation model: it is concerned with the conditions that govern a state change of the entities. Unless those above are satisfied, the event will not occur. The times at which the entities change state are known as events—hence the term discrete event simulation.

Discrete event simulation is probably the most commonly used simulation approach in management science and most of the rest of this chapter will focus on it. The approach is well suited to systems in which there appear to be classes of entities that interact with one another to produce the distinctive behaviour of the system. At some stage or other the logic of a discrete event simulation model needs to be put in some computable form. For large-scale and complex systems it will be necessary to write a computer program of some size. These may be written in a general purpose programming language such as C++ or Pascal, or in a special purpose simulation programming language such as SIMSCRIPT or MODSIM (both from CACI).

In the last ten years, software developers have produced easy-to-use discrete event simulation tools that greatly ease the process of developing and running a simulation. These tools are known as visual interactive modelling systems (VIMS, a plural or singular acronym) and they will be discussed later in this chapter. VIMS have been developed for other types of simulation too, and Stella/I Think (High Performance Systems, 1994) is an example of one developed for system dynamics.

Entities and Classes

In order to provide a useful description of discrete event simulation modelling it is important to define, more precisely, the terminology that has been introduced above. The basic building blocks used to represent the tangible components of the system are usually known as entities. An entity is an object whose behaviour within the model will be explicitly tracked as the simulation proceeds. As with all modelling, a simulation model is a simplification and there will be many candidates for inclusion within a model as an entity, but only some need be included. Those included should be those that are relevant to the reason that simulation is being conducted. In a hospital, examples of entities might be patients, doctors, nurses, items of equipment, and so on. In an airport terminal they might be passengers, staff, items of baggage, aircraft and other equipment. For each such entity, the simulation system will track their behaviour by maintaining detailed information about their current and possible future states.

In some simulation software, entities may be conveniently grouped into classes. These are permanent groupings of similar objects that, therefore, share similar features or attributes. Thus, we may refer to classes such as patients, doctors, nurses, aircraft or, in a factory, orders. The individual members of a class need not be identical, but they do have common features. Thus, an attribute of an order in a factory might be the machines (or route) that will be needed in order to meet the order. As mentioned above, many simulations nowadays are carried out using a VIMS. These may be designed for especial use in certain application areas. For example, Witness (Thompson, 1994) was originally designed for use in discrete parts manufacturing, and so users are encouraged to think about their system as a set of parts that flow through work centres. Such VIMS provide built-in classes to simulate the behaviour of common entities; in manufacturing systems examples might be conveyor systems and automatic guided vehicles.

States, Events Activities and Processes

As introduced above, entities are considered to occupy states for a period of time. It is best to assume that these states are disjoint—that is, there is no overlap and no entity can simultaneously be in more than one state. This is obviously a simplification, but it forces the modeller to think about the states that are relevant to the system and situation being modelled. Any entity included in the model must be in one state or another throughout their time in the simulation. If they are idle, then they should be regarded as in an idle state, fuzziness is not permitted. The entities persist in a state for a period of time and the time at which they change state is known as an event, or event time. State changes must also be precise and thus no entity will have states that overlap.

What goes on while an entity is in a known state? From one perspective, what is happening is that the entity is changing state and this takes time to happen. This is often known as an activity, and an activity may well be co-operative; that is, it may require the co-operation of more than a single class of entity. Thus, in the example above, unless a doctor is free and a patient is waiting, then a consultation cannot begin. Once it begins, this activity persists for some time, during which the doctor may be in the "with a patient" state and the patient may be in a "seeing the doctor" state. At the end of the consultation activity, the paths of the two entities may well diverge—but this may depend on what happens during the activity. Any activity begins with an event and ends with an event. Both events cause the entities involved to change state in some way or other.

For convenience it is often useful to think in terms of a process. A process is the chronological sequence of activities (and therefore of events) through which an entity must or may pass. Each class of entity will have one or more processes associated with it. When an entity that is a member of that class appears in the simulation, this process becomes a route through which the entity will pass. The entity's progress through the process will be delayed at times—either due to an activity in which it engages with other entities, or because the entity is in some idle state waiting for something to happen.

Figure 9.2 shows the relationship between the ideas of state, event, activity and process for two classes of entity that co-operate during their life in the system.

The Dynamics of Time

Though it may be true that, in the real world, time is "like an ever-rolling stream" (Watts, c. 1719) this is not how a discrete event

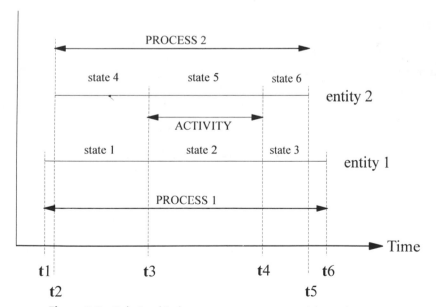

Figure 9.2   *Relationship between state, event, activity and process*

simulation works. Instead, time is controlled via what is usually known as the simulation clock and this moves forward irregularly from event to event. Thus, in Figure 9.2, the simulation clock moves as follows:

t_1 This event marks the start of state 1 which coincides with the start of process 1, because state 1 is the first state occupied by entity 1 in its process.

t_2 This event marks the start of state 4 which coincides with the start of process 2, because state 4 is the first state occupied by entity 2 in its process.

t_3 This event marks the start of state 2 (entity 1) and state 5 (entity 2) and is the start of the activity in which the two entities jointly engage. This coincides with the end of state 1 for entity 1 and state 4 for entity 2.

t_4 This event marks the end of state 2 (entity 1) and state 5 (entity 2) and is the end of the activity in which the two entities jointly engage. This coincides with the start of state 3 for entity 1 and state 6 for entity 2.

t_5 This event marks the end of state 6 for entity 2 and also the end of process 2.

t_6 This event marks the end of state 3 for entity 1 and also the end of process 1.

Thus, time within a simulation moves forward in unequal amounts depending on when the events fall due. If the simulation is driving an animated display of, for example, a factory, then the display will therefore seem jerky unless steps are taken to give it a smooth appearance.

The Executive or Control Program

In the early days of computer simulation, during the late 1950s, it was realised that it was possible to separate out a feature that is common to all discrete event simulations. This stems from the need to ensure that events happen as and when they should, and that the entities change state accordingly. This joint task of sequencing and scheduling is carried out by the control program or executive of the simulation. There are several ways in which these executives can be organised (for a thorough description see Pidd, 1992) but the various approaches are based around similar ideas. As an analogy, imagine a puppet theatre in which a puppeteer must pull strings to ensure that the puppets move around on the stage. Each puppet's possible actions are determined by the ways in which the strings are attached and their actual actions are determined by the ways in which the puppeteer pulls the strings. In a discrete event simulation, the entities are the puppets; the events, activities and processes are the strings and the executive or control program is the puppeteer.

In controlling the running of a discrete event simulation model, the control program needs access to all relevant information about all entities. In particular, the executive needs to know what state the entity is in and for how much longer it is to remain in that state. In simple terms, the executive maintains a diary (usually known as an event list or event calendar) which contains information about the simulation entities. As an entity changes state then this information is updated. These state changes may depend on one of two things. The first is that the entity will change state only when other resources (typically other entities) are available and with which it will co-operate. This activity is co-operative and the precise time when it will occur cannot be predicted because it depends on the availability of those resources. Thus, though patients are waiting at 2 p.m., an outpatient clinic will not start until the doctor appears. This, in turn, may depend on when the doctor has been able to deal with an emergency that cropped up in the late morning. Hence, until the doctor appears, the start time of the clinic is uncertain. For such activity, the event time for its start is unknown in advance and the simulation executive can take no direct action, since some other event may intervene before the expected one occurs.

The other type of event is one that will certainly occur at some known time. Hence an outpatient consultation, once begun, will come to an end. Of course, the time of that event will depend on the duration of the consultation and, it might be argued, this cannot be known in advance. In a discrete event simulation this variation in activity durations is handled by taking samples from probability distributions that are known to represent the durations. Thus, it might be believed that the duration of the consultation is normally distributed but truncated so that none takes less than five minutes and none takes more than 30 minutes. In the simulation, when the event occurs that starts the activity, a sample is taken from the distribution and this is taken as the time that the activity will end. This "end time" can then be placed on the event calendar.

In general, the first type of event will engage or consume resources that are available and must therefore await their availability. The second type, in general, will release resources at the end of the activity and these events can thus be directly scheduled. Events occur under the control of the simulation executive. As they occur, they trigger activity and this may result in future events being scheduled on the event calendar. Hence, the simulation control program maintains an event calendar on which are entered the times at which these second type of known events are due to occur. Most of these will be scheduled, or entered on the calendar, when one of the first type of events occurs. How this calendar is implemented will vary, depending on the computer software that is in use, as will the terminology used to described the two types of event. What is important is that the modeller should be able to decide which are the relevant entity classes, what are the events in which they engage and what activity will occur as a result of these events.

USING DIAGRAMS TO BUILD SIMULATION MODELS

Much of the work in building a discrete event simulation model is concerned with understanding the logic of the system to be simulated in terms of the entities and their interactions. Though this logic can be expressed verbally, many people find it simpler, at first, to use diagrams as an aid to their thinking. There is a wide variety of diagramming approaches used in discrete simulation modelling and a thorough discussion is to be found in Ceric (1996). This chapter will describe one of the simplest of these approaches—known as activity cycle diagrams. These diagrams are deliberately very simple in concept and they are not intended to represent the full complexity of any system or model. They play a part in a modelling approach that fits the principle of parsimony discussed in Chapter 4.

Activity Cycle Diagrams

An activity cycle diagram (ACD) is a network diagram that attempts to show how the processes of different entity classes interact, at least in a skeletal form. An ACD has just two symbols, as shown in Figure 9.3:

- An *active* state is one whose time duration can be directly deter-mined at the event which marks its start. This might be because the time duration is deterministic (the bus will definitely leave in five minutes) or because its duration can be sampled from some probability distribution.
- A *dead state* is one whose duration cannot be so determined but can only be inferred by knowing how long the active states may last. In

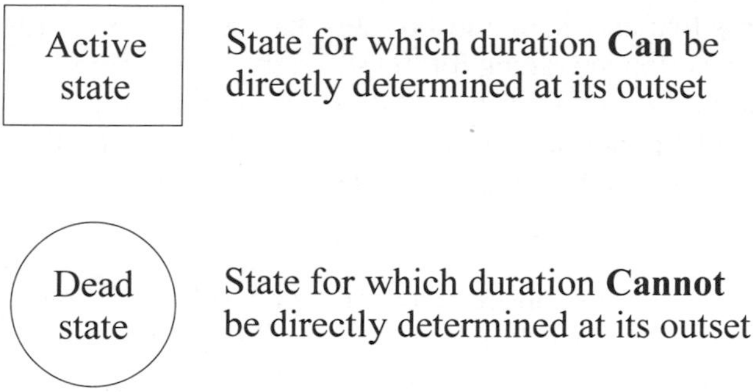

| Active state | State for which duration **Can** be directly determined at its outset |

Dead state | State for which duration **Cannot** be directly determined at its outset

Figure 9.3 *Activity cycle diagram symbols*

most cases, a dead state is one in which an entity is waiting for something to happen and, thus, some people refer to the dead states as queues.

Each entity class has an activity cycle which may be drawn on the ACD. An activity cycle is more or less equivalent to a process, as discussed earlier. To draw the diagram, the first stage is to consider the entity classes that will be needed; then an activity cycle is drawn for each entity class. The different cycles may then be combined to lead to the completed diagram which will show how the different classes of entity will interact within the simulation model. At this stage there is no need to be concerned with any statistical aspects of the model, those are considered later. As an example, consider the simple system outlined in the case study for Joe's exhaust parlour.

CASE STUDY: JOE'S EXHAUST PARLOUR

BACKGROUND

Joe owns and runs an exhaust replacement business on an industrial estate. This exhaust parlour provides a service to private motorists who are concerned about the state of their car exhaust systems. Joe has run the business successfully for a number of years, but is concerned at the competition from a national franchise that has opened up nearby. He knows that most potential customers will visit his parlour as well as that of the national competitor and he also ensures that his prices are competitive. Given this, he believes that the keys to winning an order are surroundings that are clean and businesslike, but not too plush, and also in keeping a customer waiting for the shortest possible time.

Joe's parlour is open from 9 a.m. to 7 p.m. and he and his fitters work throughout that period if there is work to be done. Meals and rest breaks are taken whenever the activity is slack. The mode of operation is as follows:

Motorists arrive unannounced and wait for Joe himself to inspect their car's exhaust system. To do this, the car is driven by Joe on to any free hydraulic ramp so that the car's exhaust system may be checked from below. Joe then advises the customer on the necessary work and 70% of customers elect to stay at Joe's parlour to have the work done. The other 30% go elsewhere.

Those drivers who choose to have the work done at Joe's sit in the lounge from which they can watch one of Joe's fitters work on their car on the ramp. When the fitter is finished, Joe inspects the work and if it is satisfactory, he prints out the bill for the driver who then pays and leaves. If Joe decides that the work is not satisfactory (which seems to happen to 10% of the jobs) then the fitter must rework the job—and this may take as long as the original work. Rework is inspected in the same way as the original job.

Joe would like some advice from you. He needs to know how many fitters and ramps he should employ in the parlour. He is very secretive about his finances and will not give you this information, preferring to carry out a financial analysis himself after you have advised him about fitters and ramps. Ideally, he would like to keep his customers waiting for rather less than 10 minutes before he inspects their vehicle after their arrival, he would also like to ensure that customers spend less than 60 minutes in total at the parlour.

ACTIVITY CYCLE DIAGRAM

Figure 9.4 shows the activity cycle of the driver/car combination—notice that this is the first simplification. We will assume that the driver always stays with the car, and never goes off elsewhere to do some shopping while the work is done. We will also simplify things by assuming that lunchbreaks are ignored and the correct parts are always available. Figure 9.4 is not a complete ACD, it just shows an annotated activity cycle for the driver/car, but it serves to illustrate some of the basic ideas. First, notice that the diagram consists of closed loops—this is an artificiality that actually can be useful as it forces the modeller to think about what

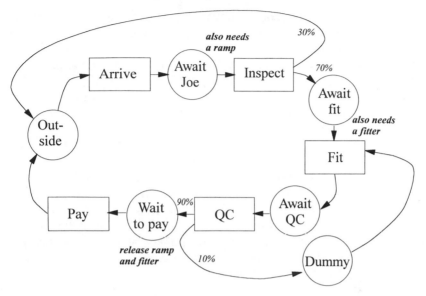

Figure 9.4 *Activity cycle diagram—Drivers and cars in Joe's Exhaust Parlour*

happens to the entity at all times. The loops are closed by the creation of an imaginary dead state Outside from which the drivers/cars enter Joe's premises and to which they return.

Secondly, notice that each loop consists of alternate active and dead states. This, too, is artificial, but once again this simplification serves an important purpose. If this alternation is observed then this means that the states fit neatly together. The durations of active states can be determined in advance but those of dead states cannot. Thus if a dead state sits between two active states, its behaviour can be inferred from the combined operation of its neighbours. Thus, the time that a driver/car will wait for the final quality control check (dead state Await QC) will depend on the time that the Fit active state ended and the time that the final quality control (active state QC) begins.

Finally, it may not be obvious why Arrive should be regarded as an active state. This actually represents another artificiality, it is an inter-arrival state. To understand this, imagine a machine that takes drivers/cars from Outside and then, a short time later, delivers them into the dead state Await Joe. Once a driver/car enters the dead state, another starts its journey from Outside. The time taken to travel from Outside to Await Joe will be variable unless people arrive according to a timetable. Also marked on the diagram are a few reminders—that 70% of drivers/cars choose to stay with Joe for the replacement work and that 10% of jobs need to be re-done. Note that the annotations indicate that extra resources are needed at certain points—namely, ramps and fitters.

Figure 9.5 shows Joe's activity cycles and these are simpler than those of the drivers/cars and also have a rather different appearance. Whereas drivers/cars follow a fairly predictable sequence, Joe has three tasks and may move from one of them to any other. For completeness sake, he is shown as passing through an Idle state as he does so.

The activity cycles of drivers/cars and Joe may be linked via their common active states Inspect, QC and Pay. These linkages make it very clear which activities are dependent upon co-operation and this is one of the points of drawing the diagram. Figure 9.6 shows the final diagram, from which we could, if we wished, write down some of the conditions that govern the activities in the simulation model. For example, for the active state QC to begin (in effect, the activity of inspecting the new exhaust on a car after it is fitted) then these conditions could be written down as something like the following:

```
If (at least one driver/car is in state Await QC) AND
(Joe is in state Idle) THEN
{
    Change Joe state from Idle to Exhaust QC;
    Take first driver/car, change state from Await QC to
    Being QC'd;
    Decide how long this QC will take;
```

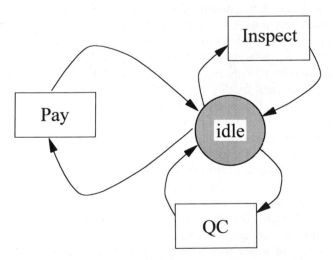

Figure 9.5 *Activity cycle diagram—Joe in his Exhaust Parlour*

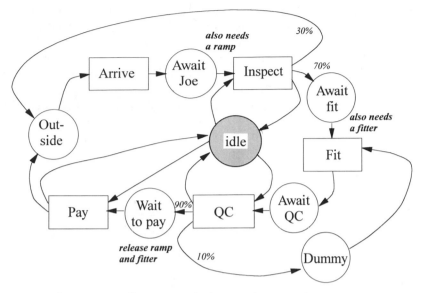

Figure 9.6 *Full activity cycle diagram for Joe's Exhaust Parlour*

    Tell the executive to end this *QC* at this time in the
    future.
}

Notice that the active state QC needs to be more detailed than the diagram might suggest if we are to enforce the desirable rule that entity classes must have unique states. Thus we may refer to the state *Exhaust QC* for Joe and to the state *Being QC'd* for the driver/car.

Entities and System Resources

One further issue has been skated over in the discussion of the ACD for Joe's Exhaust Parlour. What about the ramps and fitters? After all, Joe wishes to know how many of these are needed to run his business properly. Why are these not treated as entities in the simulation model? Figures 9.4 and 9.6 show them as annotations and these imply that they are being treated as system resources rather than as entities. A system resource is something that is used to represent things that can be measured or counted and that are, in effect, the same. This does not mean that fitters are the same as ramps, rather that all ramps are the same and all fitters are the same—that is, they are interchangeable. Thus, instead of maintaining state and calendar data about each ramp or fitter, all the program needs to do is keep track of how many are Free, InUse, or whatever other designation we choose. This can be done by the use of simple counters such as FreeRamps. If no work is in progress at the start of the simulation then, if there are five ramps, FreeRamps = 5. If FreeRamps > 0, this is one of the conditions to be satisfied for the activity Inspect to start.

Thus, the logic that governs the inspection of an exhaust on a car that has arrived at Joe's might be expressed as follows in words:

```
If (at least one driver/car is in state Await Joe) AND
(Joe is in state Idle) AND (FreeRamps>0) THEN
{
    Change Joe state from Idle to Inspect Exhaust;
    Take first driver/car, change state from Await Joe to
    Being Inspected;
    Reduce FreeRamps by 1;
    Decide how long this Inspect will take;
    Tell the executive to end this Inspect at this time in
    the future.
}
```

As with the ACD active state QC, the active state Inspect has been split into two for the two entities involved. At the end of this activity, 30% of the drivers/cars leave the parlour immediately, in which case the FreeRamps would be increased by 1. For the 70% that remain, the ramp is still occupied and thus FreeRamps need not be increased.

Hence the idea of system resources provides us with a simple way of keeping track of countable, identical items. However, if the items are not identical or if we needed to keep a detailed track of which ones are in use at any time, then the ramps and/or fitters would need to be modelled as simulation entities. For example, this would be necessary if we wished to monitor the meal breaks taken by the fitters.

MICRO SAINT—A SIMPLE VIMS

Many simulations are carried out using visual interactive modelling systems (VIMS) and this is one of the reasons that computer simulation is discussed in this book. Chapter 7 gave an overview of one such VIMS, Stella, that is used to develop system dynamics models and which may be used to simulate systems that are modelled in that way. One major technical domain for visual interactive modelling is discrete event simulation. This section of the chapter will describe a simple discrete event simulation VIMS called Micro Saint for Windows (Micro Analysis and Design, 1992). It will also show how Joe's Exhaust Parlour may be simulated using Micro Saint. Quite a variety of discrete event simulation VIMS are on the market and examples include Witness (Thompson, 1994), ProModel (Baird and Leavy, 1994) and AutoMod (Rohrer, 1994). Micro Saint is one of the simpler VIMS, but it is still surprisingly powerful, and readers of this section should gain a general insight into the use of a VIMS.

A VIMS relies on the availability of a graphical user Interface (GUI) of the type that first became popular on the Apple Macintosh, then appeared on Intel-based PCs as Microsoft Windows and has also appeared on UNIX-based systems as X-Windows. Such GUIs have a number of features that are, nowadays, entirely taken for granted. These include a keyboard, pointing device (e.g. a mouse) and a high resolution colour graphics screen. A VIMS uses these elements of the GUI to enable the user to develop a model on screen by pointing, clicking and filling in forms to parameterise the model.

Types of VIMS Network

The usual way in which a VIMS model is developed is to begin with a blank background screen and then to place icons on the screen to represent the major components of the system. These icons are then linked together by drawing lines on the screen to form a type of network which captures the logical interactions between the entities of the system. Broadly speaking, there are two approaches to this screen painting. One is machine-based networks, in which each icon represents a machine, or entity or group of entities and the links show the path that some kind of passive object follows through the system. Hence in a manufacturing example, a part might first go to an inspection centre, then to a machining centre, then to a paint booth and then to final inspection. Each of these machines would be represented by an icon on the screen, and the path of the part would be shown by a line (possibly directed with arrow heads) from machine to machine. A simple example of this is shown in Figure 9.7 taken from a Witness simulation model. The other is task-based networks, in which each entity represents a task; this task may involve one or more entities or one or more units of system resource. Hence the tasks are linked logically to show how they are dependent. Micro Saint takes this approach and its features will be illustrated by the use of Joe's Exhaust Parlour.

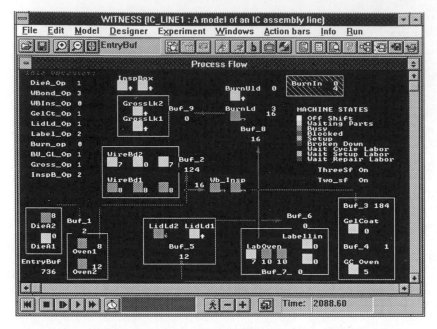

Figure 9.7   *Screen dump from a Witness model*

Machine-based networks are best suited to situations in which objects follow complex processes (sequences of activities) and in which machines may need to perform more than a single task. On the other hand, task-based networks are best suited to systems in which routing may be relatively simple but for which tasks may require the co-operation of several machines. Either approach is suitable for Joe's Exhaust Parlour.

CASE STUDY: JOE'S EXHAUST PARLOUR

THE BASICS OF MICRO SAINT

The easiest way to understand the basics of a VIMS such as Micro Saint is to use an example, and so we will use Joe's Exhaust Parlour, as introduced above. A Micro Saint task network for Joe is shown in Figure 9.8. This network was very quick to draw using the built-in functions of Micro Saint. It contains six tasks: Arrive, Inspect, Replace, Check, PayJoe, and Leave. Each task is shown on the network as a named icon, for which

Micro Saint uses a rounded rectangle. The tasks are linked by arrows that show the flow of the tasks for the main simulation objects—drivers/cars in this case. Thus, to use a task network of this type it is necessary to think in terms of the main objects that flow through the system. In essence, everything else is treated as a resource. Figure 9.8 shows the following linkages between tasks.

- Inspect follows Arrive: that is, the drivers/cars are inspected after they have arrived.
- Replace follows both Inspect and Check: that is, the drivers/cars may enter the replace task either from initial inspection or after the quality control check.
- Check follows Replace: that is, the work done is always QC-checked after replacement.
- PayJoe follows Check: that is, the customer only pays after completion of a QC Check.
- Leave follows both PayJoe and Inspect: those who pay leave, but so do those who decide not to have the work done at Joe's.

The Micro Saint network diagram has other features that are also shown in Figure 9.8. Immediately after each of the Arrive, Inspect and Check task icons are diamond shaped icons that are decision nodes at the end of the task. This example has two types of decision in use, indicated by the letter *P* (for Probabilistic) in the diamond after Inspect and Check and by the letter *M* (for Multiple) in the diamond after Arrive. Probabilistic decisions are, perhaps, the simplest to understand as they split the entity flow (drivers/cars in this case) into several flows. In the case of the probabilistic node after Inspect, 30% of the drivers/cars will go direct to the Leave task and 70% will go direct to the Replace task. Similarly, 10% of the entities will be routed back to Replace after Check and the other 90% will go to the Leave task. To set these parameters (the probabilities for each route) Micro Saint provides a screen form (in standard MS Windows format) in which the user may enter the appropriate values.

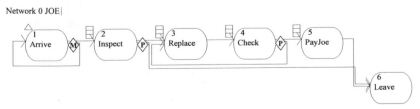

Network 0 JOE|

Figure 9.8 *Micro Saint task network for Joe's Exhaust Parlour*

The multiple node may be less clear in concept. The effect of a multiple node is to replicate entities, with equal numbers of entities going down each of the outgoing paths from the nodes. This allows the end of one task to permit the start of more than one following task. In the case of the multiple node that follows the Arrive task, the effect is to turn the Arrive task into what Micro Saint terms a "spinner" task (a task that feeds back on itself). A spinner task occurs when the multiple node is used to pass entities back into the task as well as forward to another task. The effect of this is to cause Arrive($n + 1$) to start immediately after the end of Arrive(n). That is, it causes the inter-arrival operation of entity $n + 1$ to start as soon as the inter-arrival operation of entity n ends. This provides a useful, if slightly confusing, way of modelling arrival tasks that generate new entities into the system at regular or irregular intervals. Thus, the main use of spinners is as entity generators.

As well as tasks and decision nodes, Figure 9.8 also shows a number of vertical rectangles, each with two horizontal lines, by the start of each task icon. These are queue icons that are used to indicate that a queue exists before the relevant tasks. Thus, for example, there is a queue before Check, which means that drivers/cars join this queue at the end of their Replace task. Thus, to start a Check task, the Micro Saint system checks to see if any entities are in the queue. Were there no queue before Check, then the next Replace task could not begin until the prior driver/car Check task had started because the prior driver/car would still be blocking the next Repair.

As with all elements of a Micro Saint task network, there are MS Windows-based forms on which the user may provide data to parameterise the elements of the system. These cover aspects such as task durations (which may be samples from probability distributions or might be constants), details of decision nodes and limits on queue sizes. Sensible default values are provided. The idea of a VIMS is that the user should develop the simulation model by pointing and clicking so as to draw the network using the appropriate icons, linkages and forms. In this way, a basic model can be developed without any computer programming—familiarity with the GUI (MS Windows in this case) is all that is needed. However, to be really useful, a simulation VIMS must allow the user some way to express the logic of the events that govern the behaviour of the entities and their state changes. This logic may be rather complicated.

Task Logic in Micro Saint

Each VIMS allows the user to express this logic in different ways. Those that are machine-based will inevitably look somewhat different from those that are task-based. Micro Saint is task-based and it thus allows the user to define the logic of those tasks. Specifically, the user may define the following for each task:

Release conditions. These are used to specify the conditions under which a task may begin. Thus, taking again the example of Joe's Exhaust Parlour, for Inspect, these would be that Joe is free and that at least one ramp is available. Micro Saint will automatically check that there is a driver/car in the queue, as the queue is linked by the system itself to the correct task.
Beginning effect. This defines the logic of what happens when the task starts. In the case of Inspect, this would be that Joe is no longer free and that there is one less ramp available.
Ending effect. This defines what happens at the end of the task. In the case of Inspect, this would be that Joe is now free again. As with incoming queue logic, Micro Saint links the probabilistic node after Inspect to this task and automatically deposits the driver/car into this node. From there they will proceed either to the Check queue or to Leave.
Launch effect. This is a bit more subtle and permits the user to carry out tasks *after* the task duration has been computed, which is done automatically by the Micro Saint control program. This might, for example, allow action to be taken if the task duration would take the task completion time to beyond the end of the working day.

Thus Micro Saint, and other simulation VIMS allow the user to specify the detailed event logic of the system. One problem with these VIMS is that each one seems to use its own programming language for this purpose. In the case of Micro Saint, the language uses a syntax that is rather like a cross between the C and Pascal general purpose programming languages. It might be better if the vendors of these systems could co-operate to define a language standard or adopt an existing syntax (such as C). However, this form of co-operation seems unlikely.

Running a Micro Saint Model

As well as providing an easy way to develop a model on screen, a VIMS such as Micro Saint supports parsimonious modelling. When using a VIMS there is no need to develop a complete model before running it to see how it behaves. In the case of Joe's Exhaust Parlour it would be possible to place just two tasks onscreen (Arrive and Inspect for example), to provide some parameters for these tasks and then to run the model. Once this all-too-simple model runs OK, then other tasks can be added. Similarly, the existence of default logic in the VIMS means that almost "empty" tasks can be added and the simulation may be run with these in place. The "proper" logic may then be added, a step at a time, until the model reaches the required level of detail. This step-wise development is crucial and is an entirely normal part of simulation model development. It is unlikely that the precise specification of the model can be known in advance for most simulations.

The second aspect of a VIMS is that it provides an interactive environment within which the model may be run. This means that the simulation can be carried out like a video game with interactive experimentation. As the simulation is run, the screen can be arranged to provide a display that shows the main features of this system being simulated. In some systems, these features can appear in multiple on-screen windows. Thus the user can watch the model run and might observe, for example, that queues build up very quickly and are not dissipated. This suggests a shortage of system resources of some kind and the display may make it clear where this bottleneck is occurring. Thus the user may interrupt the running simulation, may add extra resources and may then restart the simulation or may continue the run, but with extra resources. In this way the user will use the visual interactive features of the VIMS to navigate towards an acceptable system design.

Micro Saint allows the user to watch a number of different windows as the simulation proceeds. Examples include the following:

The network diagram. As drawn on screen to develop the model, so as to allow the user to check the task logic as the simulation runs. This also gives some idea of the build up of queues.

The variable catalog. All variables defined by the user are accessible and a selection can be displayed in a window as the simulation runs. This might include queue lengths, for example.

Action view. This is a different iconic representation of the model in which objects may be drawn to resemble the physical system. Thus icons may be developed for Joe, the fitters, ramps and cars. Cars may be shown arriving, waiting for service, moving on to and from ramps and the fitters and Joe may be seen attending to them. This can be useful for demonstrating the simulation to a client and convincing them of its acceptability.

The event queue. This is the technical heart of the Micro Saint control program and it shows the calendar on to which events are entered and from which they are executed at the correct simulation time. This can be very useful for debugging a model.

Thus, like other VIMS, Micro Saint provides visual tools for model development, for debugging, for client presentations and for model refinement. In addition there are analysis tools for the analysis of the results of simulation runs and the simulation output can also be exported in common formats to be read by spreadsheets and statistical analysis packages.

THE EFFECTS OF STOCHASTIC VARIATION

As was mentioned earlier, the time that an entity spends in a state (for example, being served) may not be deterministic but may be variable. That is, if we were able to observe how long a particular activity took on a number of occasions, we may find that the time taken varies and that this variation may be represented by a probability distribution. This variation through time is known as stochastic variation and is a feature of many systems simulated by discrete event methods. The inclusion of stochastic elements within a simulation model means that great care must be taken when analysing its results. This book is not the place to go into a detailed discussion of the statistical analysis of such models; excellent coverage of this is given by Law and Kelton (1991) and Kleijnen and van Groenendal (1992). Instead, some of the basic principles will be spelled out here.

The Basics of Random Sampling in Discrete Simulation

Suppose that a model needs to include some element that is governed by a probability distribution. How will samples be taken from the distribution as the simulation is run using the model? In most cases, this random sampling is achieved via a two-stage process. Sometimes the sampling process may seem rather complicated, but the underlying principles are very simple, as follows:

- Generate one or more pseudo-random numbers.
- Transform this/these into a sample from the required distribution.

Before discussing what these terms mean, it is best to consider the simplest possible approach to such sampling. This is known as top hat sampling.

Top hat sampling is used to take samples from empirical probability distributions represented by histograms. Figure 9.9 shows such a histogram which might, for example, represent the observed times, in minutes, taken by a doctor to see a patient. This tells us that no patients require less than three minutes or more that 11 minutes. The most frequent consultation time is six minutes, which is taken by 30% of the patients. To understand why this method is called top hat sampling, imagine a large, cylindrical top hat of the type worn by English gentlemen last century. In this hat, suppose that we place 100 plastic counters and on each counter we mark a number according to the probabilities shown on the histogram of Figure 9.9. Thus no counters have values below 3 or above 11. Five counters will be marked with a 3, five more with a 4, 20 with a 5, 30 with a 6, 15 with a 7, ten with an 8 and five each with 9, 10 and 11. Thus the numbers on the counters are distributed in the same way as the histogram. To take each sample we shake the hat to ensure that the counters are uniformly distributed within it and then take a counter from the hat, selecting at random. We note the number on the counter, replace it in the hat and repeat the process. In this way we should end up with samples whose proportions mirror those of the histogram.

Since no one would seriously contemplate connecting a mechanical arm and top hat to a computer, an analogous approach is used. This is based on the use of random numbers, or pseudo-random numbers to

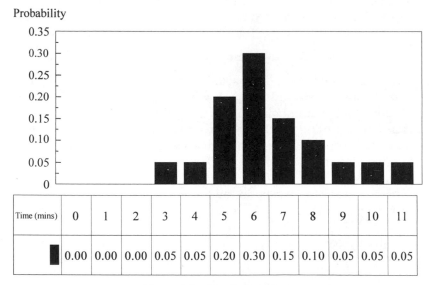

Figure 9.9   *Simple histogram*

be precise. These are numbers, distributed across some interval (usually from 0 to 1) and presented in a wholly random sequence in which all values are equally likely to occur. These pseudo-random numbers are generated by methods discussed in most books on computer simulation (for example, see Law and Kelton, 1991; Pidd, 1992). To use such a sequence of pseudo-random numbers in top hat sampling, we construct a table of the type shown as Table 9.1. This shows that the range of possible random numbers (0.000 to 0.999 inclusive) has been allocated in subranges to each possible value of the consultation time. Thus 5% of the values (0.000 to 0.049) have been allocated to a time of three minutes, a further 5% (0.050 to 0.099) to a time of four minutes, and so on. In this way, the random numbers are mapped on to the time histogram. To carry out top hat sampling in this way, all we need to do is find some suitable source of random numbers and then transform these into the required sample—the two-stage process described above.

Coping with Stochastic Variation

Suppose that a suitable stream of pseudo-random numbers is available, then these will produce the sequence of samples that are shown in Table 9.2. This shows the result of taking the first ten random numbers and transforming them into the required samples. The second column shows the random numbers and the third column is the sample produced by using Table 9.1 to transform these into the required distribution. The fourth column shows the running mean, this being the mean of all the samples produced at this stage. The true mean of this histogram is 6.5 and the running mean is an estimate of

Table 9.1 *Top hat sampling*

Time	Probability	Random number subrange
3	0.05	0.000–0.049
4	0.05	0.050–0.099
5	0.20	0.100–0.299
6	0.30	0.300–0.599
7	0.15	0.600–0.749
8	0.10	0.750–0.849
9	0.05	0.850–0.899
10	0.05	0.900–0.949
11	0.05	0.950–0.999

Table 9.2   *First ten samples of consultation times*

	Random number	Sample	Running mean	Running SE	Lower CL	Upper CL
1	0.218	5	5.000	0.000		
2	0.572	6	5.500	0.707	−3.485	14.485
3	0.025	3	4.667	1.080	0.019	9.314
4	0.779	8	5.500	1.202	1.675	9.325
5	0.576	6	5.600	0.908	3.078	8.122
6	0.798	8	6.000	0.849	3.819	8.181
7	0.269	5	5.857	0.724	4.086	7.628
8	0.750	7	6.000	0.639	4.489	7.511
9	0.888	9	6.333	0.661	4.808	7.859
10	0.376	6	6.300	0.589	4.968	7.632

the true mean. In order to show the likely accuracy of this estimate we can compute 95% confidence limits and these are shown in the last two columns. The confidence limits are computed in the standard way as follows:

$$\text{Lower 95\% CL} = \bar{x} - t_{0.05, n-1}.se$$
$$\text{Upper 95\% CL} = \bar{x} - t_{0.05, n-1}.se$$

where:

$t_{0.05, n-1}$ is the t value for a two-tailed student's t distribution with a probability of 0.05 at $(n-1)$ degrees of freedom (n is the sample size) se is the standard error of the samples (being the sample standard deviation divided by the square root of the sample size).

The student's t distribution is needed since the sample size is small. An extended set of 20 more such samples, giving 30 in all, as shown in Figure 9.10. This shows four lines: the sampled times, the running mean and the lower and upper confidence limits. We can be 95% sure that the true value of the mean (which we actually know is 6.5) is within the two confidence limits (4.97 to 7.63). Notice how the limits converge as the sample size increases. Initially the convergence is rapid, but then becomes rather slow. Repeated stochastic simulation results display similar behaviour to the simple example.

This simple example illustrates a number of important aspects of any stochastic simulation, no matter how complicated. The first is that such simulations need to be regarded as sampling experiments. The results of each experiment will depend on the random number streams that are used to produce the required samples. Different random numbers will transform into different samples and thus simulations that use different random numbers will produce different results. For confidence in the results it is important to ensure that a set of results is produced and analysed using appropriate statistical methods. The greater the number of runs then the greater the degree of confidence that the results are representative. As is clear from Figure 9.10, the confidence limits converge quickly at first and then rather slowly. The smaller the gap between the limits, the greater the precision of the results. The simulation literature includes variance reduction techniques to be employed to help speed up this convergence.

The second point is that if a stochastic simulation is being used to compare two or more policy options (for example, do we need 10 or 16 emergency beds?) then, as far as is possible, each option should be run with the same random numbers. This is to ensure that the comparison is a fair one, given that the random numbers used will affect the results. This technique, known as streaming or common random numbers, seeks to ensure that the effects of randomness are properly contained across policy comparisons.

The third point is that if a stochastic simulation is being used, any experimentation needs to be properly and carefully designed. The analysis of experiments is a statistical minefield for the unwary and a

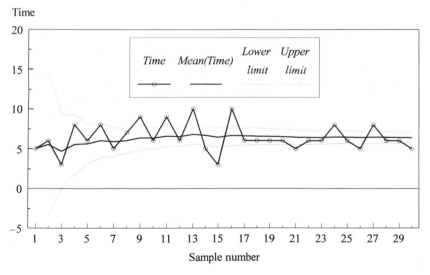

Figure 9.10 *Confidence limits in stochastic simulation*

source of some amusement among professional statisticians. Simulation modellers whose knowledge of experimental design and analysis is slight should seek statistical help in some form or another.

These points remain valid whether the simulation model is implemented in a specially written computer program or via a VIMS such as Micro Saint. If a VIMS is used, then interactive experimentation should be used to reduce the size of the set of sensible experimental options. For example, a hospital may be considering how many emergency beds are needed and it may become clear from a VIMS simulation that with fewer then ten beds the system cannot cope and that providing more than 20 beds is unnecessary. If this is so, then the options between 10 and 20 should be carefully investigated with properly designed experiments.

SUMMARY

This chapter has pointed out that many systems to be modelled are dynamic, complicated and highly interactive. One approach to modelling these is to construct a discrete computer simulation model and then to use this for experimentation to see what might happen if the system were changed or were operated in a different way. When these systems also display variability that can be statistically modelled, sampling methods may be incorporated within the simulation.

Progress within computer simulation has depended on general developments in computing. Thus, many simulations are now built and used on personal computers or workstations from VIMS which employ graphical user interfaces. These VIMS make it possible for people who are not expert computer programmers to develop discrete simulation models and also permit dynamic displays to be used to show the results of the simulation experiments. Further, these VIMS fit well with the principles of modelling discussed in Chapter 4. In particular they enable the modeller to "model simple and think complicated" and they support the principle of parsimony.

REFERENCES

Baird S.P. and Leavy J.J. (1994) Simulation modeling using ProModel for Windows. In *Proceedings of the 1994 Winter Simulation Conference*, Lake Bueno Vista, Florida.

Beadle R. (1986) Designing the control of automated factories. In R.D. Hurrion (Ed.) *Simulation Applications in Manufacturing*. IFS (Publications), Kempston, Beds.

Bhaskar R., Lee H.S., Levas A., Pétrakian R., Tsai F. and Tulskie, W. (1994) Analyzing and re-engineering business processes using simulation. In *Proceedings of the 1994 Winter Simulation Conference*, Lake Bueno Vista, Florida.

Bier I.J. and Tjelle J.P. (1994) The importance of interoperability in a simulation prototype for spares inventory planning. In *Proceedings of the 1994 Winter Simulation Conference*, Lake Bueno Vista, Florida.

Brailsford S.C., Shahani A.K., Roy R.B. and Sivapalan S. (1992) Simulation modeling for HIV-infection and AIDS. *International Journal of Bio-Medical Computing*, **31**, 2, 73–88.

Buxton J.N. and Laski J.G. (1962) Control and simulation language. *The Computer Journal*, **5**, 3.

Ceric V. (1990) Simulation study of an automated guided-vehicle system in a Yugoslav hospital. *Journal of the Operational Research Society*, **41**, 4, 299–310.

Ceric V. (1996) *Diagrammatic Approaches to Discrete Event Simulation*. John Wiley, Chichester (forthcoming).

Davies M.N. (1994) Back-office process management in the financial services—a simulation approach using a model generator. *Journal of the Operational Research Society*, **45**, 12, 1363–73.

Evans G.W., Mollaghasemi M., Russell E.C. and Biles W.E. (1993) *Proceedings of the 1993 Winter Simulation Conference*, Los Angeles, Cal.

Harrell C.R. (1993) Modeling beverage processing using discrete event simulation. In *Proceedings of the 1993 Winter Simulation Conference*, Los Angeles, Cal.

Heath W. (1993) Waterfront capacity-planning simulations. In *Proceedings of the 1993 Winter Simulation Conference*, Los Angeles, Cal.

High Performance Systems (1994) *Stella II Technical Documentation*. High Performance Systems Inc., Hanover, NH.

Kleijnen J. and van Groenendal W. (1992) *Simulation: A Statistical Perspective*. John Wiley, Chichester.

Law A.M. and Kelton W.D. (1991) *Simulation Modelling and Analysis*. (Second edition.) McGraw-Hill International Edition, New York.

Micro Analysis and Design (1992) *Getting Started with Micro Saint for Windows*. Micro Analysis & Design Simulation Software Inc., Boulder, Cal.

McGuire F. (1994) Using simulation to reduce lengths of stay in emergency departments. In *Proceedings of the 1994 Winter Simulation Conference*, Lake Bueno Vista, Florida.

Miller D.J. (1994) The role of simulation in semi-conductor logistics. In *Proceedings of the 1994 Winter Simulation Conference*, Lake Bueno Vista, Florida.

Park C.A. and Getz T. (1992) The approach to developing a future pharmaceuticals manufacturing facility (using SIMAN and AutoMod). In *Proceedings of the 1992 Winter Simulation Conference*, Arlington, VA.

Pidd M. (1987) Simulating automated food plants. *Journal of the Operational Research Society*, **38**, 8, 683–92.

Pidd M. (1992) *Computer Simulation in Management Science*. (Third edition.) John Wiley, Chichester.

Pidd M. (1995) The construction of an object-oriented traffic simulator. In *Proceedings of the 3rd EURO Working Group on Transportation*, Barcelona, Spain, September 1995.

Rathi, A.K. and Santiago, A.J. (1990) The new NETSIM simulation model, *Traffic Engineering and Control*, **31**, 5, 317.

Rohrer M. (1994) Automod. In *Proceedings of the 1994 Winter Simulation Conference*, Lake Bueno Vista, Florida.

Salt J. (1991) Tunnel vision. *OR/MS Today*, **18**, 1, 42–8.

Thompson W.B. (1994) A tutorial for modelling with the WITNESS visual interactive simulator. In *Proceedings of the 1994 Winter Simulation Conference*, Lake Bueno Vista, Florida.

Watts I. (c. 1719) O God our help in ages past. Hymn based on Psalm 90.

Wears R.L. and Winton C.N. (1993) Simulation modeling of pre-hospital trauma care. In *Proceedings of the 1993 Winter Simulation Conference*, Los Angeles, Cal.

Young W., Taylor M.A.P. and Gipps P.G. (1989) *Microcomputers in Traffic Engineering*. John Wiley/Research Studies Press Ltd, Chichester.

10
Heuristic Approaches

BACKGROUND

This final chapter of Part III considers a third approach to modelling in management science—heuristics. The term "heuristic" has a number of meanings, but here it refers to approaches that give no guarantee that they will reach the best solution. This is in contrast to the optimisation methods such as linear programming, which was discussed in Chapter 8. In linear programming, the method guarantees that an optimum solution to a correctly formulated model will be found, if it exists. As has been consistently argued in this book, this does not guarantee that the optimum solution to the model will be the best solution in practice. This can only be the case if the model is a perfect fit to the system being modelled, which is unlikely.

Heuristic approaches, like simulation approaches, give no guarantee that any solution proposed will be optimum—even in the context of the model, let alone in the context of the system being modelled. Thus they have one thing in common with simulation approaches, but there is also an important difference. A simulation approach is usually based on experiments guided by humans (see Figure 9.1). The idea is that the experimenter thinks up possible options and uses the simulation model to see what would happen if these were followed. In common parlance, this is known as a "what if" approach. Heuristic methods are different from this because they provide ways of automatically generating solutions to problems that have been formulated in certain ways. They are approximate approaches (Foulds, 1983) in that they aim to come as close as possible to some optimum—but they may fail to do so. For example, some people believe that always taking the second turn to the right is a rapid way to escape from a maze such as the one at Hampton Court. It would seem that their confidence is misplaced.

Heuristic methods are included here for two reasons. The first is that they are enjoying increasing use in management science because they seem to offer ways of coping with certain types of problem that are computationally rather complex and yet which have a practical pay-off. Examples of this might be the scheduling of transport systems, the control of emergency services or the timetabling of large events. The second reason for their inclusion is that they take management science to the edge of artificial intelligence methods. Though the honeymoon period of artificial intelligence is now over, there are great benefits in being able to design human:machine systems that are able to cope with complicated circumstances. Indeed, we take for granted that such systems will be used to help fly most commercial jet-liners. Management science practitioners can help play a part in the design and appraisal of such systems, which means that they and their customers may need to be aware of these methods.

The Basic Idea—Two Analogies

Two analogies may help to clarify the type of heuristics that are to be considered in this chapter. The first is the idea of sequential searches through a decision space. This analogy corresponds very closely with the ideas proposed by Simon and Newell (1958). As discussed in Chapter 2, Simon was concerned to understand how humans made decisions and he proposed a view that is sometimes described as linear, or sequential, search. The basic idea of this is shown as Figure 2.1 in Chapter 2 and is shown here, in a slightly revised form, as Figure 10.1. In essence it imagines that the task of a decision maker is to start from the left-hand side of the figure and move towards the right-hand side—hoping to end up at a destination that is either optimal or satisfactory. To do so, the decision maker is faced with a series of choices that constitutes the solution space of the problem. Simon points out that decision makers will not have perfect information and that for this, and other reasons, they do not actually optimise. Instead, they satisfice—they find solutions that are satisfactory in some sense or other and they employ heuristics to do so. This implies that the search starts from the left and proceeds towards the right but could go on for a very long time. The search stops when a good enough point is reached.

This idea of a heuristic, as proposed by Simon and Newell (1958), was that it should provide a rule of thumb by which choices could be made as the decision maker moves through the network of options.

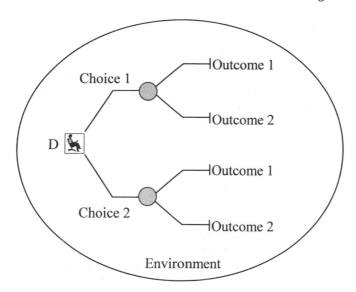

Figure 10.1 *Decision making as sequential search*

Simon (1978) was specifically interested, at one stage, in decision making in the game of chess. He suggested that experienced chess players develop heuristics which enable them to rapidly scan through possible options when faced with recognisable positions on the board. Thus, he argued, experienced (and successful) chess players learn to recognise clumps of similar situations and develop heuristics for dealing with them. As has been made clear elsewhere in this book, especially in Part II, there are many situations in which this sequential-search view of decision making breaks down. Nevertheless, it does have its uses, especially when its limitations are understood.

The second analogy is that of the explorer searching, in the dark, for the deepest valley in some terrain for which no map exists. (This is equivalent to trying to find some minimum cost solution to a problem.) A possible strategy is to always head downwards wherever possible—this can be done in the dark by the feel of the land. This is simple enough if the explorer is fortunate enough to find herself in terrain containing only a single valley. In these circumstances, all she need do is to slowly edge down the slope until the feel of the land tells her that she is at the bottom. She may then conclude, correctly, that she is at the lowest point.

However, in most such explorations, there will be more than one valley and some of these may sit above one another. This is shown in two dimensions in Figure 10.2. In it, our explorer has found the bottom of one valley, but this is by no means the lowest point in the terrain. The problem facing her is to find some way of climbing over the intervening hills so as to find her way to the lowest point. In Figure 10.2 we have a great advantage over her, we can see where she needs to get to, that is, we have perfect knowledge. But, if we were the explorer then neither we nor anyone else, has perfect knowledge and we are, figuratively, floundering in the dark. The heuristic methods that are discussed here attempt to provide strategies that enable the search to proceed until we have a reasonable assurance that we are at, or near, the minimum point. Note that there can be no certainty about this unless we know the shape of the terrain—and if we knew that, we would not need to search in this way. If the problem is one of maximisation, then the analogy is with searching for the highest point in the dark.

Simple though this analogy is to understand, it perhaps does not convey the scale of problems for which modern heuristic methods are suited. It is easy to imagine the search problem in three dimensions, which certainly complicates things. Problems to which these methods are applied have the mathematical equivalent of huge numbers of dimensions. Thus, efficient search procedures are vital.

Thus, to employ these heuristic methods, a number of things are needed. The first is that there must be some objective function. As

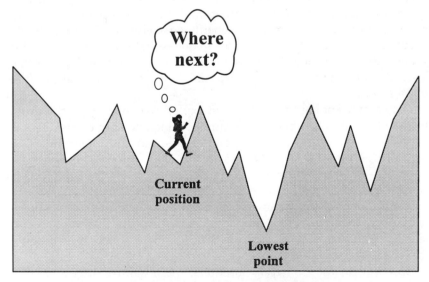

Figure 10.2　Exploring in the dark

discussed in Chapter 8 when referring to linear programming, this is simply some consistent way of working out the cost or return from any choice that is made. In terms of the search for the lowest point in Figure 10.2, the objective function measures the depth at which the search is currently located. Thus, it must relate directly to the choices and actions that are available. The notion of "cost" need not imply cash or monetary value. The appropriate measure could be, for example, distance (in a situation where vehicles need to be routed) or deaths (in a situation where a limited budget needs to be spread over a range of treatments). In a maximisation problem, the measure could be something like number of customers served (in situation in which goods need to be distributed) or number of patients within 30 minutes' travelling time of clinic (in a situation where clinics need to be located). In either case, the "cost" could be a combination of factors rather than a single value.

The second requirement for their use is that, to use the analogy of the terrain again, it is desirable to be able to get from any point to any other point. This does not mean that the journey must be straightforward, it may be very tortuous indeed. But the search procedures require the different options to be interconnected in some way or other if they are to work properly.

Why Use Heuristic Approaches?

Before looking at three meta-heuristics it is worth asking why such approaches should be used if they cannot guarantee an optimal solution. There are two answers to this question. The first stems from a comparison with optimisation methods, as typified by linear programming (see Chapter 8). To use these approaches, the model must be formulated in such a way that it fits the optimisation approach being used. Thus, in linear programming, the objective function and all of the constraints must be relatively simple linear functions. Though, as argued in Chapters 3 and 4, all models are simplifications and approximations, for many applications, such simplification may be an approximation too far. The model may have to be so distorted that its solutions are far, far removed from the real world in which they need to be implemented. In such cases, it may make much more sense to use a heuristic approach even though there is no guarantee of optimality. A near-optimal solution to a good model may be much better than an optimum solution to a bad one.

The second reason relates to the computational demands made by many optimisation algorithms. This book is not the place to discuss this in detail (for a readable and thorough account see Reeves and Beasley, 1995) but the issue is simple enough. Consider the problem of designing a laminated material with 10 distinct inner layers, sandwiched between some outer coating. If all the layers must be present once, but their order is irrelevant, then there are 3 628 800 ($10 \times 8 \times 7 \ldots \times 2 \times 1$) permutations. If the number of layers increases to 12, then the number of permutations rises to over 479 million. The problem is that the number of options may increase exponentially as the size of the problem increases. Many optimisation algorithms, though guaranteeing an optimum solution, have a solution time which increases exponentially as the size of the problem increases. Thus, for many very large problems, even if the model is a good representation of the real system, and even if very powerful computers are brought to bear, the solution times are simply too long to be of use. This is particularly true of situations in which frequent changes are made to the number and type of options being compared. In such situations, the only practicable way forward may be to use an approximate, that is, heuristic, approach.

Meta-heuristics and Heuristic Strategies

Strictly speaking, an individual heuristic is devised for a particular situation or problem. However, within management science, a number of general approaches have developed that are sometimes known as meta-heuristics. These approaches provide general guidelines that are valuable across a range of mathematically formulated problems. Useful reviews of these meta-heuristics are to be found in Eglese (1986) and Reeves (1995a). This chapter will discuss the basic ideas of three common meta-heuristics: simulated annealing, tabu search and genetic algorithms. There is clearly insufficient space here to give enough detail for you to implement them, but instead, the aim is to demonstrate their value so that you may decide whether to make the effort to find out more.

Foulds (1983) provided a four-way classification of heuristic strategies:

Construction strategies. These typically begin with the data and information that comprise the problem situation. This is examined for elements that might seem to make a valuable contribution toward some very good final solution. Successive other elements are added if they seem likely to contribute towards improvement. Thus, the starting point is an incomplete solution which is gradually completed. An example might be an attempt to produce a conference timetable by, initially, placing all the most popular sessions in non-overlapping time slots. Others are then added around them.

Improvement strategies. In these approaches, the heuristics begin with some complete and feasible solution to the problem and this initial solution is gradually modified in a progressive mode so as to improve on it. An example might be a conference timetable that fits within the time allotted to the conference but which could be improved by swapping some sessions.

Component analysis strategies. These heuristics are based on a "divide and conquer" approach and they are useful when the situation is so complicated that it has to be broken into smaller pieces. The idea is to tackle the components and then put everything together again in some acceptable way. An example of this might be to ensure that two full streams of a conference are scheduled for different days. The individual days are then assembled to form a composite timetable.

Learning strategies. These heuristics are closest to the idea of sequential search as introduced in Chapter 2 and discussed above. The different options are envisaged as mapped out like the branches of a tree and some method is devised to move through the tree while seeking to find the best solution. These are close to the ideas of improvement as discussed above.

In many practical situations, two or more of these four strategies may be combined. For example, the overall approach might be based on component analysis but an improvement strategy might be employed within each component.

Applications of Heuristic Approaches in Management Science

The field of modern heuristics is changing rapidly and so any survey of applications will be quickly out of date. An interesting review is provided by Rayward-Smith (1995) who reports on a number of successful applications from several countries. In addition, the management science journals frequently contain papers that discuss developments, both of theory and practice.

Among the applications reported in Rayward-Smith (1995) are the following:

The control of continuous chemical processes. Cartwright and Cattell (1995) report on the use of genetic algorithms to improve the control of continuous chemical processes. In such processes, feedstock is continually imported into a reactor vessel and the products and other materials are continuously pumped from the vessel at a rate equal to the input of feedstock. Such continuous plants are often much cheaper than comparable batch plants in which the vessel is filled, the reaction takes place, and it is then emptied. One important problem in continuous processes is the control of the reaction so that variations in the output product stream are minimised and so that the process is safe. Heuristics, based on genetic algorithms, were developed so as to control the reactions in a way that was superior to more conventional control systems. This is an application in which the heuristics form part of a control system.

The design of telecommunications networks. Chardaire (1995) reports on the use of simulated annealing to design computer networks that include concentrators which are used to link groups of computers into the network. In one form of "ideal" network, the computers would be organised in a star formation in which each is directly connected to a central server. The problem with this formation is that it is expensive to connect up and therefore local concentrators are employed. In one simple form of this approach, each concentrator becomes the centre of a small cluster of machines and the concentrators are then linked to the central server. Thus the network becomes hierarchical. Chardaire (1995) reports on how simulated annealing methods can help to design efficient networks that employ such hierarchical concentration. This is an application in which the heuristics are used in design.

Other applications from elsewhere include the following:

Timetabling county cricket fixtures. Wright (1994) describes how he has successfully used a form of tabu search as the basis of a computer system that organises the fixture list for first-class cricket matches in England. The fixture list needed to be one that reduced unnecessary travel for players and which met a whole series of other constraints. The situation has many complications, such as the long tradition of many first-class teams to play their home games on more than one ground in their home county. Other issues included the need to take account of international fixtures that occur in the season. Wright's efforts were successful and his system is the basis of the English County Cricket fixture list.

Timetabling sessions at a large multi-stream conference. Eglese and Rand (1987) discuss the use of simulated annealing heuristics to develop working timetables for multi-conferences so as to minimise undesirable clashes of events. In this case, their aim was to minimise the disappointment suffered by the delegates at the conference if events they wished to attend were scheduled at the same time.

Vehicle routing. Christofides (1985) discusses different approaches to problems connected with vehicle routing, the idea being to meet service criteria while not incurring excessive cost. Eglese (1990) discusses the general ideas of applying simulated annealing methods for this type of application.

SOME FUNDAMENTAL IDEAS

Iterative Improvement

The three heuristic strategies to be discussed here—tabu search, simulated annealing and genetic algorithms—have a number of features in common. The first is that they adopt an iterative approach in a quest for improvement. By iterative, we mean that the algorithms proceed step by step, each one building on the previous one—much as our explorer creeps over the terrain in pitch darkness. An iteration is equivalent to each place at which she checks height above sea level. Is she lower than she last checked or higher? The idea being to proceed in directions that will lead to the best point—whether it be the lowest in the case of minimisation, or the highest in the case of maximisation. It should, therefore, be clear that in the terms used by Foulds (1983), these three meta-heuristics are primarily to be viewed as improvement strategies. They assume that it is possible to generate some initial feasible solution from which the improvement may proceed. How long they will take to converge on a point which is near or at the optimum may well depend on the starting point as well as on their search strategy.

Neighbourhoods

A second feature of these approaches can also be understood from the analogy of our explorer. Given that the approach is iterative, it also makes sense to limit the number of options considered at each iteration to those in the neighbourhood of the current position. Hence, the terminology of these heuristics includes the idea of a neighbourhood within which immediate opportunities for improvement are sought. Thus, the algorithms need some way of recording the neighbourhood and of knowing the cost of moving from the current position to others within the same neighbourhood.

The strict definition of a neighbourhood is that it comprises the set of solutions that can be reached from the current solution by a simple operation. This is equivalent, in our analogy, to those points that our explorer can reach in her next move. Any point beyond that is not in the neighbourhood. What is meant by a simple operation will depend on the meta-heuristic itself. The solution that is better than all others within the current neighbourhood is said to be optimum with respect to this neighbourhood. Hence the search processes operate by examining the options within the current neighbourhood and then selecting one of these as the next point to move to.

Simple Neighbourhood Search

Glover and Laguna (1995) suggest that the approaches taken by some of the heuristic strategies discussed here can be generalised within a standard framework. This consists of a general algorithm with three steps, which will be illustrated by considering simple neighbourhood search. This requires the following nomenclature:

- Represent a possible solution by the variable x
- Suppose that the full set of feasible solutions is X, thus x is a member of X.
- We wish to select x from X to minimise $c(x)$, which is the cost of solution x.
- For any solution x there is a neighbourhood $N(x)$ which consists of the other solutions that can be reached from x in a simple move.
- The procedure is iterative and suppose that, at each iteration, the current solution is represented by x^{now}.

Step 1	Initialisation	• Select a starting solution x^{now} from X • Define best_cost $= c(x^{now})$
Step 2	Choice and termination	• Choose a solution x^{next} from $N(x^{now})$ such that $c(x^{next}) < c(x^{now})$ • If no solution qualifies to be x^{now}, then STOP, else proceed to Step 3
Step 3	Update	• Put $x^{now} = x^{next}$ • Put best_cost $= c(x^{now})$ • Go to Step 2

Thus, the method searches around the neighbourhood in a tentative way. It accepts moves to new points that lead to a lower value for the cost function. Once no other point in the neighbourhood leads to an improvement, then the algorithm terminates.

Neighbourhood Search with Steepest Descent

A common variation of simple neighbourhood search is to use a principle of steepest descent when choosing the next solution x^{next} from $N(x^{now})$. This is equivalent to our lost explorer attempting a search around in the neighbourhood of her current location. If she were able to visit all the locations in her neighbourhood, then an intuitively appealing strategy is to move the point that takes her deepest. Hence, she does more than just find any point in the neighbourhood which is lower. Instead she finds the lowest point in the current neighbourhood.

If the basic algorithm is modified to allow for steepest descent, then it could be expressed as follows:

Step 1	Initialisation	• Select a starting solution x^{now} from X • Define best_cost = $c(x^{now})$
Step 2	Choice and termination	• Choose a solution x^{next} from $N(x^{now})$ such that $c(x^{next})$ is $Min(N(x^{now}))$ and is less than $c(x^{now})$ • If no solution qualifies to be x^{now}, then STOP, else proceed to Step 3
Step 3	Update	• Put $x^{now} = x^{next}$ and $c(x^{now}) = c(x^{next})$ • Go to Step 2

Thus the checking of the current cost $c(x^{now})$ is shifted from Step 3 to Step 2.

CASE STUDY: THE TRAVELLING SALESMAN PROBLEM

Consider Figure 10.3. This shows seven cities in the imaginary country of Transitania. Suppose that we need to advise someone on the best route to follow, starting at Alphaville, visiting each one only once and ending up back at Alphaville. Suppose too that they wish to do this in such a way that they minimise the total distance travelled. This is a simple example of a general "problem", called the travelling salesman problem (TSP) that is often used to illustrate heuristic methods. "Problem" is in quotes because, to use the terminology of Chapter 3, this is really a puzzle to which there is, in fact, a correct solution. The example of Figure 10.3 is very small and could easily be solved by the brute force of complete enumeration. In this approach, we would simply try all the possibilities, compare them, and select the one with the lowest total distance. However, though this is possible with just seven cities to visit, the number of options to compare rises exponentially with the number of cities. Nowadays, heuristic methods are used to tackle TSPs with the equivalent of several million cities.

Suppose that this problem has arisen because the one salesman employed in Transitania by Lancaster Products Ltd has just left that company and has been replaced by Jane Wiley. She has to visit the seven cities in Transitania every Friday and would like to minimise the distance that she drives. She starts next week and would like to organise a route that starts from the base at Alphaville and returns there on Friday evening. The Transitanian Automobile Association have given her the data of Table 10.1, which shows the distance (in kilometres) between each pair of cities. Her predecessor was a likeable man, popular with his customers, but a bit disorganised. Piecing together the scraps of paper that he left her, Jane concludes that his usual route was to begin at Alphaville (A), proceed to Bean City (B), then Causeway (C) then on to Dullsville (D) and arriving back at Alphaville via Everytown (E), Friendly City (F) and Grimthorpe (G). This route is shown on Figure 10.3, which gives the clear impression that it could be improved upon.

It can be convenient to represent such a route by listing the cities in the order in which they are visited, remembering that she needs to return to the base after visiting the last city on her route. In this case, her route

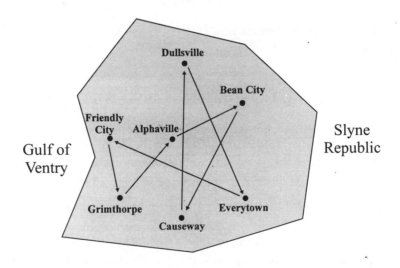

Figure 10.3 *The chaotic route in Transitania*

Table 10.1 *Distances between Transitanian cities (km)*

	A	B	C	D	E	F	G
A		30	25	32	23	25	32
B			55	33	30	60	70
C				52	37	33	18
D					45	43	57
E						52	50
F							21

could be represented by a list, or vector, of the initial letters of the cities that she will visit, presented in the sequence of her itinerary. Hence, if she were to accept her predecessor's rather odd route, then this could be represented as [A, B, C, D, E, F, G]. From Table 10.1, this route incurs a mileage "cost" of (30 + 55 + 52 + 45 + 52 + 21 + 32) km; that is 287 km.

Why should general "problems" such as the TSP be of such interest to the developers of heuristic approaches? It is not because many of them have ever been travelling salesmen or women. The reason is that it is representative of a whole class of more specific "problems" of which instances are found in the real world of organisational life. One way to appreciate this is to consider again the representation of a TSP tour by a vector that shows the places to be visited and their sequence. In the case of the problem facing Jane, her predecessor seemed to follow a tour that could be represented by the vector [A, B, C, D, E, F, G]. This form of representation can be used in a whole host of generic "problems".

For example, almost all businesses need to schedule their work in some way or other. In a manufacturing company, this might be a set of jobs that need to be in the warehouse by a certain date. The issue might be, in which sequence do we make those jobs? Clearly, this sequence of jobs could be represented in a similar manner to the tour faced by the travelling salesman. The distance function might be related to the cost of the jobs, it might be the overall lateness for some deadline or it might be some function of the expected profitability of the work. An example that might be easier to appreciate is the case of a company that needs to deliver its products to customers who are spread all over a region. It might be necessary to divide the deliveries by day of the week—for which a component analysis strategy might be used. There then remains the question of the sequence in which the sites are to be visited. This, too, could clearly be modelled in the same way. Similarly, a health care organisation may need to offer an ambulance service to non-emergency patients and some form of TSP-based analysis might help in the daily scheduling of pick ups. A rather different type of application might be the design of micro-electronic circuits in which components can occupy different places on a three-dimensional grid. This could be modelled as a TSP-like application in three dimensions.

CASE STUDY: THE TRAVELLING SALESMAN PROBLEM

NEIGHBOURHOODS

For heuristic methods based on neighbourhood search, it is important to define what is meant by the neighbourhood. This is what constrains the region of the search at each iteration. In a simple TSP it can be useful to define a two-swap neighbourhood in which it would be permissible to replace any two links (say those between A and B and between D and E) with another two links. This might be written down as remove (A, B) and (D, E) and replace them by two other links. If the current route is [A, B, C, D, E, F, G], then an alternative expression of the same move would be that the positions of cities B and D are swapped. Both expressions of this move result in a route of [A, D, C, B, E, F, G] as being the only feasible result.

The larger the neighbourhood then the larger the set of options that must be searched within the neighbourhood. The snag is, however, that a small neighbourhood may lead to a search converging quickly on a value that is a long way from the global optimum. The neighbourhood structure thus restricts the search. With simple neighbourhood search there is an implicit trade-off between neighbourhood size and the likelihood of convergence nearer to the global optimum. Small neighbourhoods result in rapid and efficient searches, but may not lead to good solutions. Large neighbourhoods are slow to search, but the search should get closer to a global optimum.

Our simple example has seven cities and, in general, for problems of this type the number of possible different tours is:

$$\frac{(n-1)!}{2}$$

Where $(n-1)!$ means multiply out $(n-1) \times (n-2) \times (n-3) \times \dots \times 2 \times 1$. Therefore, as n is 7 in this example, 360 possible tours could be devised. Hence it would be quite feasible, in such a small problem, to check all the possibilities in order to find the one that involved the shortest overall distance.

To carry out a neighbourhood search, we must first define the neighbourhood over which the search will take place. Suppose we decide that, in this case, we will take two cities and swap their positions in the list. With such a two-neighbourhood, the number of possible swaps is:

$$\frac{n(n-1)}{2}$$

This is because, in this case, each of the seven cities has six partners with which they could be swapped—hence the top line of $n(n-1)$. Also, the distance from one city to another is the same as a move in the reverse direction—which is why we divide the top line by 2. This means that, at any time, there will be 21 possible swaps in each neighbourhood for this example.

DEVISING SHORTER TOURS WITH A STEEPEST DESCENT STRATEGY

This is straightforward with the algorithm presented earlier. It works as follows if $k = 2$; that is, if pairs of cities are swapped in our attempt to find a better route.

	STEP 1	$x^{now} = [A, B, C, D, E, F, G]$ best_cost = 287 km
ITERATION 1	STEP 2	Swap cities C and E $\therefore \quad x^{next} = [A, B, E, D, C, F, G]$ and $c(x^{next}) = 243$ km
	STEP 3	$x^{now} = [A, B, E, D, C, F, G]$ best_cost = 243 km
ITERATION 2	STEP 2	Swap cities F and G $\therefore \quad x^{next} = [A, B, E, D, C, G, F]$ and $c(x^{next}) = 221$ km

	STEP 3	$x^{now} = [A, B, E, D, C, G, F]$ best_cost = 221 km
ITERATION 3	STEP 2	Swap cities A and D $\therefore \quad x^{next} = [D, B, E, A, C, G, F]$ and $c(x^{next}) = 193$ km
	STEP 3	$x^{now} = [D, B, E, A, C, G, F]$ best_cost = 193 km
ITERATION 4	STEP 2	No improvement is possible

This suggests that Jane's route should be [A, C, G, F, D, B, E] and that the distance that she can expect to drive is 193 km, a reduction of 94 km on the distance that her disorganised predecessor drove. Given that we have used a heuristic procedure, there is no guarantee that it is the one route of the 360 with the lowest total distance. However, it has only taken us four iterations to find this route, which is rather less than the 360 that would be needed to check all possibilities. It also looks a sensible route when drawn on the map (see Figure 10.4).

Avoiding Premature Convergence

Some thought about the basic method of neighbourhood search shows why the three approaches discussed in the following sections

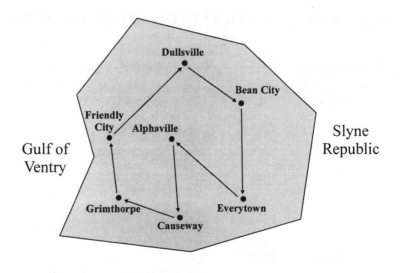

Dianistan

Figure 10.4 *A better (the best?) route in Transitania*

have been developed. This is the problem of convergence on a local optimum. Figure 10.2 shows that our explorer is currently at a local optimum, the bottom of a valley. The problem she faces is to find some way to move towards the global optimum, the lowest point overall. The following three meta-heuristics adopt different approaches to these problems. One approach would be to vary the size of the neighbourhood. Another might be to permit, in the short term at least, a move that actually makes the current situation worse, in the hope that this may lead to her climbing over the next peak en route to the lowest point. None of these ideas fully capture how the following three meta-heuristics improve on basic neighbourhood search. But they give some idea of the thinking behind the development of improved methods.

TABU SEARCH

The basic idea of modern Tabu Search seems to have been suggested by Glover (1986), who systematised and developed some common-sense notions that had been around for many years. As with the other two approaches that are discussed here, it is only possible to scratch the surface of the subject; for a thorough introduction see Glover and Laguna (1995). The basic idea is to develop procedures to guide a search process past difficult regions, attempting to avoid local optimum solutions. As with many meta-heuristics, the strategy consist of a number of principles which ought to make the search process more intelligent. It does this by storing information about past solutions as well as current ones. This storage of information is known as flexible memory in tabu search.

The idea is called "tabu" or "taboo" search, because it rests on a procedure that declares certain moves to be tabu (or taboo, meaning forbidden) even though they are part of the current neighbourhood. In simple neighbourhood search, all members of the neighbourhood are potential solutions from the current point. In tabu search, this neighbourhood set is restricted by declaring some of them to be tabu. This means that the heuristic will, normally, choose the lowest cost, no-tabu neighbour. Thus the modeller needs to decide, in advance, on a set of rules that will be used to mark certain moves as tabu according to their current status. The idea is to guide the search procedure so that clearly bad moves are not made and also to ensure that moves (or their components) are not attempted time after time in a vain attempt at improvement.

The idea of flexible memory is introduced into tabu search as a way of keeping track of some aspects of the history of the search. The precise way in which this memory is organised will depend on the tabu procedure in use and also upon the way in which the heuristic is programmed for computer use. Glover and Laguna (1995) suggest that this flexible memory may have four aspects: recency, frequency, quality and influence

Recency

This refers to some way of keeping track of how many iterations have occurred since a particular element of a solution was last altered in some way or other. There are many ways of representing this, but one way is in a simple matrix as shown in Table 10.2. This relates to Jane Wiley's problem in Transitania and shows a way of representing recency at the start of the fourth iteration. It is based on a strategy that requires moves to be tabu for three iterations after they have occurred. Thus, a non-zero value indicates that a move is tabu and this value is decreased by one at every subsequent iteration. Three iterations after its last move, the move becomes non-tabu and may be used in a new solution. Thus, when considering candidates for moves in the neighbourhood search, the basic idea is that only moves which are non-tabu should be considered. This is to prevent swaps being continually made and then quickly reversed as the heuristic hunts for a new solution. It helps to prevent the heuristic from thrashing around in vain.

Frequency

The second aspect of flexible memory often employed in tabu search is that the heuristic should keep track of how many times that particular move has taken place. In most cases the frequency notion is

Table 10.2 *Recency matrix at the start of iteration 4*

	A	B	C	D	E	F	G
A			3				
B				1			
C							
D							
E							2
F							

employed when the descent has reached a local optimum. This happens when no move in the neighbourhood offers an immediate improvement. Frequency is employed as a way to diversify the search—in terms of the analogy of our lost explorer, it may permit her to climb uphill in order to find her way over an intervening peak into the next valley. If the basic principle of the recency tabu is to restrict the search, the basic principle of frequency is to diversify the search.

A simple implementation of frequency-based search would deploy a similar memory structure as that used in recency-based memory. Thus, one method might be to employ a matrix similar to the one shown in Table 10.2. However, this time, the cells would show how often that the particular move or swap had occurred. Thus, if cell (A, B) contained the value 5 and cell (D, E) contained the value 3, this would indicate that the (A, B) move had occurred five times and the (D, E) move had happened three times since some defined cut-off point. The essence of the approach then is to allow a move among non-tabu candidates that have a low-frequency score. The lower the frequency value, the less often that this move has been considered in the past. Thus this use of frequency serves to diversify the search into regions that have not yet been considered. In essence, both recency and frequency serve to influence the choice of neighbour from a current solution. How this will be implemented will depend on the application.

Breaking the Tabu—Influence, Quality and Aspiration Criteria

The third aspect suggested by Glover and Laguna (1995) is that of influence. This becomes important when the tabu status of a move may need to be overridden in the interests of attempting to shift from some local optimum. The idea is to permit a move that may be tabu if it may lead to a solution that is much better than the current one, or which offers the potential to be much better. The concept of aspiration criteria is introduced to specify the circumstances under which the tabu may be broken. Such a criterion is used to encourage moves that may have a great influence.

A move is considered to be influential if it shifts the solution substantially—that is, to a degree beyond that offered by non-tabu moves. In conceptual terms, this may be equivalent to being able to leap over an intervening peak into the next valley. This opens up whole new possibilities for the search to proceed and may avoid it getting stuck at some local optimum. The modeller thus needs to specify these aspiration criteria, which may be static (i.e. wholly determined in advance) or might be dynamically computed as the search proceeds. This relates to the fourth concept of solution quality, which is a measure of the way in which a particular move contributes to a shift towards a global optimum.

A Basic Tabu Search Algorithm

An earlier section of this chapter presented a general algorithm for neighbourhood search and for its steepest descent variant. This same general scheme may be employed to capture the essence of tabu search as follows:

Step 1   Initialisation
- Select a starting solution x^{now} from X
- Define best_cost $= c(x^{now})$
- Create an empty history record, H

Step 2   Choice and termination
- Choose a solution x^{next} from $N(H, x^{now})$ to minimise $c(H, x^{now})$ over this set
- After a specified number of iterations STOP, else proceed to Step 3

Step 3   Update
- Put $x^{now} = x^{next}$
- Revise H
- If $c(x^{now}) <$ best_cost then best_cost $= c(x^{now})$
- Go to Step 2

As stated earlier, the effect of the history record is to influence the move by taking account of what has gone before with the intention of improving the search.

SIMULATED ANNEALING

The Physical Analogy

This second way of trying to avoid convergence of local optima owes its name to an analogy between the physical operation of annealing and a search process. Annealing is the name given to a process of heat treatment that is commonly applied to metals and also to other materials such as glass. When metals are heated, their physical structure can be modified by careful control over the ways in which they are heated and then cooled. Annealing is used to soften metals that have grown hard and less ductile due to attempts to reshape them at low temperatures. The effect of the process is to change the crystalline structure of the metal in such a way that it can be worked without the breaking and cracking that would occur had it not been annealed. The essence of this physical process of annealing is careful temperature control.

Perhaps the best way of understanding this annealing analogy is to relate it to the earlier analogy of the lost explorer who is stuck in a valley higher than the point she is seeking. How can her search proceed beyond this point? In physical annealing, the idea of the process is to avoid the points at which the metal would normally harden and break—this is analogous to a local optimum. When the metal is approaching the point at which it might start to fail, then it is reheated to permit further work to continue. In simulated annealing, this "reheating" permits the search to continue beyond an apparently local optimum. In a physical annealing process, the amount of extra work that is possible will depend on the temperature of the annealing and this is carefully controlled. In simulated annealing, the same concept is used to control the search that occurs around some local optimum.

The method itself was proposed, in a form relevant to management science, by Kirkpatrick et al (1983) and readable accounts can be found in Eglese (1990) and Dowsland (1995). As with all of the meta-heuristics described here, the approach has been considerably enhanced since its introduction and there are many variants in use. The basic idea is that the heuristic selects moves at random within the current neighbourhood. Whereas local search would only permit such moves if they lead to immediate improvement, simulated annealing permits some uphill moves in an attempt to shift the search to new ground.

The Usual Terminology

In its original form, simulated annealing employed an equation from statistical thermodynamics. The use of this equation in this way is usually attributed to Metropolis et al (1953). This equation is usually presented as follows:

$$\Pr(\delta E) = \exp(-\delta E/kt) \qquad \text{Equation 10.1}$$

where E represents Energy, δE represents a change in Energy, t represents temperature and k is known as Boltzmann's constant. Metropolis et al were simulating what happens to metals as they were cooled and heated in a heat bath. Their simulation generated a small change and, from it, computed the change in energy. In their model of the physical world, if the energy has decreased then the system moves to a new state. But if the energy has increased, then it *may* move to a new state, depending on a probability given in the equation. That is, increases in energy may, possibly, lead to new states. Dowsland (1995) suggests the analogy between the terminology of thermodynamics and simulated annealing that is shown in Table 10.3.

Perhaps the most important part of the analogy to understand is that, in its original form, simulated annealing employed an exponential probability function. An example of the shape of such a function is shown in Figure 10.5. This shows that the function has a sharp decline when x is small, but that it levels off as x increases. Relating this back to the probability equation, this means that the probability is high when the temperature (t) is high or the cost increase is low. Thus, applying this to simulated annealing, a high control parameter means that there is a high probability of accepting an uphill move. The usual approach is to allow such an exponential decay in the probability as the number of iterations increase. The idea of this is that, in the early iterations, the search should be encouraged to roam widely. As it proceeds, the search should get increasingly restricted. This strategy aims to remove the effect of the starting solution.

A Basic Simulated Annealing Algorithm

As with tabu search, the general scheme presented earlier may be used to show the essential features of a simulated annealing algorithm. There are considerable differences between this and the algorithm for neighbourhood search with steepest descent as follows:

- The algorithm requires a control parameter (temperature) function to be established. This has the form:

Table 10.3 *Analogy between thermodynamic simulation and simulated annealing*

Thermodynamic simulation	Simulated annealing
System rate	Feasible solution
Energy	Cost
Change of state	Move to a neighbouring solution
Temperature	Control parameter
Frozen state	Heuristic solution

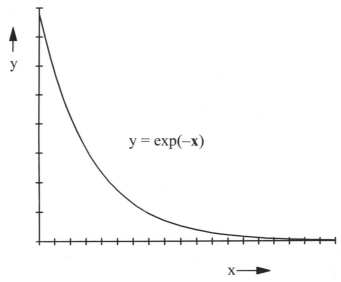

Figure 10.5   *An exponential function*

$$t_{next} = f(t_{now});$$

that is the control parameter t is recalculated at each iteration, based on a function of its previous value. The control parameter must be given some initial value t_0.

- The value of x^{next} is selected from its neighbourhood $N(x^{now})$ and is accepted as the new value of x^{now} if it produces a lower cost. The selection may be random or the choices may be considered in some defined sequence.
- If x^{next} produces a higher cost, then it may be accepted as a new value of x^{now} if it meets a probability criterion. This usually involves taking a sample from a uniform probability distribution on the range 0 to 1. This random sample is then compared with a function based on equation 10.1.
- If this comparison results in a rejection of the x^{next} value then the process is repeated until an acceptable value is found or until some predetermined number of attempts is reached. This latter condition is needed, otherwise the algorithm would circle forever.

Step 1   Initialisation
- Select a starting solution x^{now} from X
- Define best_cost $= c(x^{now})$
- Set $t_{now} = t_0$, some initial value

		• Specify n_rep, the maximum number of attempts • Set n = number of attempts so far
Step 2a	Choice	• If $n >= n\_rep$ then STOP • Select x^{next} from $N(x^{now})$ • Compute $\delta = c(x^{next}) - c(x^{now})$ • If $\delta < 0$, then proceed to Step 3, else proceed to Step 2b
Step 2b	Accept	• Generate u from Uniform $(0, 1)$ distribution • If $u < \exp(-\delta/t_{now})$ then proceed to Step 3, else return to Step 2a
Step 3	Update	• Put $x^{now} = x^{next}$ and $c(x^{now}) = c(x^{next})$ • Compute $t_{next} = f(t_{now})$, put $t_{now} = t_{next}$ • Go to Step 2a

Comparison with Tabu Search

Comparing the two basic versions of these approaches presented here, one major difference is apparent. Though both strategies have been devised to reduce the risk getting stuck at some local optimum, they tackle this in completely different ways. In tabu search, the history of the search so far is used to guide the search in future. In basic simulated annealing, there is no attempt to do this, instead obviously good moves are accepted automatically without regard to their history. If no obviously good move exists, then a potentially bad one is accepted at random according to a probability based on equation 10.1. A second difference is that, in the forms presented here, tabu search is more "conservative" than simulated annealing. Tabu search tries to choose lowest cost neighbours, whereas simulated annealing uses a random element in the hope that this will eventually lead to improvements.

Which of the two basic strategies is better? The two camps each have their own advocates and the answer will depend on the precise problem on which they are being used. However, it does seem reasonable to ask whether the two approaches could not be combined in some way or other. This is clearly the case and, for example, a simulated annealing approach could be modified to include some form of tabu.

GENETIC ALGORITHMS

The Genetic Analogy

The third heuristic strategy discussed here is also based on an analogy—this time from population genetics. It stems from the belief that random mutations at genetic level can, in the right circumstances, lead to a healthy population that contains those genes. The notion being that the circumstances (the environment) temper the random mutation by selecting some individual mutations as better suited to survival and prosperity than others. Thus, like simulated annealing, genetic algorithms rely on some kind of randomness.

A readable but fairly detailed introduction to the basic idea of genetic algorithms as they might be used in management science is given in Reeves (1995b). The method was first suggested by Holland (1975) and an in-depth coverage of the topic is provided by Goldberg (1989). The basic concept is that of a chromosome, which is usually represented as a binary string, such as the following example:

$$[1\ 0\ 1\ 0\ 0\ 1\ 0]$$

This example chromosome has seven variables and these are often known as alleles. Each of these alleles has a position in the string and this is often known as its locus. Thus an allele with locus 2 in a chromosome of length 9 is occupying the second position in a string of nine (0, 1) variables. Each solution in the search needs to be represented by such a chromosome if a genetic algorithm is to be used. Strictly speaking, the alleles need not be restricted to (0, 1) variables, but most straightforward algorithms are based on this representation. In the strict terminology of genetic algorithms, the coded chromosome structure processed by the algorithm is known as the genotype. The decoded version of the chromosome string is known as the phenotype. Thus different problems with the same structure may share genotypes while having different phenotypes.

The Basic Approach

Though, like simulated annealing, genetic algorithms use randomness to improve upon simple neighbourhood search, the way that this is done is very different. The first difference is that, whereas simulated annealing methods move from single solution to single solution, genetic algorithms maintain a population of solutions. In genetic terms, this is a population of potential parents within which breeding will occur. The assumption being that alleles present in the parental chromosomes will find their way into the chromosomes of the offspring. Thus, the intention is to encourage the best fitted offspring to survive each generation to become the next generation of breeding parents. The second difference is that the basic form of algorithm representation shown earlier for neighbourhood search, steepest descent and tabu search is not a suitable way to represent the approach.

Instead, it is more helpful to envisage the basic approach as consisting of a series of generations stemming from reproductive activity. Each phase of reproduction develops as three steps:

1. *crossover*: the mating of two parents to produce a new chromosome
2. *mutation*: in which random changes with low probability are introduced into the chromosomes
3. *selection*: deciding which chromosomes will survive.

These three stages are repeated as the basis of the algorithm.

Crossover and mutation

Crossover is the normal way of simulating breeding between two parent chromosomes and its mechanism is best illustrated by an example. Suppose there are two parents, which are represented by the following chromosomes, each of length 7:

$$[1\ 0\ 1\ 0\ 1\ 0\ 1]\qquad\qquad[0\ 0\ 0\ 0\ 1\ 1\ 1]$$

These will be mated by the exchange of alleles around some randomly chosen crossover point. Suppose that the crossover point will be at 3, which means that it lies between the third and fourth allele in each string. Hence the chromosomes in loci 1, 2 and 3 are swapped for those in loci 4, 5, 6 and 7. Such a crossover would result in the following pair of offspring:

$$[1\ 0\ 1\ 0\ 1\ 1\ 1]\qquad\qquad[0\ 0\ 0\ 0\ 1\ 0\ 1]$$

The crossover point is often selected by sampling from a uniform probability distribution as part of the randomness of the algorithm. Operators other than simple crossover are sometimes employed in these algorithms, an example would be having more than one crossover point in the breeding process.

Mutation occurs when one or more of the alleles is changed at random. If binary strings are used as the chromosomes, then this simply means that a 0 becomes a 1 or vice versa. The idea of mutation being to introduce new attributes into the genetic make-up of the population and to thus reduce its dependence on its starting chromosomes.

Selection

During each cycle, the population completes its mating phase and some of the candidate offspring are selected to survive as the next generation of breeding parents. Thus, the algorithm must specify a selection mechanism that includes some measure of fitness. This fitness function is equivalent to a cost function or an objective function. That is, offspring which make the greatest contribution to the objective function will be selected for survival. Having set a fitness function, there are several possible inter-generational mechanisms which could be used in selecting survivors from the breeding and mutation. In discussing this issue, Reeves (1995b) lists the following options:

- Replace each generation en bloc after breeding, which was the mechanism originally proposed by Holland for genetic algorithms. Thus, selection is automatic.
- Replace incrementally after breeding. That is, only keep those offspring that do not duplicate chromosomes present in the parent population. This helps avoid recessive breeding.
- Employ elitist selection by forcing the best member of the current population to be a member of the next. This ensures that good chromosomes pass forward.
- Use termination with prejudice, an approach that removes members of the parent population that have below-average fitness. They are replaced by a randomly selected member of the offspring.
- Employ parental selection, by encouraging breeding between parents with the highest fitness values.
- Finally, some algorithms employ speciation. This is a way of avoiding indiscriminate mating between different "species".

Other Coding Methods

In the basic approach, the chromosome is a binary coding of the solutions. There are many problems in which this is not a convenient form of representation. One example is the travelling salesman problem, in which it is much more normal to use a string representation of the type shown earlier for the simple, seven-city trip of Jane Wiley. In this case, we might have two parents such as the following:

[A, B, C, D, E, F, G]   [C, A, B, F, G, E, D]

Simple crossover mechanisms are not suited to this form of representation and various others have been suggested. However, it may be that genetic algorithms are not well suited to this form of sequence representation but, instead, are better suited to other types of application in which fitter parents are likely to create fit offspring. Simple crossover will not guarantee this in TSP.

SUMMARY

The argument in this chapter is that, in many of the cases in which some form of mathematical search is a useful way to proceed, optimisation approaches of the type exemplified by linear programming in Chapter 8 are unsatisfactory. This is because, for large-scale problems, the solution methods may take far too long to converge on the optimum. In addition, there are other problems for which search is needed but for which no optimising algorithm exists. Hence, for these types of problem, heuristic search is a sensible way to proceed. The discussion employed the travelling salesman problem as a simple to understand generic application that needs heuristic approaches for problems of a reasonable scale. Many situations to which these methods are applied are much more complicated than the simple TSP and do not lend themselves to simple visual representation.

The heuristic search methods discussed here proceed towards a solution in an iterative manner, each step hoping to find a better solution, though with no guarantee that it will be optimal. They usually employ a form of neighbourhood search at each iteration, rather than examining all possibilities. Strategies such as tabu search and simulated annealing have been devised to avoid early convergence on very suboptimal solutions. A rather different approach is taken in genetic algorithms, the expectation being that aspects of good solutions will be propagated from generation to generation, each time getting better.

REFERENCES

Cartwright H.M. and Cattell J.R. (1995) Studies of continuous-flow chemical synthesis using genetic algorithms. In V.J. Rayward-Smith (Ed.) *Applications of Modern Heuristic Methods*. Alfred Waller, Henley-on-Thames.

Chardaire P. (1995) Location of concentrators using simulated annealing. In V.J. Rayward-Smith (Ed.) *Applications of Modern Heuristic Methods*. Alfred Waller, Henley-on-Thames.

Christofides N. (1985) Vehicle routing. In E.L. Lawler, J.K. Lenstra, A.H.G. Rinnoy Kan and D.B. Shmoys (Eds) *The Travelling Salesman Problem. A Guided Tour of Combinatorial Optimisation*. John Wiley, Chichester.

Dowsland K.A. (1995) Simulated annealing. In C. Reeves (Ed.) *Modern Heuristic Techniques for Combinatorial Problems*. McGraw-Hill, Maidenhead, Berks.

Eglese R.W. (1986) Heuristics in operational research. In V. Belton and R.M. O'Keefe (Eds) *Recent Developments in Operational Research*. Pergamon Press, Oxford.

Eglese R.W. (1990) Simulated annealing: a tool for operational research. *European Journal of Operational Research*, 46, 271–81.

Eglese R.W. and Rand G.K. (1987) Conference seminar timetabling. *Journal of Operational Research*, 38, 591–8.

Foulds L.R. (1983) The heuristic problem solving approach. *Journal of the Operational Research Society*, 34, 927–34.

Glover F. (1986) Future paths for integer programming and links to artificial intelligence. *Computers and Operations Research*, 5, 533–49.

Glover F. and Laguna M. (1995) Tabu search. In C. Reeves (Ed.) *Modern Heuristic Techniques for Combinatorial Problems*. McGraw-Hill, Maidenhead, Berks.

Goldberg D.E. (1989) *Genetic Algorithms in Search, Optimization and Machine Learning*. Addison-Wesley, Reading, Mass.

Holland J. (1975) *Adaptation in Natural and Artificial Systems*. University of Michigan Press, Ann Arbor, Michigan.

Kirkpatrick S., Gellat C.D. and Vecchi, M.P. (1983) Optimization by simulated annealing. *Science*, 220, 671–80.

Metropolis N., Rosenbluth A.W., Rosenbluth M.N., Teller A.H. and Teller E. (1953) Equation of state calculation by fast computing machines. *Journal of Chemical Physics*, 21, 1087–91.

Rayward-Smith V.J. (Ed.) (1995) *Applications of Modern Heuristic Methods*. Alfred Waller, Henley-on-Thames.

Reeves C. (Ed.) (1995a) *Modern Heuristic Techniques for Combinatorial Problems*. McGraw-Hill, Maidenhead, Berks.

Reeves C. (1995b) Genetic algorithms. In C. Reeves (Ed.) *Modern Heuristic Techniques for Combinatorial Problems*. McGraw-Hill, Maidenhead, Berks.

Reeves C. and Beasley J.E. (1995) Introduction. In C. Reeves (Ed.) *Modern Heuristic Techniques for Combinatorial Problems*. McGraw-Hill, Maidenhead, Berks.

Simon H.A. (1978) On how to decide what to do. *The Bell Journal of Economics*, **9**, 3, 494–507.

Simon H.A. and Newell A. (1958) Heuristic problem solving: the next advance for operations research. *Operations Research*, **7**, 1–10.

Wright M.B. (1994) Timetabling county cricket fixtures using a form of tabu search. *Journal of the Operational Research Society*, **45**, 7, 758–71.

PART IV

Model Assessment and Validation

Introduction

If models are intended to be used to think through the consequences of possible actions, it seems important that some form of quality assurance is applied to them. This final part of the book, which applies to both "soft" and "hard" approaches, aims to introduce ideas relevant to this theme. As will become clear, the apparently simple question of model validity turns out to be rather complicated.

11

Model Assessment and Validation

INTRODUCTION

The theme which runs through this book is that modelling is a great help in facing up to complex issues. Part I introduced some general ideas that affect virtually all types of model employed in management science. Part II described the basics of some commonly used interpretive approaches to modelling and Part III covered similar ground for quantitative modelling. Whatever the type of model in use, it seems important to ensure that it is suitable for the purpose for which it was built. This process goes under a range of names, of which model assessment and model validation are probably the most common. The purpose of this final chapter of the book is to discuss how management science models might be assessed and validated.

First, some of the general issues that seem to be important when considering the validation of any type of model in management science will be introduced. Following this is discussion on some general principles for the validation of quantitative models. Then, the slightly more vexing question of the validation of interpretive approaches will be looked at. As will be clear, the validation of quantitative and interpretive models rests on rather different assumptions. Finally, the different threads will be drawn together.

FOUNDATIONS OF VALIDATION

A naive approach to validation would be something like the following:

A model is a representation of the real world, or of at least part of it. Therefore the validation of the model is really quite straight-forward—in principle. All we have to do is check that the model behaves as the real-world does under the same conditions. If it does, then the model is valid. If it doesn't, then it isn't.

Though this view is appealing in its simplicity, there are reasons why it is described as naive. To understand this requires some consideration of epistemology, the subject concerned with human knowledge—how do we know what we know? In two fascinating papers, Déry et al (1993) and Roy (1993) show that validation is more complex than might be seemed at first sight.

Epistemology

Déry et al (1993) argue that, if management science is to be viewed as a scientific or even a technological activity, the dominant epistemologies of science ought to be seriously considered when thinking about the question of validation. They discuss three different perspectives on this, as outlined below.

Philosophical perspective

This has mainly been concerned with the relationship between scientists, the objects they observe, and the ways that those observations are captured as knowledge or scientific truth. Déry et al point out that three threads are woven into this philosophical garment:

- A view, based on logical empiricism, that a statement is an addition to scientific knowledge if it is an objectively correct reflection of factual observations that are translated into logico-mathematical terms. Thus objectivity and rigorous quantification are crucial to the development of scientific knowledge.
- A later view, credited to Popper (1959, 1964) that all scientific knowledge is, in one sense, conjectural because no experiment could conclusively prove a theory to be true. This does not mean that all theories or conjectures are equally valuable. In this view, truly scientific experiments are ones that could disprove a theory or part of a theory rather than ones that seek to confirm it.
- Alongside this, the commonplace notion of utilitarianism, that scientific and technological knowledge is that which is practical. Thus a theory that does not have any consequences in the real world may be interesting, but it is not scientific. This provides a partial explanation of why theories may continue in use even

though they have been refuted. Thus, Newtonian mechanics are widely used despite their replacement by relativistic notions.

Combining these three views might therefore lead us to suppose that a valid management science model is one that is based on objective research, expressed mathematically, shown to be useful and which passes tests designed to show its inadequacy. These are all technical issues.

Historical perspective

This is mainly concerned to account for the ways in which different theories have dominated scientific communities. Thomas Kuhn (1970) is perhaps the best-known historical analyst of scientific epistemology. He argues that a scientific community is bound together by a disciplinary matrix which defines its interests. This comes to define what it regards as scientific knowledge. In a period of "normal science" the members of a scientific community share a stable matrix and most research is devoted to activity which confirms the validity of the matrix. During periods of "revolutionary science" the matrix is threatened by alternative paradigms and this may result in periods of fierce conflict and argument. In this sense, validity relates to the acceptability of an idea, theory or model to the expert community of scientists who are operating with a dominant paradigm. Thus validation is the concern of the professional community of management scientists who ought to define rules for validation. In "normal science", validation is, therefore, partly a test of whether the theory fits the paradigm. Interestingly enough, Gass (1993) makes a plea for a quantitative measure of model acceptability, which seems to imply that management scientists operate within something equivalent to normal science.

Sociological perspective

This takes a yet wider view and looks at scientific communities in the same way as any other group of social system. From this perspective, scientific knowledge is defined by social processes that include conflict, power-play and other social activity. This is in addition to its definition by the ways in which individual scientists observe and describe the world. Thus, in these terms, a theory becomes knowledge when it is accepted by the community and that much the same range of ploys are used to achieve this acceptance as in any other social group. This accounts for peer group pressure, for power play and the rest. However, if the community of scientists gets too far out of kilter with the rest of society then it ceases to be effective because it has no wider franchise. Thus the social processes operate within the scientific communities and between them and other groups. This provides one reason why utilitarian views may be espoused to justify scientific activity.

These three viewpoints illustrate why the naive approach to validation might indeed be considered naive. The naive approach seems to stem from philosophical views about scientific knowledge that take little account of the history of the development of scientific knowledge or of social analyses of the process of development. From the historical perspective it is clear that the scientific community sets the validation rules and that these may shift over time as new problems are faced. Hence, though the naive approach might be fine for quantitative models, it could be wholly inappropriate for interpretive approaches that are aimed at quite different targets. From a sociological perspective we see that the scientific community is not immune to the same pressures as the rest of society. Social relations affect scientific work and are part of what scientists have to say about the objects that they observe. Irrelevance will be rewarded by indifference.

The Declaration of Independence

Underlying the naive approach is what might be termed "The declaration of independence", an implicit view that the problems on which management scientists work are independent of the observer or of other people. They are somewhere "out there". This is the target which Roy (1993) attacks in his discussion of validation from the perspective of multi-criteria decision making (MCDM). MCDM is an approach that seeks to find ways to express differing preferences within a common framework. Roy accepts that, like social scientists, management scientists form part of the systems with which they are concerned. This applies just as much to quantitative modelling as to interpretive work. This makes validation a difficult issue.

Chapter 3 argued that problems are social and psychological constructs, and that these need to be negotiated between the management scientist and the client or user. The management scientist is not separate from the context of the problem. The problem situation, as Checkland (1981) defined it, includes the analyst. Roy (1993) analyses this by considering three paths, or quests, towards scientific knowledge. The first he calls the "realism" path, which aims to describe what the world is really like. This, he points out, may lead to a belief that the elements of a model represent real objects. But "some costs which play critical roles in numerous models refer to virtually unspecifiable realities". For example, what does "cost of capital" mean in an investment calculation?

His second path is called "axiomatic", by which he means the view that a science needs a consistent set of axioms (frames of reference) by which to make sense of things. This seems to correspond to "normal science" with a dominant paradigm. Thus validity may be assessed against these axioms. For example, there are highly consistent theories of choice based on expected subjective utility (see Chapter 2). These theories may be employed to model how decisions should be taken. This view is related to the idea of logical empiricism discussed above and is open to exactly the same criticism.

His third path is that of "constructivism", in which models are not used in an attempt to discover truth but in an attempt to discover useful "keys" that might help to organise a situation. In this sense, models become working hypotheses. This is close to a utilitarian view but also close to the idea running through this book that models can be interpretive tools.

Validation is Impossible, but Desirable

The preceding argument leads us to a sombre conclusion. This is that validation, if this is taken to mean a comprehensive demonstration that a model is fully correct, is impossible. What, then, is possible, and is this better than nothing? It would perhaps be best to answer the second question first. Validation is best regarded as an ideal towards which we must strive if we are to be at all faithful to the idea that management science aims to support action in the real world. It actually matters whether our models are wrong, as this may cause people to embark on action that has very negative consequences. Hence, management scientists have a responsibility to aim at some form of validation, but recognising that this may be limited. Among many scientists it is recognised that theories and knowledge can never be comprehensively demonstrated to be true, and yet these same theories turn out to be very useful. They also have an impact on the world outside the scientific community, especially if they resonate with wider social concerns and needs.

What then is possible in the way of validation? That depends on the type of model and the use to which it is put. This is the subject of most of the rest of this chapter, after a short diversion into the world of validation errors.

VALIDATION ERRORS

Statistical Inference

One of the commonly applied areas of statistical theory is that of statistical inference. In many areas of life it is neither possible nor desirable to test a complete population about which we wish to know something. In a different example, the only way to know how long a light bulb will last is to test it to destruction. Thus any manufacturer of light bulbs will wish to test only a sample of the output, otherwise none would be left for sale. There is, therefore, often a need to make inferences about a population by examining a sample of items from that population. However, most members of populations vary somewhat and thus we may choose to estimate a statistic of some kind. The statistic being measured might belong to the items themselves, such as the expected life of a light bulb, or it might be the result of a comparison, such as knowing whether one light bulb type lasts longer than another. To provide support in making these inferences, statisticians have devised a whole armoury of tests and approaches that can be employed. If all members of the population were clones of one another there would be no problem, for a sample of any size (one, say) would contain all the information about the population.

What all of these tests have in common is the simple fact that inferences are made from samples and these inferences may, in the light of full and complete information, turn out to be wrong. For instance, a comparison of samples of two types of light bulb may suggest that, on average, type A lasts longer than type B. However, even though the samples might have been selected at random from the available production, this inference may be wrong. It could be that the random sampling led us, unwittingly, to a set of type B bulbs which was unaccountably bad. Thus the sample comparison was not a fair one. To cope with this possibility, statistical theory suggests confidence levels for the statistic that fixes boundaries on the likely values of the statistic. Thus a statement that the 95% confidence limits for the expected life of a bulb are 2010 hours and 1850 hours gives an upper and lower bound for this expected life. The 95% figure simply implies that there is a probability of 0.95 that the true average life of the whole population of bulbs lies within those limits.

Type I and Type II Errors

One application of statistical inference is hypothesis testing. We may, for example, wish to know, as mentioned above, whether two different types of light bulbs have different lives. One way to check this would be to take random samples of each type, measure how long each lasted, and then compute the average life for each sample. To test whether type A lasts longer than type B, we need to decide whether the difference between the two average values is greater than zero. Thus we have a null hypothesis that the difference between the two average lives is zero, and an alternative hypothesis that there is a positive difference in favour of A. Hypothesis tests, like confidence intervals, allow a statistically trained person to compare the two hypotheses by estimating how likely it is that the difference between the means is a true difference which reflects the entire population. Thus these tests result in statements such as "Reject the null hypothesis at a confidence level of 95%", which means that there is a probability of 0.95 that the difference observed in the samples is actually greater than zero in the whole population.

This statement of statistical confidence reflects the fact that there is a risk of drawing the wrong conclusion. The difference might be very small in the whole population, effectively zero, despite a reasonably large difference in the samples taken. To cope with this risk, statisticians use the terms type I and type II errors. A type I error occurs, in classical hypothesis testing, when a correct hypothesis is wrongly rejected. In the light bulb example, the application of statistical theory may lead us to conclude that there is a significant difference between the average lives of the two types of light bulb. If we had access to the entire population of these bulbs then we might know that this conclusion from the samples was wrong, because their average lives are effectively the same. This would be a type I error. The higher the level of significance, then the lower this risk will be—but this may require very large samples. A type II error occurs, by contrast, when an incorrect hypothesis is wrongly accepted. Thus we might accept, at some confidence level, that the average lives of the two types of light bulb are effectively the same. If this turns out to be an error, then it would be a type II error.

It is sometimes naively assumed that the validation of a model involves the straightforward application of these ideas of statistical inference to a sample of results from the model against a sample from the real world. As will be seen later, this is a gross oversimplification for both quantitative and interpretive models. However, the general notion is still a useful one. In general validation terms, a type I error is the risk of wrongly rejecting a valid model. A type II error is the risk of wrongly accepting an invalid model.

Type Zero Errors

A type zero error (called a type III error by Balci, 1994) occurs when the modeller sets out on the wrong track altogether. The result is a model that does completely the wrong thing and is of no value at all. This can happen with the cleverest and most complicated of models and is the most important error to avoid in any modelling. It can also happen when a model, which in overall intention is sensible, ends up with detail in irrelevant places and sketchy coverage of things which turn out to be important.

The best way to avoid these fundamental type zero errors is to pay careful attention to problem and model formulation. This is one aspect that comes across very clearly in Willemain's (1995) study of expert modellers and their modelling referred to in Chapter 4. Although the experts studied might have been expected to focus almost exclusively on the technical aspects of their modelling, they spent about 30% in careful consideration of the problem context and in thinking about model assessment and validation. This time was devoted in the short space of the 60 minutes they were given to think aloud. Thus, experts recognise the importance of avoiding these type zero errors.

THE ASSESSMENT AND VALIDATION OF QUANTITATIVE MODELS

Some Relevant Concepts from Computer Simulation

Perhaps the most attention to the question of validation in management science has been paid in the discrete computer simulation community, with notable contributions from Balci (1987, 1994), Sargent (1988) and Zeigler (1976, 1984). A thorough discussion of some issues related to validation and validity is to be found in Zeigler (1976), who is careful to distinguish between the following (shown in Figure 11.1):

The real system. This is defined as the source of observable data. Even if we do not understand the real system, we can still observe its behaviour. The observable data consists of a set of input:output relations which need not be simple.

An experimental frame. This is defined as the limited set of circumstances under which the real system is to be observed or experimented with.

The base model. This is defined as some hypothetical model which would account for all of the input:output behaviour of the real system. This may not exist in any tangible form, though it must do so if there is no real system, such as when a new system is being developed from scratch.

A lumped model. This is defined as an explicit and simplified version of the base model and is the one that will be used in the management science.

A computer program. In this the lumped model is implemented and is intended to generate the input:output relations of the lumped model.

Thus, the idea is that, when faced with the need to develop a model of some complex system, we begin with a conceptual or base model which we have in mind as we try to build the lumped model which may then be implemented in a computer program. The intention is that the models should be used in relation to the purposes defined by the experimental frame.

Validation and Verification Defined

Zeigler (1984) develops a notation system, based on set theory, which allows the convenient expression of some useful ideas. In this chapter I will just use one of these ideas, that of an input:output relation. This embodies the idea of a reference system (Zeigler's real system) as a form of black box that can be observed and from which we can relate inputs to outputs. This is known as the input:output relation of the real system. Zeigler points out that we wish to know the true

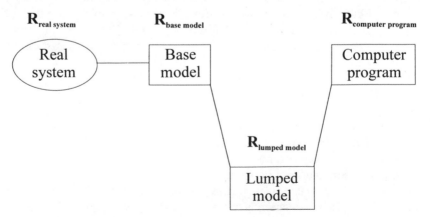

Figure 11.1 *Zeigler's view of modelling (adapted from Zeigler, 1984)*

input:output relation of this system but that in fact we can only observe it at some point of time t (of which there may be many). Ideally, the input:output relation of the model should be the same as that of the computer program and the same as that of the real system. Defining some nomenclature:

$R_{real\ system} | \varepsilon =$ input:output relation, subject to some experimental
frame ε.

$R^t_{real\ system} | \varepsilon =$ input:output relation at time t, subject to some
experimental frame ε.

Thus, for the real system we wish to know $R_{real\ system}$ (the full input:output relation) but we can only know $R^t_{real\ system} | \varepsilon$, the input:output relation at time t and subject to some experimental frame ε. This emphasises that validation involves the comparison of observations and that any notion of validity can only be subject to some intended purpose, that is, some defined experimental frame. $R^t_{real\ system} | \varepsilon$ is a sub-set of $R_{real\ system}$.

As shown in Figure 11.1, Zeigler argues that each component except the experimental frame has an input:output relation R. Zeigler postulates that:

$$R_{base\ model} = R_{real\ system}$$

but that, as mentioned above, the real system is known only at some time point t and the base model is only hypothetical and exists in people's minds, if at all. Validation and verification as activities are concerned with the relationship between these various Rs.

Verification is a process by which we try to assure ourselves that:

$$R_{lumped\ model} = R_{computer\ program}$$

that is, we are trying to ensure that the lumped model is properly realised in the computer program. This is, in one sense, straightforward since the lumped model is, by definition, fully specified and the computer program exists in a tangible form.

Validation is a process whereby we assess the degree to which:

$$R_{lumped\ model} = R_{real\ system}$$

that is, the degree to which the base model input:output relations map on to those of the real system. This implies the existence of the experimental frame.

The Importance of Process and Other Aspects

Balci (1994) points out that computer simulation studies are cyclic, in that models are refined gradually and thus simple models are refined to as time progresses. This fits well with the principle of parsimony espoused in Chapter 4. In a proper sense, therefore, assessment and validation are activities which should continue throughout a simulation project. The same should be true of any quantitative modelling in management science that follows the principle of parsimony. Therefore it would be wrong to focus all the assessment and validation effort at the end of a modelling project. Instead it should be a fully-fledged part of all stages of the modelling work, part indeed of a critical approach. Balci (1994) suggests tests and assessments that can be made at each point of the simulation modelling cycle. He suggests that many of these could be built in to simulation support environments.

Also writing about computer simulation, Robinson (1996) points out that "Three terms are often used in the context of simulation model and simulation study assessment: validity, credibility and acceptability". He quotes Schruben (1980) as arguing that "*credibility* is reflected in the willingness of persons to base decisions on the information obtained from the model". This is clearly as much a feature of the trust that the model user or client places in the analyst or group building the model, as it is in the credibility of the model itself. Acceptability is usually a reference to the entire study, which includes the model and is also clearly a reflection of the relationship between the modeller(s) and the user or client.

Black-box Validation: Predictive Power

There are many different approaches to model validation, but they can be divided into two groups: black-box and open-box validation. In black-box validation, the model is treated as if it were an input:output system of unknown internal construction—hence the term, black box. Chapter 1 introduced the idea of a Turing Test and Figure 1.2 showed the basic idea of such a test, which is the essence of black-box validation. In such an approach the idea is to test the model by the degree to which its results resemble those produced by the system(s) being modelled. This assumes that both model and system(s) operate under the same circumstances. Hence, it is assumed that if the model output is indistinguishable from that of the system, this implies that the model is in some sense a valid representation of that system. In one sense, black-box validation focuses on the predictive power of the model.

It is important to realise that any black-box validation is based on the comparison of two sets of observations. The first set comes from the model and the second from the system with which it is being compared—its reference system. As with all observations, those used in validation are open to errors due to recording, transcription, analysis and interpretation. It is highly unlikely—indeed, it would be very suspicious—if the model observations were identical to those from its reference system. Hence, the aim of black-box validation is not to test whether model and reference system produce the same results. Rather, the aim is to test whether the two sets of observations are close enough to be confident that the model has adequate validity. Thus, the usual armoury of statistical test may be brought to bear on this comparison in order to make some statement about the degree of confidence that may be placed in the similarity between the performance of the model and its reference system.

Open-box Validation

The opposite extreme from black-box validation is the realisation that the model is not really a black box with an unknown internal structure. Instead, this model is a deliberate creation of human minds and it includes relationships which ought to be understood by its creators, if not by its users. Thus, the box can be opened—hence the name of this type of approach, which is sometimes known as white-box validation (Pidd, 1984). A closed white box is just as hard to peer into as a closed black box, hence the term open box seems preferable. The idea of this approach is that the detailed internal structure of the model should be compared with that of its reference system. It should be apparent that there is an immediate problem here, because the reason for building the model may be to help understand the structure of the reference system. Nevertheless, there are ways for open-box validation to proceed, depending on the type of model being built. In the case of quantitative models it is possible to check a number of key features.

If any probability distributions are employed are they reasonable, given the phenomena being modelled? For example, in queuing-type systems it is often reasonable to assume that a distribution based on Poisson process may be used to model the arrival pattern of customers. This is true when there is believed to be no relationship, other than a random one, between the arrival of successive customers. As another example, certain distributions such as the Weibull have particular value in modelling the ways in which items of equipment tend to fail in service. It is much better to think about the process which the probability distribution is representing than to just collect some data try to fit any old distribution to it. The analytical probability distributions are all derived from different assumptions about the process that generates the results. At its most basic, some distributions assume a continuous variable (such as the weight of an item) whereas others assume a discrete variable (such as the number of people arriving during a time interval). Continuing with the same point, some distributions assume that the variable covers an infinite range, that is it has no limits; some assume that the value can go negative and others that the range is strictly bounded by a maximum and minimum value.

A related issue might be whether the model employs what is believed to be appropriate theory. For example, a model for air traffic control might need to track aircraft as they move through some three-dimensional airspace. The time taken for an aircraft to get from one point to another may therefore be of great importance and may depend on the aircraft's type (for example, a wide-bodied Boeing 747) and also its load. It will also depend on whether the departure and arrival points are at the same altitude and on any wind patterns. It is important to ensure that any well-known behaviours in these circumstances are embodied in the model. In essence, these are submodels within an overall model.

Clearly, this type of open-box validation is not a once-and-for-all exercise conducted by the management scientist after the model is built. It is part of the modelling process itself and needs to be carried out throughout the modelling. It should also be conducted hand-in-hand with the client for the study or user of the model. The modeller may be skilful at modelling, but the other parties are more likely to be well informed about the problem domain.

Validation Difficulties

In a way, validation is one of those things that everyone favours but which is less straightforward than might be imagined at first sight. There are a number of possible reasons for this. The first might be because the model is being built to help investigate how something works or how something might work. In this sense, the model is a theory about the operation of its reference system. Hence, there is no fully understood reference system with which the model may be compared. As a simple example, it is increasingly common for complex manufacturing systems to be simulated so as to find better ways to operate them. Because these manufacturing plants are very complex it is not uncommon for them to perform below their specified levels of output and efficiency. Rather than experiment with the plant itself, which might be dangerous, costly or even illegal, it may be better to experiment with a computer simulation model. Thus, in such cases, any complete validation may be impossible.

A second difficulty, closely related to the first, occurs in the common case that a model is built in some known circumstances. In this sense, the model may be validated against its reference system. However, then the problems start. It is very common for the purpose of the modelling to be to find better or new ways of operating the reference system. Though the management scientist and the client may be happy that the model is a valid representation of the system as it now is, there can be no such certainty about its operation in new modes. Note that this is not an argument about whether the model is slapdash, simply a statement that its extension into uncharted territory is a process of exploration in which trust may gradually be built up.

A third problem, closely related to the second, occurs when the model will be used to predict the future. A golden, if somewhat cynical, rule among forecasters is "when asked for a forecast always give a number or a date, but never both". The future is uncertain and unknown, that is why it is being modelled. Therefore the future is the reference system. As an example, newspapers are fond of competitions to find the best economic forecaster or the best investor. In the former case, distinguished economic commentators are asked to estimate various statistics about economic performance (such as percentage growth in gross domestic product). In the latter case, investors are given a hypothetical amount of cash and are invited to "invest" this over a year, so as to produce the maximum return. The winners are lauded a year later as the best economic forecaster or the canniest investor. A pause for thought reveals that in a race, someone must win unless all perform identically. Suppose that economic performance or the stock market were entirely random, then someone would still win—but this would not be a reflection of their ability, simply a result of their luck on two more of life's lotteries. In other words, even predictive success is no guarantee of a model that is valid. If, on the other hand, the same person were to win the competition year after year, then it begins to look as if their model is rather good. But hindsight always helps when dealing with the future.

Program Verification

Validation is the process of assuring that the simulation model is useful for its intended purpose. It needs to be distinguished from verification, a term usually applied to a computer program, given that many management science models are implemented in computer programs. Program verification is the process of ensuring that the program embodies the model correctly—that is, it assumes that the model has been correctly specified. With this in mind, Law and Kelton (1991) suggest eight aspects to consider when attempting to verify a computer simulation program:

1. Write and debug the program in modules. Develop and add submodules as needed until the model is complicated enough.
2. With large models, have other people read through the code or walk it through to avoid the programmer getting stuck in a rut.
3. Run the simulation under a variety of conditions for input parameters and check that the output is reasonable.
4. Make use of variable traces, especially to check the program's behaviour under extreme conditions. Make use of interactive debuggers if they are available.
5. Run the model under simplifying assumptions for which true characteristics are known or can easily be computed.
6. If it seems sensible, watch an animation of the output from the model.
7. Check the observed sample moments against those specified for the input distributions.
8. Where possible, use a simulation language/package to reduce the lines of code.

Though items 3 and 8 refer directly to computer simulation applications, they apply just as much to other types of model in management science. Only item 6 may be inapplicable in many other types of management science model since it refers to dynamic models in which the time dimension is a major concern.

THE ASSESSMENT AND VALIDATION OF INTERPRETIVE MODELS

Part II of this book is devoted to three "soft" modelling approaches commonly used in interpretive management science. That is, they are used with the deliberate intention of helping to support a debate among people who have differing views and make different interpretations of the way things are, or of the way that things might be. As Checkland (1995) points out, one of the fundamental differences between the quantitative management science models and interpretive models is in their approach to validation. The first section of this chapter pointed out that there might be approaches to validation other than attempts to see how well the model maps on to a chunk of the real world. The argument presented by Déry et al (1993) suggests that these other approaches are, in fact, necessary for all types of model. Certainly they are important for interpretive models. Roy (1993) points the way forward by suggesting that validation might be related to axiomatic or constructivist ideas.

Validation in Soft Systems Methodology

Checkland (1995) points out that the type of quantitative validation discussed above is based on a view which is close to that espoused in the physical sciences. He describes this as based on the three Rs.

Reductionism. As discussed in Chapter 5 this is the notion that a complex system may be decomposed into its constituent parts without any loss of information, predictive power or meaning.

Repeatability. This is the idea, dominant in the scientific literature, that any experiment ought to be, in concept at least, repeatable. Most scientific journals require enough detail in their papers to enable other investigators to replicate any experiment. Thus, they may check the work that led to the claims of the paper.

Refutation. As mentioned earlier, this notion is mainly due to the philosopher of science Karl Popper (1959, 1964), who argued that no experiment could conclusively prove a theory to be true. Thus, truly scientific experiments were ones that could disprove a theory or part of a theory. In this sense, all scientific theory is conjectural—which does not mean that all theories are equally valuable.

In Checkland's terms, one aspect of physical science is that its practitioners have developed a social process of enquiry that rests on these three Rs. The three Rs themselves rest on logical empiricism, an outlook that is suspicious of any thought (including would-be scientific hypotheses) which is incapable of being reduced to direct observation.

Hence, in these terms, the approaches to model assessment and validation discussed previously are attempts to devise tests that measure how close a fit a model may be to the system being modelled. This is because these models are intended to be used in efforts to decide how to improve these real systems. In one sense they are intended as surrogates for those systems. In Checkland's terms, they are "would-be representations of the world". By contrast, Checkland (1995) argues that, in soft systems methodology (SSM—see Chapter 5), the idea of a model is more subtle. Figure 5.1 shows that SSM makes use of conceptual models developed from a consideration of root definitions of relevant systems. These conceptual models are attempts to show the relationships between those activities that must, in concept, be present in any system which could realise the root definition. That is, they are not intended to be models of the "real" world.

As Figure 11.2 shows, rather than being attempts to develop a model of some real system X, models in SSM are devices that are relevant to a debate about X. They are developed in an attempt to support a debate intended to lead to agreed action. The same claim could certainly be made about cognitive maps and the SODA methodology, and could easily be extended to system dynamics when used in the mode discussed in Chapter 7. What are the implications of this claim?

Checkland (1995) argues that "the validity question becomes the question of how we can tell a 'good' device from a 'bad' one". According to Checkland, this "good" or "bad" notion includes two aspects. First, is the model as developed in any sense "relevant"? Secondly, is the model competently built?

Before looking at these two issues it may be necessary to stand slightly further back and recall that SSM is a *systems* methodology. This means that it employs systems ideas and is itself systemic, a learning system. The employment of systems ideas might lead one to assume that conceptual models in SSM must be based on systems ideas. As mentioned briefly in Chapter 5, Checkland and Scholes (1990) feel this is no longer necessary. That is, there is no need to employ any formal systems ideas in assessing whether a conceptual model is acceptable. Instead they suggest that a conceptual model needs to be defensible in the sense that its activities each follow directly from words or concepts in the root definition. The same should be true, argues Checkland (1995), of any measures of performance suggested for a conceptual model. Nevertheless, it should be clear from a cursory examination of Figure 5.4 that most of the concepts of a root definition stem from a simple input:output view of a system contained in an environment. Thus, even when checking the linkage between a conceptual model and a root definition in SSM, there is implicit recourse to formal systems ideas. That is, the validation is, in part at least, related to an axiomatic view.

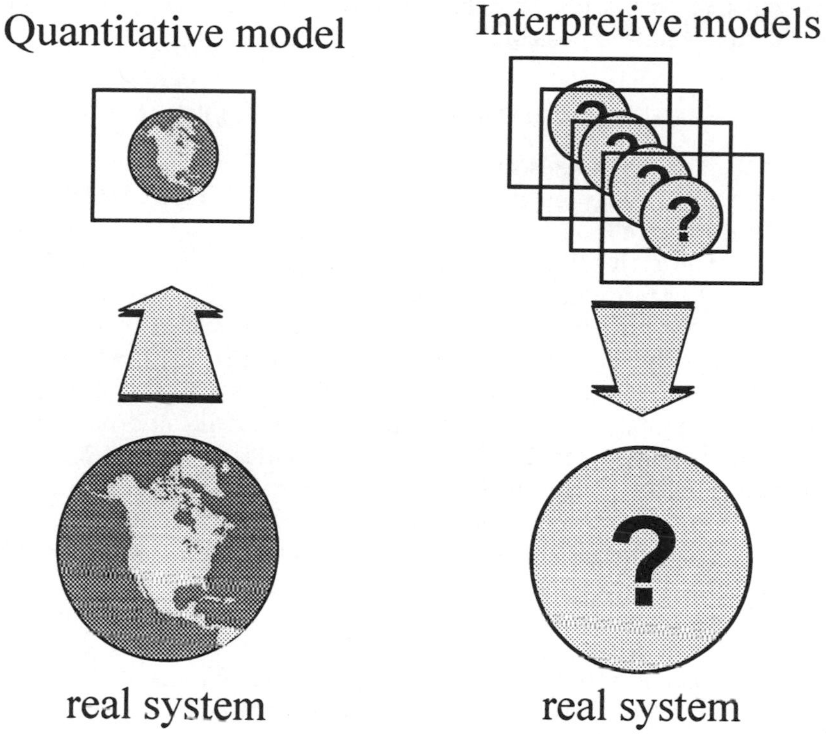

Quantitative model   Interpretive models

real system   real system

Figure 11.2 *The nature of models in SSM*

Checkland's (1995) own two suggestions are to ask whether the model is relevant and whether it is competently built. Both of these ideas could themselves be interpreted in two ways. The first interpretation relates to the previous paragraph. That is, it addresses the degree to which the models are relevant to, and competently built from, the root definitions that have been produced. That is, once again, the validation is related to an axiomatic approach. The second interpretation would be that of its relevance to the outcome of the work and the competence of the analyst in the eyes of the client group. This relates to a constructivist view in that the question is whether the models provide any keys and also to an instrumental view about whether the models were of any use.

Thus we see that model validation can be attempted in SSM, provided we forsake the view that these models are intended as would-be representations of the real world. If instead we view them as ways of supporting a debate about systemic issues, then some validation is indeed possible.

Validation in Cognitive Mapping and SODA

What then of the models that characterise cognitive mapping and the SODA methodology as discussed in Chapter 6? How can they be validated, if at all? According to its developers, cognitive maps are "tools for reflective thinking and problem solving" (Eden et al, 1992). As tools, their design stems from personal construct theory and its notions about how people, individually, make sense of their worlds. Hence, as with conceptual models in SSM, some form of validation is possible with cognitive maps and, as with SSM, this validation is based on axiomatic, constructivist and instrumentalist approaches.

Cognitive maps can be validated axiomatically by checking the degree to which they conform to the underlying ideas of construct theory. To give an obvious example, this theory views constructs as psychological opposites. That is, it is based on notions of anti-thesis—the dichotomy corollary mentioned in Chapter 6. Thus, to be valid in axiomatic terms, the map must be expressed as a set of these psychological opposites. If there is ambiguity about the concepts on the map, then it is presumably invalid in axiomatic terms.

The analysis of these maps, which was discussed in Chapter 6, can also be assessed in these axiomatic terms. The analysis aims to identify clusters of related concepts according to some ideas about organisation. For individuals, this organisation is based at least partially on the idea in construct theory that constructs are hierarchically ordered—the organisation corollary. If no such organisation can be detected in a map then it seems reasonable to question its validity in axiomatic terms—it appears not to correspond to construct theory. A similar argument could be made about the merging of maps prior to a SODA workshop. This depends on the commonality and sociality corollaries. If people appear to have no concepts in common and if the theory itself has any validity, either the maps are invalid or the people at the SODA workshop truly have nothing in common.

As in SSM, it seems reasonable to invoke the constructivist and instrumentalist approaches to the validation of cognitive maps. They are developed as a means to an end and not as an end in themselves. If they serve to move a group towards commitment to action then they have, in some instrumental sense, demonstrated their validity. If they provide insights previously hidden or unknown, they are acting as keys that unlock things. They may thus be regarded as valid in a constructivist sense.

Validation in System Dynamics

System dynamics models are a little different from conceptual models in SSM or cognitive maps. This is because they can be used pretty much in the same way as other quantitative models or as interpretive models. Writing about validation in system dynamics, Lane (1995) points this out and captures it in the idea of a folding star, shown in simplified form in Figure 11.3. The star is an extension of a simpler tetrahedron model proposed by Oral and Kettani (1993) and it can be imagined as a tetrahedron whose sides have been unfolded. The faces of the tetrahedron represent four different ways in which a system dynamics is put to use. The vertices represent different aspects of a system dynamics modelling process:

AoS. This represents an "Appreciation of the Situation" and is the result of the efforts of a group of people who collect data from, and reflect on, the "world". It is thus a conceptualisation which provides data that will be used later. In some senses it resembles Zeigler's notion of a real system as a source of data. When the star is folded into a tetrahedron, the three AoS vertices coincide.

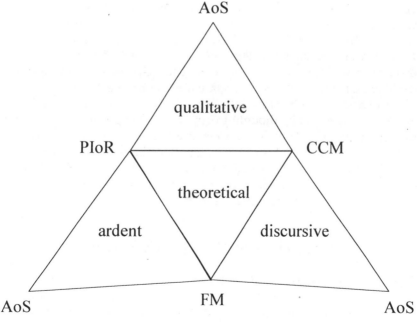

Figure 11.3 Lane's folding star (adapted from Lane, 1995)

CCM. This is the "Communicated Conceptual Model" which is the expression of the AoS within some ordered framework so that it can be communicated to, and understood by, other people. This is close to Zeigler's idea of a lumped model.

FM. The "Formal Model" is the representation of the CCM, probably using a computer package such as Stella (see Chapter 7). It may be used for experimentation.

PIoR. This vertex represents "Policy Insights or Recommendations", which are the results, in qualitative or quantitative terms, of the use of a system dynamics model.

The faces emphasise the fact that system dynamics may be put to a range of different uses, only some of which are properly interpretive. They are labelled as follows:

Ardent system dynamics. This links the AoS, FM and PIoR vertices. It represents the use of a formal model, captured in computer software to develop a set of recommendations for change in the real world. This is indistinguishable from the type of modelling discussed in Part III of this book, and thus the techniques for validating quantitative models may be applied.

Qualitative system dynamics. This links the AoS, CCM and PLoR vertices. In this mode of use, system dynamics provides a language in which people may discuss their views of the systems under considera-tion. In a limited sense, this is therefore an interpretive mode of use.

Discursive system dynamics. This links the AoS, CCM and FM vertices. It represents the use of a formal model to help understanding and to develop learning. This, too, has some interpretive features.

Theoretical system dynamics. Note that none of the vertices of this face are AoS. This might be thought to imply the worst kind of speculative modelling in which there is no concern whatsoever with a real system, in the terms that it is used by Zeigler. Lane uses it to describe work done for the system dynamics community to demonstrate the power of the approach, or models for which there is no obvious client or user. This has some interpretive features.

REFERENCE POINTS FOR VALIDITY

The argument so far might lead a critical reader to one of two false conclusions. The first would be that the use of interpretive models is so far from notions of rationality that they have no place in manage-ment science and can be dismissed out of hand. The second would be that validation of these models is irrelevant as long as they seem to be useful. Neither of these conclusions is justified. To understand why, we need to think about the role of frameworks or presuppositions.

Chapter 2 was a brief tour of rationality as the idea is often used in management science. It began in the pleasant foothills of the classical rationality of choice, as espoused by many economists. In this terrain, routes were found through the meadows by a map containing every feature of the terrain, and the only problem was to decide which way to go. The tour climbed into the steeper slopes of procedural rationality as proposed by Simon, in which it becomes clear that there is no complete map of the terrain, but it can be surveyed—at a cost. Individuals or groups may decide that they have only so much resource to expend on the survey and may thus settle for a route that is pleasant but which could be bettered—if perfect information were available. The bus then took us to the steeper slopes of non-rational and intuitive ideas as espoused by Mintzberg and his colleagues. These might seem, at first sight, to support a view that the best way to select the route is to choose one that looks immediately appealing from where we happen to find ourselves. In fact it is more subtle than this, for it is more concerned to argue that there are more things in life than can be measured or assessed—positivism is a false god or guide. There are times when an inspired leader may choose a route which, with helicopter vision, we might see is a relatively bad one, yet the group may get there due to the tour guide's personal qualities. Finally, the tour ended on the high peaks of Damasio's suggestion that emotion and reason are in fact closely linked in the brains and bodies of healthy people. Put together, they allow routes to be chosen that are pretty good and permit emotion and social processes to keep the tour together.

Figure 11.4 shows the interpretive and quantitative approaches as extreme points on a spectrum—which they are, since even a quantitative model can be clearly be used in an interpretive way. Underneath the spectrum are three wedges, which attempt to show the importance of the three "paths" suggested by Roy (1993). The thickness of the wedge is intended to show its importance for the two extremes. With quantitative models it may be very important to demonstrate that they are valid "would-be representations of the real world". Hence realism is very important. This is less so for interpretive models, but it would be dangerous to argue that all concepts of reality have no importance. Axiomatic validation is crucial for interpretive models, for the aim is provide a language that will enable debate to flourish at a new level. Thus, the models need to be checked

Interpretive models

Quantitative models

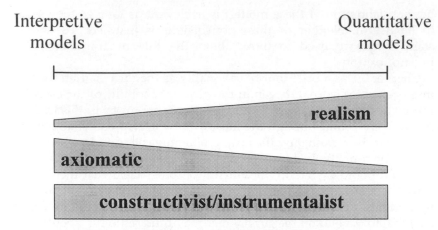

Figure 11.4   *A spectrum of approaches*

against the language. This might also be true of quantitative models when they are being used in an attempt to shed new light on something—and it may also be part of open-box validation. Constructivist validation is also important, especially for interpretive models, as the idea is to provide new keys that might unlock new insights.

SUMMARY

Validation is an important issue in management science modelling and should not be ignored, though this often happens due to the pressure of time. The validation of quantitative models of short-term operational problems is relatively straightforward, though it can be time-consuming in practice. The validation of other models is not so simple.

When models are to be used in an interpretive mode, then the modeller must go way beyond the simple Turing-type tests that dominate much thinking about validation in management science.

REFERENCES

Balci O. (1987) Credibility assessment of simulation results: the state of the art. In *Proceedings of the Conference on Methodology and Validation*, pp. 19–25, Orlando, Florida.

Balci O. (1994) Validation, verification and testing techniques throughout the life cycle of a simulation study. In Balci, O. (Ed.) *Annals of Operations Research*, **3**, 53, Simulation and Modelling. J.C. Baltzer AG, Basel, Switzerland.

Checkland P.B. (1981) *Systems Thinking, Systems Practice*. John Wiley, Chichester.

Checkland P.B. (1995) Model validation in soft systems practice. *Systems Research*, **12**, 1, 47–54.

Checkland P.B. and Scholes, J. (1990) *Soft Systems Methodology in Action*. John Wiley, Chichester.

Déry R., Landry M. and Banville C. (1993) Revisiting the issue of validation in OR: an epistemological view. *European Journal of Operational Research*, **66**, 2, 168–83.

Eden C.L., Ackermann F. and Cropper S. (1992) The analysis of cause maps. *Journal of Management Studies*, **29**, 3, 309–24.

Gass S.I. (1993) Model accreditation: a rationale and process for determining a numerical rating. *European Journal of Operational Research*, **66**, 2, 250–8.

Kuhn T.S. (1970) *The Structure of Scientific Revolutions*. (Second edition.) University of Chicago Press, Chicago, Ill.

Lane D.C. (1995) The folding star: a comparative re-framing and extension of validity concepts in system dynamics. In *Procedures of the 1995 International System Dynamics Conference*, 30 July–4 August, Tokyo.

Law A.M. and Kelton W.D. (1991) *Simulation Modelling and Analysis*. (Second edition.) McGraw-Hill International Edition, New York.

Oral M. and Kettani O. (1993) The facets of the modelling and validation process in operations research. *European Journal of Operational Research*, **66**, 2, 216–34.

Pidd M. (1984) *Computer Simulation in Management Science*. (First edition.) John Wiley, Chichester.

Popper K.R. (1959) *The Logic of Scientific Discoveries*. Hutchinson, London.

Popper K.R. (1964) *Conjectures and Refutations*. Routledge, London.

Robinson S. (1996) Service quality management in the process of delivering a simulation study. Paper presented to the 14th Triennial Conference of the International Federation of OR Societies, July 8–12, 1996, Vancouver, BC.

Roy B. (1993) Decision science or decision aid science? *European Journal of Operational Research*, **66**, 2, 184–203.

Sargent R.W. (1988) A tutorial on validation and verification of simulation models. In *Proceedings of the 1988 Winter Simulation Conference*, pp. 33–9. San Diego, Cal.

Schruben L.W. (1980) Establishing the credibility of simulations. *Simulation*, **34**, 3, 101–5.

Willemain T.R. (1995) Model formulation: what experts think about and when. *Operations Research*, **43**, 6, 916–32.

Zeigler B.P. (1976) *Theory of Modelling and Simulation*. John Wiley, New York.

Zeigler B.P. (1984) *Multi-facetted Modelling and Discrete Event Simulation*. Academic Press, New York.

Author Index

Subject Index